SAGE has been part of the global academic community since 1965, supporting high quality research and learning that transforms society and our understanding of individuals, groups and cultures. SAGE is the independent, innovative, natural home for authors, editors and societies who share our commitment and passion for the social sciences.

Find out more at: **www.sagepublications.com**

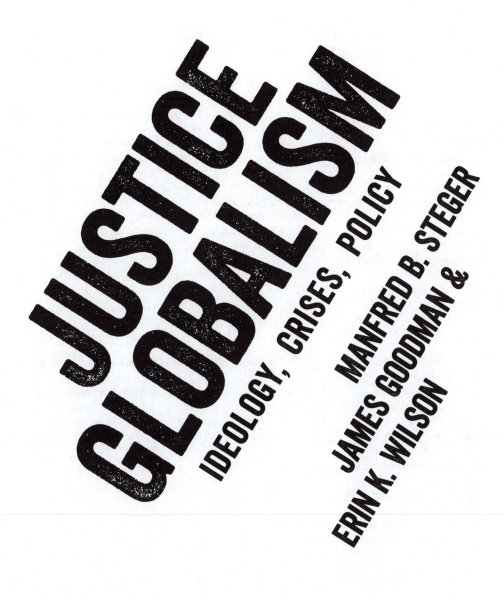

JUSTICE GLOBALISM

IDEOLOGY, CRISES, POLICY

MANFRED B. STEGER
JAMES GOODMAN &
ERIN K. WILSON

SAGE

Los Angeles | London | New Delhi
Singapore | Washington DC

Los Angeles | London | New Delhi
Singapore | Washington DC

SAGE Publications Ltd
1 Oliver's Yard
55 City Road
London EC1Y 1SP

SAGE Publications Inc.
2455 Teller Road
Thousand Oaks, California 91320

SAGE Publications India Pvt Ltd
B 1/I 1 Mohan Cooperative Industrial Area
Mathura Road
New Delhi 110 044

SAGE Publications Asia-Pacific Pte Ltd
3 Church Street
#10-04 Samsung Hub
Singapore 049483

© Manfred B. Steger, James Goodman and Erin K. Wilson 2013

First published 2013

Library of Congress Control Number: 2012939733

British Library Cataloguing in Publication data

A catalogue record for this book is available from the British Library

Editor: Natalie Aguilera
Editorial assistant: James Piper
Production editor: Katie Forsythe
Copyeditor: Elisabeth Rees Evans
Proofreader: Imogen Roome
Marketing manager: Sally Ransom
Cover design: Francis Kenney
Typeset by: C&M Digitals (P) Ltd, Chennai, India
Printed by MPG Books Group, Bodmin, Cornwall

MIX
Paper from
responsible sources
FSC
www.fsc.org   FSC® C018575

ISBN 978-1-4462-4090-8
ISBN 978-1-4462-4091-5 (pbk)

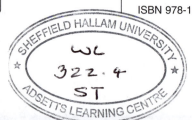

CONTENTS

DETAILED TABLE OF CONTENTS

ABOUT THE AUTHORS

Manfred B. Steger is Professor of Political Science at the University of Hawai'i-Manoa and Professor of Global Studies at the Royal Melbourne Institute of Technology (RMIT University). He is also the Research Leader of the Globalization and Culture Program of RMIT's Global Cities Research Institute. He has served as an academic consultant on globalization for the US State Department and as an advisor to the PBS TV series, *Heaven on Earth: The Rise and Fall of Socialism*. He is the author or editor of over twenty books on globalization, global history, and the history of political ideas, including: *The Rise of the Global Imaginary: Political Ideologies from the French Revolution to the Global War on Terror* (Oxford University Press, 2008); the award-winning *Globalisms: The Great Ideological Struggle of the 21st Century*, 3rd edn. (Rowman & Littlefield, 2009), and the best-selling *Globalization: A Very Short Introduction*, 2nd edn. (Oxford University Press, 2009).

James Goodman is Associate Professor in the Social and Political Change Group at the Faculty of Arts and Social Sciences, University of Technology, Sydney. He researches social movements and globalization with a focus on global justice and climate change. He is co-author of *Disorder and the Disinformation Society* and co-editor of *Crisis, Movement, Management: Globalising Dynamics* (both forthcoming with Routledge). He has edited several books on the politics of globalization, including *Nationalism and Global Solidarities: Alternative Projections to Neoliberal Globalisation* (Routledge, 2007); *Nature's Revenge: Reclaiming Sustainability in an Age of Corporate Globalism* (Broadview, 2006); *Protest and Globalisation: Prospects for Transnational Solidarity* (Pluto, 2002); *Moving Mountains: Communities Confront Mining and Globalisation* (Zed, 2002); and *Stopping a Juggernaut: Public Interests versus the Multilateral Agreement on Investment* (Pluto, 2001).

Erin K. Wilson is the Director of the Centre for Religion, Conflict and the Public Domain, Faculty of Theology and Religious Studies, University of Groningen, the Netherlands. She has previously worked in the Globalism Research Centre, RMIT University, Melbourne, Australia, and received her PhD from the University of Queensland in 2008. Her research focuses on the relationship of religion with various dimensions of politics and public life, including globalization, political ideologies, migration, global justice, human rights, and the post-secular turn. Her first book, *After Secularism: Rethinking Religion in Global Politics*, was published by Palgrave Macmillan in 2012.

ACKNOWLEDGEMENTS

This book represents the culmination of a three-year research project conducted jointly at RMIT University, Melbourne and the University of Technology, Sydney. The research was funded by a 2009 Discovery Grant awarded by the Australian Research Council (ARC). The authors first and foremost wish to gratefully acknowledge the support of the ARC.

The success of the project depended crucially on those who provided translation and transcription of interviews and texts for analysis. We would particularly like to thank Louise Byrne, Kevin Wood, Marc Storms, and Geoffroy Laptes for their assistance in this area. Our special thanks go to Stefan Siebel, who worked as a research assistant on the project. His assistance with the data analysis, in particular the quantitative data, was invaluable. We also extend our sincere thanks to Dr Andy Scerri, who assisted us with conducting interviews during the 2011 World Social Forum. Professor Heikki Patomäki played an important role in shaping the project in the early stages. We thank him for his insights.

A key aspect of the development of this book was the debate and discussion of the findings of our research with other academic colleagues and practitioners from government, non-government, and private sectors. We are grateful to all the participants in the policy workshop on 1 July 2011 for their insights and feedback that have helped to shape the contents of this book.

James and Erin would like to thank participants of a panel at the 2012 International Studies Association Annual Convention where the policy aspects of the second half of this book were discussed. Manfred would like to thank the Global Studies Association for inviting him to their 2012 annual conference to present on the core concepts and claims of justice globalism, drawing on this book.

Portions of Chapters 1, 2, and 3 appeared as part of an article published in *International Studies Quarterly* in 2012. Permission to reprint that material here is granted by John Wiley and Sons publishers. Manfred and Erin thank the reviewers and editors of *International Studies Quarterly* for their insights. They would also like to acknowledge the support of colleagues in the Globalism Research Centre and the Global Cities Research Institute at RMIT.

James would like to thank the UTS Social and Political Change Group and the Research Centre for Cosmopolitan Civil Societies, also at UTS, for ongoing support for research into social movement and global politics, much of which underpins his contribution to this book.

Table 5.1 – A fate worse than debt – originally appeared in Manfred Steger's (2009) *Globalization: A Very Short Introduction*. Permission to reprint the table is granted by Oxford University Press.

Figure 7.1 – The South's Dilemma – originally appeared in EcoEquity (2008) *The Right to Development in a Climate Constrained World: the Greenhouse Development Rights Framework*. Permission to reprint the figure here is granted by EcoEquity.

1

JUSTICE GLOBALISM AND GLOBAL CRISES

The Problematic

The breakdown of the Cold War order organized around the opposing ideological poles of capitalist liberalism versus state-controlled communism and the ensuing wave of globalization have unsettled conventional political belief systems. Across political, economic, and cultural dimensions, the expansion and intensification of social relations across world-space and world-time both generate and respond to new 'global crises' beyond the reach of conventional political institutions and their associated ideologies. These new challenges include worldwide financial volatility, climate change and environmental degradation, increasing food scarcity, pandemics such as AIDS, SARS, and H1N1, widening disparities in wealth and wellbeing, increasing migratory pressures, manifold cultural and religious conflicts, and transnational terrorism. Intrinsically connected to these complex global problems, we have witnessed a noticeable shift away from state-based international governance mechanisms to transnational networks, NGOs, and non-state actors often referred to as 'global civil society'. The current transformation of nation-centered political ideologies is part and parcel of these powerful globalization dynamics.

However, much-needed assessments of the current makeover of the ideo-logical landscape have been largely confined to what has been variously referred to as 'neoliberalism', 'globalization-from-above', 'market globalism', and the 'Washington Consensus' (Falk 1999; Rupert 2000; Barber 2001; Stiglitz 2003; Mittelman 2004; Harvey 2005; Schwartzmantel 2008; Steger 2009). To some extent, this research focus makes sense. After all, market globalism has remained the most dominant global political ideology in spite of the serious challenges posed by the global financial crisis and the EU debt crisis. The chief codifiers of market globalism have been transnationally networked elites, most of whom are frequent attendants of the annual meeting of the World Economic Forum (WEF) in Davos, Switzerland. These include corporate managers, executives of large transnational corporations, corporate lobbyists, high-level military officers, journalists and public relations specialists, and prominent intellectuals writing to large audiences, high-level civil servants, and politicians. Confining the meaning of their core concept 'globalization' to the allegedly 'inexorable' formation of a single global market, these power elites assert that, notwithstanding the 'cyclical downturns' of the world economy, the global integration of markets is a fundamentally 'good' thing for it represents the 'natural' progression of (Western) modernity.

Drawing on the economic doctrine internationally known as 'neoliberalism', market globalists argue that state interference with the global economy should be minimal, confining itself to providing the legal framework for contracts, defense, and law and order. Public-policy initiatives should be limited to measures that liberate the economy from social constraints: privatization of public enterprises, deregulation instead of state control, liberalization of trade and industry, massive tax cuts, strict control of organized labor, and the reduction of public expenditures. State-regulated models of economic organization are discredited as 'protectionist' or 'socialist'. Ultimately, market globalists seek to enshrine economic neoliberalism as the self-evident and universal doctrine of our global era by claiming that the liberalization of trade and the global integration of markets will 'inevitably' lead to rising living standards and the reduction of global poverty. Enhancing economic efficiency and expanding individual freedom and democracy, market globalism is said to usher in a global age of prosperity and unprecedented technological progress.[1]

Despite its hegemonic status as the dominant ideology of our time, market globalism has been challenged by new global movements on the political Left, which project alternative visions of a global future based on values of 'social justice' and 'solidarity with the global South'. For more than a decade, this 'global justice movement' (GJM) has demonstrated its popular appeal on the streets of major cities around the world. Yet, prominent market globalists – and even some influential reformists like Joseph Stiglitz – have dismissed the GJM as unreflectively 'anti-globalization'. They allege that its agenda amounts to little more than a superficial shopping list of complaints devoid of conceptual coherence and a unifying policy framework capable of responding to the global challenges of the 21st century (Friedman 2000, 2005; Stiglitz 2003; Wolf 2004; Bhagwati 2004; Greenwald and Kahn 2009). Testing the validity of these highly influential allegations, this book undertakes as the *first* of its two principal research objectives a thorough examination of the under-researched *ideological* framework of the GJM – an ideational constellation we call 'justice globalism'. Indeed, this study engages in the first in-depth mapping and analysis of core ideological concepts and claims that span across a wide range of actors connected to the GJM.

The Evolution of the Global Justice Movement

As far back as 1994, Zapatista rebels in Southern Mexico called for the creation of a worldwide network of resistance to neoliberalism. In the following decade, a number of events served as additional catalysts for the emergence of the GJM: the 1997–98 Asian Financial Crisis, the mass strikes in France in 1995 and 1998, the debt crisis in the global South, the growing power of the World Trade Organization (WTO) and other international economic institutions based in the North, and the US-led 'global war on terror', following the al-Qaeda attacks of 11 September 2001. Since then, progressive thinkers and activists have gradually developed and articulated ideological claims that connect local and global issues. This expanding 'network of networks' demonstrated its popular appeal on the streets of cities around the globe where the WTO, the International Monetary Fund (IMF), and other key institutions of global capitalism held strategic meetings. Although market globalists quickly branded the movement as 'anti-globalization', most organizations emphasized that they were actually 'alter-globalization' – in the sense that they envisioned alternatives to corporate-led globalization. Rallying around the slogan 'Another World is Possible', the 'anti-globalization movement' gradually came to be known as the 'global justice movement'.

Progressive academics and activists tracing these new social movement developments posited the emergence of a 'new cosmopolitanism' anchored in 'the worthy ideals of justice and equality' as well as solidarity with people in the disadvantaged global South (Held 1995; Nussbaum 1996: 4). These scholars also identified what Sidney Tarrow (2005) would later call 'global framing' – the act of connecting local problems to broader contexts of global injustice, inequality, and unsustainability (Bello 1999; Klein 2000; George 2004). However, despite the continuing attention from these social movements scholars (Tarrow 2005; Della Porta (ed.) 2007; Smith et al. 2007; Moghadam 2008; Cumbers and Cumbers 2009; Pleyers 2010), the GJM has escaped close academic scrutiny with regard to its ideological structures and its role in generating policy alternatives.

As noted above, our first research objective is to fill the vacuum of scholarship on the ideological dimensions of the GJM by mapping and analyzing its core political ideas and claims. The relevance of this research effort seems to be even more obvious in the second decade of the 21st century when, after a temporary setback caused by the attacks of 11 September 2001, the combined forces of justice globalism have gathered political strength. This has been evident not only in the massive demonstrations against bank bail-outs during the global financial crisis, the global impact of WikiLeaks and its radical 'informationism', but also in the worldwide proliferation of the 'Occupy Wall Street' network.

One ideational inspiration of this new wave of global justice activism can be found in informal global forums such as the World Social Forum (WSF), a key ideological site of the GJM. To this day, the WSF still draws to its annual meetings tens of thousands of delegates from around the world. These proponents of justice globalism established the WSF in the global South as a 'parallel forum' to the influential WEF in the global North. Similar to market globalists who treat the WEF as a platform to project their ideas and values to a global audience, justice globalists have utilized the WSF as one of the chief sites for developing their ideological vision and policy alternatives. The abiding relevance of such massive informal 'think tanks' reinforces not only the increasingly globalized nature of political contestation but also underlines the academic imperative to move beyond the conventional research focus on state-based political actors.

The Significance of Ideology

Political ideologies are comprehensive belief systems comprised of patterned ideas and values believed to be 'true' by significant social groups (Freeden 1996; Schwartzmantel 2008; Steger 2009; Sargent 2009). Codified by political elites who contend over control of political meanings and offer competing plans for public policy, ideologies play a key role in consolidating social forces as political groups. The perpetual struggle over meaning and control places ideologies at the heart of the political process. Consequently, scholars have highlighted the importance of the comparative and transdisciplinary study of ideologies (Zizek 1994; Ball and Dagger 2008). For many years, the pioneers of ideology studies have used various qualitative methodologies to analyze and evaluate the historical evolution and conceptual structures of political belief systems. Their efforts have yielded familiar ideal-types: liberalism, conservatism, socialism, anarchism, communism, and fascism/Nazism. Ideology is often viewed as a tool of power, and certainly all ideologies engage in simplifications and distortions, but their functions should not be reduced to such a 'critical conception' (Thompson 1990). A more 'neutral conception' would also affirm their constructive and integrative functions as indispensable shared mental maps that help people navigate the complexity of their political environments (Mannheim 1936; Althusser 1969; Gramsci 1971; Ricoeur 1986; Freeden 1996; Steger 2008).

During the last two decades, political and social theorists have researched the impact of globalization on existing ideational systems, arguing that the contemporary transformation of conventional ideologies is linked to the rise of a new social imaginary that casts the world as a single, interdependent place (Robertson 1992; Albrow 1996; Appadurai 1996; Giddens 2000; Sassen 2006; Steger 2008). Like all social imaginaries, the rising global imaginary fosters implicit background understandings enabling common practices and identities (Taylor 2004) as well as providing common background understandings for our daily routines (Bourdieu 1990). But the thickening consciousness of the world as a single, interdependent place neither implies the impending 'death of the nation-state' (Ohmae 1995; Guehenno 1995) nor suggests the disappearance of localisms and tribalisms (James 2006). As we emphasized above, the local, national, and regional persist in hybrid symbolic markers, identities, and socio-political systems, but these are increasingly reconfigured and recoded around the global.

Political ideologies translate the largely prereflexive social imaginary – and their associated social forces – into concrete political agendas. Conventional political ideologies have been predominantly linked to national imaginaries, such as Italian fascism, American liberalism, Russian 'socialism in one country', 'communism with Chinese characteristics', 'Swedish democratic socialism', and so on (Anderson 1991; Steger 2008). Since the late 20th century, however, political ideologies have been articulating the emerging *global* imaginary into political programs. Variants of political Islamism, ecologism, and transnational feminism are obvious examples of how the rising global imaginary has provided a novel frame of reference that increasingly destabilizes nationally based ideologies and introduces new ideational formations assembled around the global.

This unsettling dynamic is reflected in a remarkable proliferation of qualifying prefixes adorning conventional 'isms': *neo*-liberalism, *neo*-conservatism, *neo*-fascism, *neo*-Marxism, *post*-Marxism, *post*-modernism, and so on. These semantic add-ons point to the growing public awareness that something 'new' is pushing conventional worldviews 'post' their traditional meanings and categories. An underlying force generating such novelty, we argue, is globalization manifesting itself subjectively in the form of a rising global imaginary – a globalizing reflexivity – and its associated ideological articulations. Conditioning the norms and interests of actors, competing globalisms both shape and are constituted by the contemporary global order and its many fissures. However, rather than adding prefixes to conventional political ideologies rooted in the national imaginary, globalization researchers need to develop new typologies of political ideologies that more adequately recognize an important source of their ideational novelty. A central factor in this process is the increasing prominence of the *global* in contemporary political belief systems.

Recent attempts to sketch the conceptual structures of today's political belief systems have so far focused on market globalism, and, since 9/11, religious globalisms like political Islamism (Kepel 2004; Karam (ed.) 2004; Mandaville 2007). As we noted, the considerable lack of research on justice globalism has fueled confusion and speculation over the main claims, objectives, and policy alternatives of the GJM. Previous conceptual mapping exercises have been carried out chiefly to track organizational flows and processes, the geography of global civil society, and the intricacies of North–South relations (Rupert 2000; Bleiker 2000; Carroll 2007). General forays into the ideational composition of justice globalism can be found in the burgeoning literature on new global justice movements (Tarrow 2005; Della Porta et al. 2006; McDonald 2006; Pleyers 2010). But even in these very useful studies, the focus is more on 'issue framing' than on the analysis and evaluation of politically potent ideas and claims, leading one observer to describe ideology as the neglected 'orphan' of social movement theory (Buechler 2000).

One possible explanation for this neglect of ideology within social movement theory may be the long shadow cast by the 'end of ideology' debates. Erupting in Europe and the United States in the late 1950s (Waxman (ed.) 1968), the first wave of these debates postulated the exhaustion of both Marxist socialism and classical liberalism. Proponents argued that modern political belief systems were rapidly displaced by a non-ideological pragmatism associated with the Keynesian welfare state. A side effect of this argument was that the already pejorative concept of 'ideology' accumulated further negative connotations. Professionals working in areas of policy development and provision viewed ideology with suspicion and skepticism, a view that continues to be held even by members of the GJM (Wilson 2009a, 2009f, 2009i; Steger 2011a).[2]

After the upsurge of ideological politics and cultural protest in the 1960s and 1970s discredited the end of ideology thesis, it was unexpectedly resurrected with the 1989 collapse of communism. A number of influential scholars argued that the passing of Marxism-Leninism marked the disappearance of viable ideological alternatives to capitalist liberalism from the stage of world history, which signified the unabashed victory of an increasingly information and communication technology-driven liberal capitalism (Fukuyama 1989, 1992; Furet 2000). However, the emergence of the GJM and the significance of globalized Islam have once again cast severe doubt on the validity of this thesis.

As we noted earlier, a globally articulated political ideology of the Left centered on 'social justice' and 'solidarity with the global South' emerged forcefully during the 1990s in response to market globalism's unfulfilled promises (Steger 2008: 197; Wilson 2009b, 2009c). But rather than looking for new ways of folding social justice issues back into nationally-based political ideologies, many GJM activists sought to link their normative commitments to concrete policy alternatives capable of tackling the global problems of our age. The universalist claims of market globalism, and the global crises they create, have required a dramatic rescaling and transformation of justice questions. The GJM has responded, as we shall see, with an insistence on multiplicity against the singularity of market globalism, framed by a distinctly global set of alternative values and claims. Our assessment of the connection between ideology and policy initiatives related to global crises constitutes the second principal research objective of this study.

Research Questions and Book Structure

Taking the WSF as our primary research focus, Chapters 2 and 3 draw on relevant data and textual evidence from 45 organizations linked to the WSF as well as 24 semi-structured interviews conducted with representatives from 22 of these organizations.[3] After mapping the core ideological concepts and claims of the GJM, we offer an analysis of the political ideological structure that underpins the global justice movement. Here are our central research questions:

- Does the GJM possess a coherent political ideology?
- If so, what is the conceptual structure of that ideology?
- In particular, what are the core ideas, key values, and claims (decontestation chains) that make up justice globalism?

As we discuss in more detail in the methodology section below, we also ascertain the extent to which these concepts and claims are distinct from other ideologies. The determination of ideological uniqueness allows us to assess whether justice globalism should be considered a maturing political ideology that offers clear conceptual alternatives for collective political action.

In Chapter 4, we examine how organizations strategically operationalize ideological values and claims into policy proposals emanating from the GJM. In particular, we consider the extent to which these policy alternatives reflect the core concepts and claims of justice globalism, the points of rupture (incoherence) between justice globalism's ideological structure and its apparent policy preferences, alongside continuity and dissonance that exists at the policy level within the GJM. We explore the process of generating alternatives – the process of responsiveness – and how it produces proposals that address global crises. In the final three chapters centered on responses to global crises, we then ask the following questions:

- How has the GJM sought to translate values into policy proposals?
- What programmatic frameworks have been put forward and how can such alternative policies be implemented?
- Are these policy proposals and action programs consistent with the espoused ideological commitments of the GJM?

Thus, we outline how the GJM brings its values to bear, through its strategic engagement with the social field. Engagement across the values and claims of global justice groups is documented, to demonstrate strategic engagement against emergent power structures. In Chapters 5–7, we pursue these policy-oriented questions through an examination of the GJM's responsiveness to three major global crises of our time: the 2008–09 global financial crisis; the crisis of food production and distribution (from 2008 onwards); and the ongoing crisis of climate change linked to global energy supply. We explore the emergence of each of these crises, the mainstream neoliberal political and economic responses, and the alternative interpretations and responses offered by major GJM organizations connected to the WSF.

Throughout the book, we elaborate on our broader argument that political ideologies are no longer purely nationally focused, but increasingly articulate a rising global imaginary (Steger 2008). We want to understand if and how justice globalism articulates the underlying social imaginary in global context. We are also interested in how major geographical scales (local/national/regional/global) are situated and represented within justice globalism.

Finally, in addition to mapping the ideology and policy alternatives of the GJM, our research efforts are intended to contribute to the important process of self-clarification within the movement. In our interviews, members of the GJM frequently expressed their desire to find out whether there exists a significant ideological overlap among the organizations linked to the WSF. Moreover, there is now a widespread acknowledgement across the GJM that it cannot confine itself to pointing out the shortcomings of neoliberal measures but must offer constructive policy alternatives. This perspective is very clearly expressed by Focus on the Global South as follows:

> Focus on the Global South ... search policy analysis, organizing, conferencing, networking, even joining mobilizations, publications, ... in pursuit of our ideal, ... *to come up with viable alternatives to the kind of world that we have right now.* Of course that's the strategic aim, but a big part of the work that we are doing at the moment – that we have been doing – is exposing and explaining what is wrong with the present dispensation. This is the deconstruction part of our work or the resistance part of our work. But *the strategic aim really is the reconstruction of an alternative path.* (Wilson 2009e, emphasis added)

Additional Themes

We interweave four additional themes with our key focus on ideology and policy. The first theme relates to the question of geographic scales at which both the political ideology and the policy proposals of the GJM are targeted – the local, regional, national, or global. But we refrain from analyzing justice globalism according to such rigid geographical scales that suggest the separation of the 'global' from the 'national' or 'local'. Leading global studies scholars like Saskia Sassen (2001, 2006) have long argued that with the intensification of globalization dynamics and the related rise of global cities in the late 20th century, these spatial scales should no longer be conceived of as vertically nested hierarchies, but as overlapping horizontal spaces.

The significance of Sassen's work for this project lies in producing a theoretically sophisticated and empirically sound analysis of how these spatial scales interpenetrate each other on both the ideational and policy levels. For example, it is important to note that the main focus of the GJM's policy proposals is democratic participation of a vast majority of populations and a shifting of power

from corporations and governments to local communities, regional organizations, and development banks and national cooperatives. As such, the policies
form part of a global agenda that is usually implemented and enacted on all
levels simultaneously, which, in turn, amplifies the mutual interpenetration of
geographical scales, a phenomenon referred to as 'multiscalarity' (Steger 2005).
Thus, the spatial dynamics involving the GJM should be characterized as a
'global-local nexus' constituted by the intermingling of the local, national,
regional, and the global.

A second additional theme in this book relates to the firmly entrenched conceptual binary of singularity versus multiplicity. Given the rather monolithic
conceptual framework of market globalism centered on the ideal of the 'free
market', it seems sensible to expect that its ideological challengers also need to
put forward a similar singular vision and set of proposals in order for these to
be seen as 'legitimate', 'feasible', and 'viable'. Yet, there exist alternative models
of conceptualizing coherence based on the common acceptance of multiplicity
and diversity. Here, the 'carnival of resistance' is a deliberate exercise, a dialogue for transformation, defined against the singularity and authoritarianism
it opposes. In short, coherence and unity in social movements can be predicated
upon a common embrace of difference as much as it might arise from privileging singularity. At the same time, however, social movements like the GJM face
the political challenge of articulating multiplicity in the form of clear normative
principles and social demands.

The popularized WSF slogan, 'Another World is Possible' – the irresistible
desire for a 'world where many worlds fit' – suggests that many members of
the GJM are aware of this crucial political challenge. Insisting that the dominant model of market globalization is not the only one, they envision alternative forms of globalization rooted in diversity and difference that incorporate
more transparent and participatory models of decision-making, as the following quotes from the World Council of Churches (WCC) and OneWorld representatives demonstrate:

> In terms of globalization, it is about alternative globalization. We have a new earth
> community developing that is so wired to each other that things happen fast, and
> that's exciting. It could also go crazy, but so far it is really helping the develop-
> ment of global movements. And of course we are part of that. I think we wouldn't
> have had something as successful as the World Social Forum without electronic
> communication ... But most of all it really is about emphasizing the need for a new
> paradigm of economic development, which is fair, compassionate, wealth. So this
> is now policy ... and what patterns, good governance, diversity, vitality, all those
> good things. (Wilson 2009h)

> It is a profoundly different paradigm. The word ideology often has a negative ideol-
> ogy. And I think ideologies become fixed very quickly, and everyone has to follow
> the doctrine, and it becomes very dogmatic. The whole point of this [new paradigm]
> is that it is not dogmatic. It is about inviting in different voices, with different points
> of view, and diversity. (Wilson 2009f)

It is important to note that the GJM leaders cited above do not argue that there exists only one alternative. Their valorization of diversity includes the recognition that 'one-size-does-*not*-fit-all'. Globally networked communities will need to develop their own responses to global problems and crises. On the surface this seems to present a fundamental contradiction – how can an ideology be *global* yet be promoting diverse, specific solutions to local problems, national and regional sovereignty and autonomy? Resistance to singularity produces a world of multitudes – no singular multitude – presenting a deepening praxis to be pursued. We explore this paradox in greater depth throughout the ensuing chapters.

The singularity-multiplicity binary relates closely to a third theme raised in this study – the contrast between bottom-up and top-down modes of operating. As we shall see, justice globalists actively promote the values of transparency, dialogue, and openness while resisting secrecy, authoritarianism, and the impulse to push for closure on policy initiatives. Recently, this emphasis on transparency within the GJM has been on global display in the war on secrecy waged by WikiLeaks and similar cyberspace-based groups committed to what they call 'informationism' (Sifry 2011; Leigh and Harding 2011). This commitment marks a significant difference between the practices and methods employed by justice globalists and those of market globalists. The GJM openly embraces dialogical, bottom-up modes of operating, while market globalism's expressed sympathies for 'democracy' seem to coexist rather comfortably with a preference for top-down decisions made in closed-door meetings.

The fourth theme addresses the centrality of socioeconomic discourse in the GJM. As we will discuss, this is a surprising finding given the fact that many of the examined organizations consider themselves primarily as cultural organizations. Yet, GJM members often speak in a decidedly socioeconomic tongue rather than use language that would correspond more closely to their central cultural concerns. While our quantitative data establishes that issues related to racism, sexism, and indigenous rights are clearly eclipsed by keywords related to social and economic issues such as rights, trade, and economy, our qualitative analysis offers an explanation for why the GJM, on the whole, has focused on the socioeconomic discourse of market globalism. Finally, our analysis also establishes that the socioeconomic idiom is gradually shifting in a socioecological direction, with profound consequences for how political community is understood. This has occurred not merely within the GJM but, more broadly, within a global public discourse increasingly focused on the social, environmental, and health impacts of disasters such as the 2011 earthquake in Japan and the ensuing meltdown of the nuclear reactors in Fukushima.

In this context we are confronted with the magnitude (and asserted magnificence) of the natural world, which can so dramatically re-position the meanings of consumer capitalism. The reality of embeddedness, and of the global linkages that shape our existence, is reflected in the following quote from the OneWorld representative comparing economic problems with natural disasters impacting vast regions of our planet:

> The economic crisis is small beer; it's really small beer. It's a first sign, it's a bit like you sneeze once but that's not the cold. The [2006 Christmas] tsunami is another sneeze, but that's not the cold. And that's one of the things that really upset me a lot. The tsunami made people wake up a lot, even though it wasn't in one sense about climate change. (Wilson 2009f)

Methodological Issues

This study utilizes morphological discourse analysis (MDA) to map and critically evaluate the core ideological structure of justice globalism. This methodological approach was introduced by Freeden (1996; 2003) and later refined by Steger (2002; 2009). As noted, language is critical to how ideologies distort, legitimate, integrate, and, most importantly, 'decontest' their core values and claims. Successfully decontested ideas are held as truth by large segments of a given population with such confidence that they no longer appear to be assumptions at all. Freeden (2003: 54–5 emphasis in original) explains 'decontestation' in the following way:

> An ideology attempts to end the inevitable contention over concepts by *decontesting* them, by removing their meanings from contest. 'This is what justice means', announces one ideology, and 'that is what democracy entails'. By trying to convince us that they are right and that they speak the truth, ideologies become devices for coping with the indeterminacy of meaning ... . That is their semantic role. [But] [i]deologies also need to decontest the concepts they use because they are instruments for fashioning collective decisions. That is their political role.

Ideological morphologies can thus be pictured as decontested truth-claims that facilitate collective decision-making. Their interlinked semantic and political roles suggest that control over language translates directly into political and social power. Consequently, any analysis that attempts to identify, map, and critically evaluate core ideological claims must focus on the use of language. Ultimately, these claims give each ideology its unique conceptual configuration or 'morphology'.

Morphological discourse analysis is a qualitative method for a contextually sensitive mapping and assessing of the structural arrangements of political ideologies (in terms of core claims) that attribute meanings to a range of mutually defining political concepts. The key difference between Freeden's methodology and that developed and applied by Steger (2002, 2009) concerns the proper conceptualization of basic ideological units that carry meanings. Unlike Freeden, who disaggregates ideational systems into relatively static elements according to levels of decreasing contestation (from 'core concepts' to 'adjacent concepts' to 'periphery concepts'), we evaluate the ideological status of justice globalism on the basis of its ability to arrange concepts of roughly equal significance into meaningful 'decontestation chains' or 'central ideological claims'. This adjustment better captures the dynamic and changeable character of ideational systems as well as the contested and evolving process of concept formation and contextual responsiveness (Steger 2009). For this study, we have made additional methodological innovations by complementing the qualitative analysis with a quantitative word frequency count and in-depth semi-structured interviews with senior representatives from our sample organizations.

But what criteria should be used to distinguish a conceptually thin and rather incoherent ideational cluster from a coherent and mature political ideology? Following Michael Freeden (1996: 485–6), we argue that maturity of ideologies should be assessed according to three cardinal criteria: (a) their degree of *distinctiveness*; (b) their context-bound *responsiveness* to a broad range of political issues; and (c) their ability to produce *effective conceptual decontestations*. Thus, the ability of justice globalism to distinguish itself from other ideologies through distinct core concepts and core claims, respond to a broad range of political issues (such as, in our case, global climate change, the global financial crisis, or the global food crisis), and its ability to present decontested explanations of the current global context provide evidence for whether justice globalism may be considered a mature (and thus coherent) political ideology.

This book assesses the political ideology and practice of the global justice movement using these three criteria as a guide. If the ultimate test of any ideology is its responsiveness to concrete political problems and its capacity to offer meaningful answers to these problems, then our analysis has to address the dynamics of creative transformation. An assessment of the policy capacity of justice globalism to produce alternatives thus provides the main focus of Chapters 5 to 7 of this book. Indeed, the conceptual mapping accomplished in the first three chapters offers an evaluative framework for various types of political action under contemporary globalization (Goodman (ed.) 2002, 2006). Never before have the policy proposals of justice globalists been systematically and holistically assessed and situated within their corresponding ideological framework. Rare attempts to assemble the policy proposals of the GJM have been conducted mainly to investigate dynamics of transnational networks, rather than to address ideological coherence (Reitan 2007). Our study represents an encompassing attempt to evaluate the range of GJM policy positions set against its overarching ideological architecture. Moreover, our evaluative synthesis has been grounded and verified with a select range of in-depth investigations into the emergence, relevance, and effectiveness of key policy proposals emerging from the GJM in response to global crises. Ultimately, this book thus tests the successful translation of ideological claims into policy analysis and institutional contexts. Such forays into the theory–practice connection are especially significant with regard to the hotly debated issue of alternative forms of global governance (Goodman (ed.) 2002, 2006; Goodman and Ranald (eds) 2000).

Why the WSF?

It is important to emphasize that this study is not concerned with the WSF as such but with its constituent organizations that are part of the GJM. The WSF was chosen as a key site of the GJM for a number of reasons. Although there may be disagreements over the future significance of the WSF, there is virtual unanimous agreement in the authoritative literature on the importance of the WSF as the intellectual and organizational epicenter of the GJM in the first decade of the 21st century (Conway 2004; Patomäki and Teivainen 2004a, 2004b; Sen et al. 2005; Della Porta (ed.) 2007; Smith et al. 2007). Supported by influential organizations within these global justice networks, such as the Transnational Institute and Focus on the Global South, the first WSF meeting was held in January 2001, in Porto Alegre, Brazil. It attracted 5000 participants from 117 countries and thousands of Brazilian activists. Attendance at subsequent meetings skyrocketed, reaching over 100,000 participants in 2003. Since then, the WSF has met in Mumbai, Nairobi, Porto Alegre (again), and Dakar, Senegal in 2011. Around the globe, numerous regional, national, and local 'social forums' have also taken place.

Secondly, the WSF constitutes the largest and most diverse organizational umbrella of the GJM. While other large global justice networks exist (for example, the International Confederation of Free Trade Unions, the Amsterdam-based Transnational Institute, or Friends of the Earth International), these organizations are focused on particular sector concerns. The WSF brings together a vast diversity of social sectors, spanning North and South, crossing a range of linguistic divides. The WSF is also politically diverse: unlike other global justice formations (such as People's Global Action), it draws together a broad range of political orientations and tendencies. Although much of the WSF's membership is in Latin America, Europe, and North America, there is also significant involvement from African and Asian groups. Indeed, no other global justice coalition comes close to the WSF's geographical, ethnic and linguistic reach and diversity.

Thirdly, unlike other large global justice coalitions, the WSF was consciously established as an ideational alternative to the market-globalist World Economic Forum (WEF). Designed as an 'open meeting place' (as stated in the first clause in its Charter of Principles (WSF 2002), the WSF was intended to encourage and facilitate a free exchange of ideas among justice globalists. As the representative from Associazione Ricreativa Culturale Italiana (ARCI) expressed it, 'The WSF ... offers itself more as a common ground, an open forum for common research. So it's more the idea of a big laboratory, and the place of convergence, and the meeting of different cultures, that can together look and try to define a possible global alternative in terms of policies' (Steger 2011a). Hence one would expect to find a particularly rich source of ideological materials among its membership. Moreover, there has been an animated debate within the GJM as to whether the WSF should remain an open meeting place or become a political action-oriented 'movement of movements' (Keraghel and Sen 2004; Patomäki and Teivainen 2004b; Funke 2008). While the WSF played a critical role in mobilizing at the grassroots level and educating communities and individuals on issues that are generally hard to communicate, some activists have argued that it did not go far enough in engaging with and utilizing dominant political forces for social change. As a result, some affiliated organizations, such as the Global Progressive Forum (GPF), contemplate developing their own alternative politically focused forums and political parties outside the WSF (Wilson 2009c).

Why these Organizations?

Our sample includes 45 out of the over 150 organizations affiliated with the WSF (see Table 1.1). We specifically selected 20 organizations because of their membership in the WSF International Council's Liaison group, which indicates their high level of involvement and commitment to the Forum. The remaining 25 organizations were randomly selected from the list of groups affiliated with the WSF International Council displayed on the WSF website (WSF n.d.). As far as was possible, we endeavored to obtain a broad geographic and linguistic spectrum within the organizations selected. Thus, we were able to gather a snap-shot of the GJM in its various local, national and regional iterations that reflects the views of justice globalists from both global North and South.[4]

We conducted background research on each organization through examination of their websites and publications. Three representative texts from each organi-zation were chosen and subjected to morphological discourse analysis. These included the website – chiefly the organization's homepage and sections related to the history and identity of the organization – a press release, and a public statement or declaration. These documents were also used as sources of data for the analysis of policy proposals although we made sure to add longer and more detailed publications that focused on specific policy issues. We provide additional detail regarding data in subsequent chapters.

In addition to the wealth of textual data that has been collected for this project, the three authors of this study – plus two research assistants – interviewed 24 leading members of 22 organizations. These individuals expressed their deep commitment to the pursuit of a more just world – or, more accurately, their ideal of a more just world – while also displaying critical awareness of shortcomings of the WSF and the GJM at various stages of their development and across a broad range of issues. The insights gained from these interviews provided us with a plethora of 'insider' perspectives on the GJM, its history, and its future.

Our selected organizations provide a representative snapshot of the diversity of issues, organizations, *modus operandi*, and geographic locations that make up the membership of the GJM. The groups we sampled included international, regional, and national trade union confederations, which were particularly concerned with how the global finance and climate crises impact on jobs amongst their members, and agitate for proactive innovation on these issues, particularly climate change.[5] A further important insight is that some of the trade unions see themselves as both part of and distinct from other groups in the GJM (Wilson 2011).

Other organizations sampled included cultural and religious organizations, which focus on a broad array of issues, with a particular concern for the recognition of economic, social, and cultural rights.[6] These groups would highlight the ways in which they believed the richness of the human experience in a number of different areas was slowly being devalued and limited by the influence of neoliberalism around the world. The sample also included a number of networks concerned with communication and democratization of media and access to information, including OneWorld and AIDC. We also included research-centered organizations such as International Forum on Globalization and the Latin American Council for Social Services (CLACSO).

Feminist organizations such as the World March of Women and Articulacion Feminista Marcosur also formed a key part of the sample. Single-issue groups, such as Food First International Action Network (FIAN), Palestinian Grassroots Anti-Apartheid Wall Campaign (PGAAWC), People's Health Movement (PHM), Friends of the Narmada River, Jubilee South, World Fair Trade Organization (WFTO), and Association pour une taxation des transactions financières pour l'aide aux citoyens (ATTAC) were also included. It is important to emphasize that while these organizations focus primarily on one issue – such as global financial reform, the right to food or the right to health – they nonetheless consider how a broad range of global problems has an impact on their respective single-issue areas.

Human rights organizations such as Terre des Hommes (TDH), Federacion International Direitos Humanos (FIDH), and Poor People's Economic Human Rights Campaign (PPEHRC) also formed part of the sample. Several groups concerned particularly with inequalities in trade relationships, such as Third World Network and the Africa Trade Network, were also included. A final category of organizations were multi-issue networks that engaged not only with a broad range of issues, but also focused on research and policy development alongside political advocacy and grassroots activism. As one Transnational Institute (TNI) representative put it, 'It's not a think tank … it's not completely academic; it's not completely activist. It's not a single-issue organization. It has a lot of pieces of the wheel, and there are a lot of interactions' (Wilson 2009i). These groups included Focus on the Global South and TNI, who, along with ATTAC and peasant movements such as La Via Campesina and Movimento dos Trabalhadores Rurais Sem

Terra (MST) (also included in the sample) are especially prominent within the GJM. It is important to note also that a large number of the organizations that are members of the WSF International Council Liaison group are so-called 'representative organizations', which means that they represent a vast number of other member groups. Hence, the popularity of the terms 'association of associations', 'network of networks', or 'movement of movements' (Steger 2011a). Such 'representative organizations' include ARCI, all of our selected trade unions, Hemispheric Social Alliance, Global Progressive Forum, and Jubilee South. Table 1.1 provides a brief description of each organization included in this study.

Table 1.1   Names, Locations and Areas of Focus for 45 Organizations Included in Analysis

Name of Organization	Location	Areas of Concern/Focus
Australian Council of Trade Unions (ACTU)*	Melbourne, Australia	Workers' Rights
Association pour une taxation des transactions financières pour l'aide aux citoyens (Association for the Taxation of Financial Transactions for the Aid of Citizens) (ATTAC)*	Paris, France plus multiple regional offices	Tobin Tax, reform of global financial institutions and infrastructure
American Federation of Labor – Congress of Industrial Organizations (AFL-CIO)	Washington DC, USA	Workers' Rights
Articulacion Feminista Mercosur (Southern Common Market) (AFM)*	Montevideo, Uruguay	Rights of women, indigenous people, and marginalized people
Alternative Information Development Centre (AIDC)	Cape Town, South Africa	Promote social justice through the production and dissemination of alternative knowledge
Associazione Ricreativa Culturale Italiana (Italian Cultural Recreational Association) (ARCI)*	Rome, Italy	Social development organization which uses the arts to promote democracy
Africa Trade Network (ATN)	East Legon, Accra, Ghana	Trade and investment issues in Africa; reform of global financial system
Comissão Brasileira Justiça e Paz (Brazilian Commission/Organization for Justice and Peace) (CBJP)*	Rio de Janeiro, Brazil	Catholic Church initiative promoting research and action on social change, human rights, democracy, and justice
Confédération Européenne des Syndicats/European Trade Union Confederation (CES/ETUC)	Brussels, Belgium	Workers' rights
Coordenadora de Centrais Sindicais do Cone Sur (Coordinator of Trade Unions of the Southern Cone) (CCSCS)	Montevideo, Uruguay	Workers' rights, democracy, human rights, representation of trade unions in economic integration of South America
Consejo Latinoamericano de Ciencias Sociales (Latin American Council of the Social Sciences) (CLACSO)*	Buenos Aires, Argentina	Collaborative research network promoting good governance, equality, and democracy
Canadian Labour Congress (CLC)	Ottawa, Canada	Workers' rights

Name of Organization	Location	Areas of Concern/Focus
Council of Canadians (CoC)	Ottawa, Canada	Protecting Canadian independence in policy areas of trade, clean water, energy security, health care
Corpwatch	San Francisco, California, USA	Human, environmental, and worker rights at the local, national, and global levels; transparency and accountability into global finance and trade
Congress of South African Trade Unions (COSATU)*	Johannesburg, South Africa	Workers' rights, protection of democracy, promoting African development at an international level
Central Trabajadoes Argentina (Argentina Workers' Centre) (CTA)	Buenos Aires, Argentina	Workers' union concerned with international relations, health, migration, disability, human rights, poverty, famine, energy, culture, and youth
Central Unica dos Trabalhadores (Central Workers' Union) (CUT)*	Sao Paulo, Brazil	Workers' rights, equality, and democracy
Environmental and Development Action in the Third World (ENDA)*	Dakar, Senegal	Development in Africa, economy, rights of women and children
Food First International Action Network (FIAN)	Heidelberg, Germany	Promote the right to food, food sovereignty, and food security around the world
Federation Internacional Direitos Humanos (International Federation for Human Rights) (FIDH)	Paris, France	Promote human rights around the world as outlined in international human rights treaties, declarations, and covenants
Focus on the Global South*	Manila, Philippines; Bangkok, Thailand; Delhi, India	Policy research, advocacy, activism, and grassroots capacity building; critique of corporate-led globalization, neo-liberalism, and militarization
Friends of the Narmada River	India and global	Campaign against dam project on Narmada River; rights of indigenous people, environmental degradation; democracy and transparency
General Union of Oil Employees in Basra	Basra, Iraq	Workers' rights; equality between workers and administrators
Grassroots Global Justice (GGJ)	California and Florida, USA	Rights of workers and the poor locally and globally
Global Progressive Forum (GPF)	Brussels, Belgium	Political organization promoting justice, equality, sustainability, rights of workers in policy circles
Hemispheric Social Alliance Alianza Social Continental (ASC/HSA)*	Rio de Janeiro, Brazil	Strengthen civil society, promote rights, especially workers' rights
Institute Brasiliero de Analises Sociais e Economicas (Brazilian Institute for Social and Economic Analysis) (IBASE)*	Rio de Janeiro, Brazil	Promote democracy, active citizenship and economic, social and cultural rights

(Continued)

Table 1.1   (Continued)

Name of Organization	Location	Areas of Concern/Focus
International Forum on Globalization	San Francisco, USA	Think tank providing critique of neoliberal globalization; emphasize developing alternative global trade and commerce that promotes interests of people and environment
Institut Panos Afrique l'Ouest (Panos Institute West Africa) (IPAO)	Dakar, Senegal	Free speech, participatory democracy, active citizenship
Instituto Paulo Freire (IPF)*	Sao Paulo, Brazil	Right to education globally
International Trade Union Confederation (ITUC)*	Brussels, Belgium	Promotion and defense of workers' rights and interests globally
Jubilee South	Manila, Philippines	Debt cancellation, reform of global financial rules and institutions, redistribution of wealth and resources
Korean Confederation of Trade Unions*	Seoul, South Korea	Promote and protect workers' rights; democracy; support reunification of North and South Korea
Movimento dos Trabalhadores Rurais Sem Terra (MST)*	Brazil	Reform of land use; rights of indigenous people and marginalized poor; promote equal access to food, shelter, health care, education, a healthy, sustainable environment, and gender equality
OneWorld	London, UK	Information organization; facilitate networks amongst organizations committed to justice, equality, democracy, action on climate change, poverty, development, and resource distribution
Palestinian Grassroots Anti-Apartheid Wall Campaign (PGAAWC)	Jerusalem	End construction of wall in West Bank; promote global action against imperialism, racism, and human rights abuses. Focus on violations of economic rights of Palestinians
People's Health Movement (PHM)	Cairo, Egypt	Advocacy for provision of public health care and circumstances that enable good health – clean water and sanitation, shelter, electricity, education, and food
Poor People's Economic Human Rights Campaign (PPEHRC)	Minneapolis, USA	Promote access to basic public services such as health care, education, welfare for the homeless and traditionally marginalized in US – African-American and Hispanic communities
Terre des Hommes (TDH)*	Brussels, Belgium and Geneva, Switzerland	Focus on the rights of children globally

Name of Organization	Location	Areas of Concern/Focus
Transnational Institute (TNI)	Amsterdam, The Netherlands	Network of activist-scholars promoting democracy, equality, and environmental sustainability on a global scale
Third World Network (TWN)*	Penang, Malaysia	Non-profit international network focused on needs and rights of peoples in the Third World, fair distribution of resources, and forms of development which are ecologically sustainable and fulfill human needs
Via Campesina*	Jakarta, Indonesia	Promote the rights and entitlements of peasants, landless people, rural women and youth, indigenous people, and agricultural workers around the world
World Council of Churches (WCC)	Geneva, Switzerland	International body representing the Christian ecumenical movement. Focus on rights, poverty, climate change, unequal economic and political relationships
World Fair Trade Organization (WFTO)	Culemborg, The Netherlands	Focus on building relationships of respect, dialogue, and partnership across trade pathways from production to sale; promote sustainable agricultural production practices and investment in social welfare provision
World March of Women (WMW)*	Sao Paulo, Brazil	International feminist action movement; seek to address structural inequalities that keep women oppressed and marginalized through advocating political, economic, and social change

*Member of WSF Liaison group/specifically chosen organization

Justice Globalism Versus Market Globalism

As this book will demonstrate, the GJM critique of market globalism is multi-faceted and addresses a multitude of issues. Before delving into the specifics of the conceptual structure of the GJM in Chapter 2, we outline in general terms three fundamental disagreements between justice globalism and market globalism over processes and meanings of 'globalization', the nature of 'development', and the question of 'power'. Each side has offered opposing definitions and views on these subjects and how they are related. Especially critical to the arguments are conflicting understandings of power – and where power is located or should be located in the emerging global order of the 21st century.

Organizations and individuals belonging to the GJM have long contested the central ideological claims of market globalism (Steger 2009). They have insisted that neoliberal policies have actually increased inequality and disparities in wealth throughout the world. They have suggested that market-driven globalization does *not* benefit everyone (George 1976; Bello 1999). They have pointed to the growing power and influence of Transnational Corporations (TNCs), hedge funds, and financial institutions such as the IMF and the World Bank to argue that, rather than being led by neutral techno-economic forces, globalization is fueled and directed by corporate elites and pro-business governments of the global North whose main goal is the maximization of profits at the expense of the wellbeing of people, communities, and the environment. Members of the GJM have emphasized that globalization should not focus on the liberalization and integration of markets. Instead, they argue for a world founded on a global ethic of planetary co-responsibility towards each and all.

With regard to the nature and purpose of 'development', there has been a clear discursive shift in the pertinent debate from the national to the global arena (McMichael 2004: xviii, 154–7). Codifiers of conventional political ideologies like liberalism or socialism argued over the best model for future growth and stability pertaining to particular national states. Today, market globalists clash with members of the GJM over the best way to manage global resources in the immediate and long term for the benefit of humanity in general. Market globalists hold that economic growth is the central defining feature of development, although they have begun to use the term 'sustainable' alongside their market model to indicate their awareness of serious obstacles in the path of 'development-as-usual'. Still, economic growth has remained their credo along with an emphasis on wealth accumulation, consumption, and ever-rising living standards (Sachs 2005). Once a pattern of strong and consistent growth has been established, neoliberals argue, then countries can begin to focus on 'soft issues' such as adherence to human rights standards, education, health care, and the environment.

The GJM has challenged neoliberal meanings of 'development' based upon the primacy of economic growth. They insist that factors other than economic growth must be taken into consideration when measuring a society's level of 'development' such as democratic participation and equitable patterns of income distribution. Consider the following remarks made by GJM leaders in interviews with the project team:

We … have a critique of the word development, because development is actually something that has progressed in history from civilization to progress, and then came to development, and this was used by the World Bank for the first time in 1949 to mean growth. So from there people talked about then just to qualify development as not just to grow things, it has to be distribution, it has to be people's participation. (Goodman 2010a)

When we say development we talk about the eradication of poverty, we talk about gender development, equality, food security, food sovereignty and these things. (Scerri 2011a)

As discussed in subsequent chapters, the GJM does not simply present an alternative development model, but instead insists on public participation in defining what is meant by global development, encompassing both the North and the South. This reflects what Jan Nederveen Pieterse (1998) calls 'reflexive development' where the movement produces its own critical perspectives, defined against top-down programs for maximizing economic growth in the name of 'lifting people out of poverty'. Through debates within the GJM 'development' is thereby redefined as reflexive in a social and political sense – a *participatory, popular reflexivity*, which takes the form of 'broad social debates and fora on development goals and methods' (Pieterse 1998: 369).

Finally, a key GJM criticism relates to the intensification of asymmetrical power relations on a global scale. Marketization, the argument goes, promises a more open, free, competitive trading system while deepening class divisions. Thus, corporate-driven globalization and its profit-based vision of development actually exacerbate conventional inequalities or power imbalances. In addition, members of the GJM have castigated market globalism as a hierarchical and authoritarian regime, which allows little space for dialogue and negotiation:

> What's difficult with neo-liberalism is that there is no dialogue … . So first there is no longer any dialogue between the governments and the social society … . CUT has been investing a lot in studying the social dialogues, and the social responsibility of the companies. We always try to dialogue. But dialogue is a two-sided thing, it's not only to say 'Yes Sir'. (Steger 2010c)

Complaints about the lack of dialogic space and negotiation are raised at all levels of the GJM and across different geographic locations. Their impression is that decisions are made by political and corporate elites that affect the livelihoods and daily experiences of vast swathes of the global population with little to no discussion about those decisions, the reasons for them, or the possible consequences of them.

Thus, one of the key demands put forward by the GJM has been to permanently alter worldwide power networks spun by global corporate and political elites in the global North. In the last decade, this demand has become even more pressing with regard to top-down decision-making processes in relation to global crises. As part of the condemnation of what they perceive as the opaque, authoritarian, and rigid structures of market globalism, GJM organizations have advocated for the empowerment of individuals and communities generally marginalized from global decision-making processes. Encouraging more participatory and transparent styles of global democratic governance, the GJM has argued that decision-making power should increasingly involve local communities, and indigenous populations, particularly in the global South. This does not mean that GJM organizations claim to 'speak for' or 'represent' indigenous populations and groups. Rather they endeavor to open up space in which these groups can speak for themselves.

Much is known about the core ideas, key values, and central claims that constitute the morphology of market globalism. But the ideological status of the
political vision of justice globalism, connected to the GJM, has not yet been
clearly identified. The next chapter performs this important task.

Notes

1 For a detailed discussion and analysis of market globalism and its central ideological
   claims, see Steger (2009).
2 Interviews have been referenced according to the surname of the interviewer (a member
   of the project team), the year in which the interview was conducted, and then assigned
   a letter indicating their chronological order for that year. For example, Wilson (2009a)
   indicates that the interview was conducted by Wilson in 2009 and was the first interview she conducted that year. Full interview details may be found in the reference list.
3 At the beginning of the research project, the three authors developed a list of 17 questions around the key themes of core ideological concepts, claims and policies. These
   questions were then used as a basic structure for each interview, whilst also allowing
   space for other avenues of enquiry as they arose during the course of the interviews
   themselves.
4 To some extent, this broad snapshot sheds some light on claims of elitism within the
   GJM. Some authors and critics have questioned whether the political views expressed
   by the GJM are actually the views of the people they claim to represent. This is not a
   question which our research engages with directly and as such we are not able to offer
   a definitive comment. The diversity of issues, geographical locations, socio-economic
   and cultural contexts represented by the sample group do suggest that there is a deepening of justice globalism beyond its intellectual elite, permeating grassroots movements in a variety of areas around the world. However, this is an issue that requires
   further investigation, which is presently beyond the scope of this project.
5 The trade union confederations included the International Trade Union Confederation
   (ITUC), European Trade Union Confederation (ETUC), American Federation of Labor
   and Congress of Industrial Organizations (AFL-CIO), Australian Council of Trade Unions
   (ACTU), Canadian Labor Congress (CLC), Congress of South African Trade Union
   (COSATU), Korean Confederation of Trade Unions (KCTU), Central Única dos
   Trabalhadores (CUT), Coordenadora de Centrais Sindicais do Cone Sul (CCSCS), Central
   de Trabajadoes Argentinos (CTA), General Union of the Oil Employees of Basra.
6 For example, the World Council of Churches, ARCI, CBJP, Council of Canadians, IPAO,
   ENDA, and Ibase.

2

JUSTICE GLOBALISM: CORE CONCEPTS

Introduction

In this chapter, we present our analysis of the ideological configuration associated with the GJM. As noted in Chapter 1, this mapping exercise represents a crucial step in the process of assessing the maturity and coherence of an ideational cluster according to three main criteria developed by Michael Freeden (1996: 485–6): its *distinctiveness* in relation to other political ideologies (specifically market globalism); its *context-bound responsiveness* to a broad range of political issues; and its ability to produce *effective conceptual decontestations*. Chapters 2 and 3 of this book directly address Freeden's criteria of the *distinctiveness* and *effective conceptual decontestation* of core concepts and claims. Our policy analyses that follow in Chapters 4 to 7 speak primarily to the *responsiveness* of the GJM's ideological vision to a range of political issues.

Ultimately, our findings presented in this chapter suggest that the main ideas of the GJM project meanings that distinguish them clearly from other political ideologies. This alternative vision of globalization puts the wellbeing of ordinary people around the world above the creation of largely unfettered and globally integrated markets. Disconnecting the meaning of 'development' from neoliberal notions of 'economic growth' and living standards measured purely in material terms, the 45 WSF-affiliated organizations covered in our analysis assemble an ideational arsenal directed against the 'corporate-led' expansion and intensification of asymmetrical power networks across national borders.

We begin this chapter by outlining the main assumptions and theoretical commitments connected to the methodology of morphological discourse analysis (MDA). Next, we provide a detailed discussion of the core concepts drawn from key texts and transcriptions of semi-structured interviews. Our close analysis of these texts reveals that some core concepts of justice globalism – for example, sustainability and transformative change – are unique. Other key ideas such as democracy, justice, and equality seem to be identical to important concepts utilized by (neoliberal) market globalists. However, what makes these overlapping core concepts of justice globalism quite distinct from those of market globalism are their associated meanings – that is, the ways they are understood and applied. For example, justice globalists argue that 'democracy' should be participatory, not merely representative. 'Justice' is understood to be more than a formal procedural justice. It is meant to refer also to social, restorative, and redistributive justice involving generations and communities, not just individuals. 'Equality' is supposed to connote both opportunity and outcome. The existence of such significant differences points to conceptual distinctiveness, thus suggesting the presence of a coherent and mature ideological structure we refer to as 'justice globalism'. Finally, the core concepts identified in this chapter also provide the ideological building blocks utilized by justice globalists to formulate their claims about the global political context – the subject of Chapter 3.

Morphological Discourse Analysis (MDA)

MDA is a form of critical discourse analysis, which requires that analysts engage in close, repeated, and independent readings of selected texts for the purpose of mapping core concepts and central ideological claims. For this research project, we focused on key texts generated by 45 GJM organizations (out of over 150) associated with the WSF. We analyzed these materials by following five sets of guiding questions:

1 What are the core concepts of the organization?
2 How are these concepts used?
3 How is narrative used? What ideological claims are being made?
4 How is metaphor used?
5 What are the main policy proposals of the organization?

These guiding questions were designed to fulfill three main purposes. First, in order to positively identify core concepts, the project team needed to find and interpret key ideas that were used and emphasized repeatedly throughout the texts or were explicitly identified by organizations themselves as central values. Examples of such core concepts included equality, justice, democracy, solidarity, sustainability, rights, and so on. Second, we looked for less prominent recurring values and ideas – 'adjacent concepts' (Freeden 1996) that formed an additional meaning component of core concepts, such as diversity, planetary citizenship, autonomy, transparency, governance, and freedom. Finally, as we discuss in Chapter 3, we examined how core and adjacent concepts get linked together into ideological claims – often in the form of linked metaphors, slogans, narratives, or stories. Such claims constitute 'decontestation chains' – statements and assertions that insist on particular ways of understanding relevant political contexts and environments.

To ensure methodological consistency, the three members of the research team who were trained in MDA analyzed independently four sets of texts (12 texts taken from four different organizations). An additional eleven sets (33 texts taken from 11 different organizations) were independently analyzed by at least two researchers. The findings from each analysis were then compared to ensure consistent application of the methodology. This follows Coe and Domke's (2006) model for ensuring methodological consistency in discourse analysis. A high degree of correlation was found across the analyses, with only occasional minor discrepancies involving, typically, discussions over slightly different wordings of the main claims of an organization. This excellent outcome suggests that MDA methodology was applied consistently, thereby increasing the reliability of the findings.

Three main types of texts were utilized in the morphological discourse analysis:

- websites (including sections that talked about the history, goals, and values of the organization);
- press releases (usually one that related to one of the three major crises selected as case studies for the policy section);
- statements or declarations (related to the financial, food, and/or climate crises).

The website is the main text through which an organization defines and advertises itself and its activities to the world. It is the primary vehicle through which an organization communicates its core values, main goals, and priorities. This makes the website a rich environment for identifying underlying ideological meanings and assumptions that contribute to the identity, aspirations and actions of civil society actors. Press releases and statements were chosen for similar reasons. Both types of texts are relatively short and thus require concise articulation of goals and priorities. Any policy outlines or recommendations in these documents are also likely to be linked tightly with the overarching goals and values of the organization. This again makes press releases and statements key sites for the articulation of ideas and translation of ideology into political practice.

Our emphasis on texts and on language is consistent with previous studies of political ideologies, particularly those of Freeden (1996) and Teun A. van Dijk (1998). Moreover, a number of our interviewees also emphasized the significance of language in their activities linked to the GJM. They recognized that language and discourse are potent social forces capable of contributing to significant political changes. Joy Kennedy, a member of the World Council of Churches, puts it well:

> We must also be about changing the discourse, because when you change the world you change the discourse, you change how people perceive and how they believe. Because if we really believe that we are the all-powerful, we will act that way. If in fact we believe that we are one small part of nature, and that we have roles and responsibilities, and gifts – we have amazing gifts of creativity, of consciousness, of perception – if we use those collectively and engage this marvelous creation. If we do it with humility, and that is one of the other values that we really need to be upholding, it is going to be a very different kind of place ... we are a people of the book, so texts are important to us. (Wilson 2009h)

Paolo Beni, President of ARCI, also emphasized the importance of language. Indeed, one of ARCI's more recent campaigns focused on altering dominant understandings of justice and social equity, encouraging people to reclaim these concepts, to 'give a new sense, a new meaning to words' so that these concepts become more fully realized and more aligned with an alter-globalization worldview (Steger 2011a).

Our analysis presents the core concepts as they occur within the selected texts and interviews as a coherent and decontested set of key ideas. But we need to emphasize that most organizations usually arrived at such settled meanings only in the course of long and sometimes difficult internal discussions about how these concepts and values should be understood and defined. Moreover, the ideological coherence presented in this chapter might not necessarily be the final iteration as many organizations are involved in ongoing processes of meaning formation. Although core concepts acquire a high degree of solidity in order to serve as reliable building blocks of ideological claims, they nonetheless retain a good dose of dynamism and flexibility as GJM activists continue to reflect on these ideas, particularly in the context of their ideological struggle with market globalism. This process of ongoing meaning evolution was obvious even during some interviews when GJM activists engaged consciously with their use of the key terms and sometimes reassessed what they meant and how they understood them:

> I think the notion of justice would be embodied within my understanding of equality ... [the two are] distinct in my mind. You see, I would tend to think of justice as the ideological structure around equality. But I'm not sure now. And justice as the instrument through which equality is attained ... . Obviously there are differences. I think in the climate debate, when you say climate justice, what does it mean? It can't just mean equality. It can't just mean we want an equally polluted world for everybody. It has to refer to basic human values that are fundamental to us being human beings ... so equality and justice are very different in that respect. So you would have to just assume that justice really has a foundation and a basic premise, which relates to the quality of life for everyone, a minimum quality of life for everyone that is human and healthy. (Wilson 2011)

Emerging Core Ideological Concepts

Initially, each analyst's list of core concepts contained only often-repeated words, for example, democracy, justice, equality, and so on, without links to any descriptive or qualifying terms. This produced a list of core concepts that most proponents of conflicting ideologies would have no difficulty identifying with. Consequently, it was unclear exactly how, if at all, the ideational cluster associated with the GJM differed from that of market globalists. Yet as further results of the MDA were compiled, it became clear that our selected organizations utilized some unique ideas in their narratives while also endowing the aforementioned overlapping concepts with meanings that were quite distinct from those of their ideological competitors. By including a descriptive term or qualifier that often appeared in pertinent textual passages, we were able to make clear what is distinctive and unique about justice globalism.

The concepts we provide in Table 2.1 were consistently and forcefully present in the texts of our selected organizations.

Unsurprisingly, the most frequently used core concept was 'social justice', identified as a core concept for a substantial 35 of the 45 organizations. 'Universal rights' was the next most common value, identified for 33 organizations, followed by democracy and sustainability (29 each), equality (28), change and solidarity (27 each). Other values that emerged in the study included 'diversity', 'decent work', 'citizenship' (usually global/planetary), 'peace', 'autonomy/sovereignty', and 'freedom/liberty'. These concepts, while central for some organizations, tended more generally to be assumed or implied within broader overarching concepts – diversity within equality, freedom/liberty within democracy, peace as part of justice, and so on. This finding suggests that while a common set of values exists within justice globalism, organizations differ with regard to the priority given to those values. Following Freeden's (1996) framework, we argue that concepts that are core or central for one organization may be adjacent or peripheral for another, yet nonetheless constitute critical components of the ideological constellation.

In this chapter, we discuss only those ideas and values that emerged as core concepts for a majority of the 45 organizations. As Rafaele Salineri from Terre des Hommes indicated, core concepts might serve different purposes for social activists: '"Participation" is a tool, for example. "Equitable justice" is a value' (Steger 2011b). In other words, some of our concepts may be seen by GJM activists as substantive norms, whereas others are associated with the methods or means the movement is willing to use to operationalize its values.

Most importantly, all of these concepts tend to be mediated by terms like 'global', 'globalization', or 'international', thus highlighting the growing significance of the rising global imaginary. This finding is dramatically confirmed by the quantitative content analysis, discussed in Chapter 3. Let us now turn to our analysis of seven core concepts of justice globalism.

Table 2.1 Summary of Core Concept Distribution across Organizations

	Transformative Change	Participatory Democracy	Equality of access to resources and opportunities	Social Justice	Universal Rights	Global Solidarity	Sustainability
ACTU							●
AFL-CIO	●		●	●	●	●	
AFM	●	●	●	●	●	●	
AIDC		●		●	●	●	●
ARCI			●	●	●		●
ATN		●	●				●
ATTAC	●		●	●			
CBJP		●			●		●
CCSCS	●	●		●	●		
CES/ETUC	●	●	●		●	●	●
CLACSO		●			●	●	
CLC	●	●	●	●	●		●
CoC	●	●		●	●		
CorpWatch	●	●		●	●	●	●
COSATU	●	●	●	●	●	●	
CTA	●	●		●	●	●	
CUT	●	●	●	●	●	●	●
ENDA			●				●
FIAN	●			●		●	●
FIDH				●	●	●	
Focus[1]	●			●		●	●
Friends[2]		●					
General Union[3]		●	●	●			●
GGJ	●			●	●	●	
GPF	●	●	●	●	●	●	●
HSA		●					
Ibase	●	●		●	●	●	
IFG	●	●	●	●	●		●
IPAO			●	●	●	●	●

	Transformative Change	Participatory Democracy	Equality of access to resources and opportunities	Social Justice	Universal Rights	Global Solidarity	Sustainability
IPF	●	●		●	●	●	●
ITUC	●	●	●	●	●		●
Jubilee South	●	●	●	●	●	●	●
KCTU		●	●	●	●	●	
MST	●	●	●	●	●		●
OneWorld		●	●	●	●	●	
PGAAWC					●		●
PHM					●		
PPEHRC							
TDH	●	●	●	●		●	●
TNI			●	●	●		●
TWN							●
Via Campesina	●	●	●	●	●	●	●
WCC	●		●	●	●	●	●
WFTO	●	●	●	●		●	●
WMW	●	●	●	●		●	●
Totals	27	29	28	35	33	27	30

1 Focus on the Global South
2 Friends of the Narmada River
3 General Union of Oil Employees in Basra

Transformative/Paradigmatic Change

Twenty-seven organizations explicitly emphasized the urgent need for trans-formative change in global politics, economics, culture, and ecology. These organizations decontested 'paradigmatic change' in unique ways that emphasized both the unprecedented severity and global dimension of the problems facing humanity at the outset of the 21st century. Hence, they insisted that profound social, political, economic, and cultural changes were urgently required – for instance to prevent irreversible climate change:

> If we are to *avert calamitous climate change*, we know we cannot continue 'business as usual'. We must end our addiction to nonrenewable fossil fuels and learn how to live in harmony with the natural systems that we depend on. *This transformation will require deep restructuring, not just the adoption of green lifestyles by those who can afford it.* It will require systems that do not depend on the exploitation of nature and people. *It will require a shift from a throw-away consumer culture*, in which certain peoples and lands are seen as expendable. It will require new ways of defining wealth and the American Dream that de-link our well-being from over-consumption of Earth's resources. (Grassroots Global Justice 2009, emphasis added)

According to some organizations, there exists a strong moral imperative to change. 'People need to rethink and change their lifestyles so that everyone may have life with dignity within a context of respect for the creation' (World Council of Churches 2009a). Change has to occur not only at the policy level, but, most importantly, at the deep normative level that drives decision-making by individuals, institutions, and governments. Such transformational change must be reflected within the very paradigms and frameworks through which we make sense of the world.

> [W]e need a bigger economic, cultural social transformation to really get justice. I think we get that. I think for the [GGJ] alliance, if we were to answer that question, I would say that there are three veins of our work that we seek to make a movement intervention, bring a frame, and do some work around … .

> I think we can get justice by winning a campaign, or win some impact, but true justice is never accomplished until those situations are also dealt with. So I think that for us justice needs a complete transformation of the economic political system. (Steger 2010a)

While still calling for fundamental change, other organizations expressed their willingness to accept the fact that the pace of change might be slow and gradual. For example, FIAN argued that while an alteration in the modes of production, labor, and access to property ownership would be essential for a realization of the right to food for all, these changes did not need to occur immediately through revolutionary processes, but could take place in piecemeal fashion over a longer period of time (Wilson 2009d). Furthermore, FIAN members conceded that change might not be about taking action or doing something new or different, but rather 'abstain[ing] or refrain[ing] from doing something. They just have to not evict people from their land and those kind of things' (Wilson 2009d). Yet, the FIAN representatives also expressed their dissatisfaction with governments that are often afraid to implement change of any kind, thus maintaining the status quo and resisting any real reform (Wilson 2009d).

Like FIAN, other organizations, such as the ITUC, are not necessarily aiming at a fundamental transformation of society as a whole but rather seek to facilitate reform measures that make existing systems fairer, more just, and more ecologically sustainable (Wilson 2009a). But even within reformist organizations, reform is often understood as prefiguring a paradigmatic shift away from the currently dominant social arrangements rather than preventing it.

In discussing the concept of change, interviewees were sometimes reluctant to refer to their political vision as 'ideology'. This reflects the prevalence of pejorative connotations of the term in mainstream public discourse (Steger 2008). Although interviewees expressed their misgivings about the term 'ideology', they nonetheless affirmed that they were actively promoting an 'alternative way of seeing the world, or a different worldview' (Wilson 2009i; Goodman 2010a).

Finally, the conceptual significance of 'change' relates mainly to altering dominant understandings of globalization and fundamentally reversing the balance of power in contemporary global politics (Jubilee South 2009). Our organizations called for a major shift in who exercises power in global politics and economics away from corporations, political elites, and consumers to a more decentralized, dispersed power structure, where individuals, communities, and nation-states have control over the decisions that affect their lives on a daily basis. In short, the GJM's expressed desire for paradigmatic change is rooted in this perceived imbalance of power on a global level.

Participatory Democracy

Our selected organizations offered three perspectives of democracy: a method of political organization (representative democracy); a philosophy or normative principle fueling active political engagement (participatory democracy); or a combination of the two (Wilson 2011). Democracy is also seen as a vital source of legitimacy not only for these organizations and the larger GJM, but also for national and local governments and international regimes.

Of the 29 organizations that adopt 'democracy' as a core concept, 20 define it in strong 'participatory' terminology. They cherish democratic engagement as a principle that should underpin all areas of society, not just politics. In particular, this includes democratic control and regulation of financial markets. In this context, democracy is closely tied to principles of transparency and accountability:

Basic concepts of *participatory democracy* and community empowerment should be at the heart of all international decision-making structures and processes. (Corpwatch 2002, emphasis added)

ETUC thinks that democracy is necessary to control the economy. So if you have strong economic politics then you need a strong politics to control this, so you need a strong parliament. (Wilson 2009b)

Demanding *transparency* from elected representatives and managers of public funds; insisting on *ethical behavior and social accountability* from business sectors; *and establishing strategic alliances to promote democracy and to strengthen civil society and planetary citizenship, linking the global to the local*: these too are fundamental steps in *building a truly democratic society*. (Ibase 2009, emphasis added)

Our textual analysis suggests that GJM organizations want principles of participatory democracy and transparency to govern relationships amongst workers and business owners, religious organizations, local, regional, national, and international governing bodies, as well as civil society organizations (Steger 2010c). In a nutshell, participatory democracy should be the main principle around which relationships at every level of society should be organized. Once again, the correction of asymmetrical power relations emerges as the key reason for this widespread emphasis on participation and transparency. Many of the GJM organizations we studied insist that power should move away from global and local elites. Decision-making processes must be made more inclusive, primarily by returning power to people who have been marginalized by dominant neoliberal forces.

We also found a strong link between participatory democracy and rights such as access to information and the right to protest. Rights are considered fundamental to democracy in the same way participatory democracy is viewed as critical to protecting and promoting individual rights. By extension, then, participatory democracy and rights are mutually reinforcing: 'Until people living in marginalized communities are empowered through *participatory* media supporting *participatory* politics, their *human right* to a climate-friendly future will be at risk' (Vittachi 2007, emphasis added). Such comments also suggest a strong link between participatory democracy, rights, and alternative approaches to 'development' within the GJM. A similar, but perhaps somewhat less pronounced, link exists between the ideas of democracy and justice. Justice is often considered the backbone of democracy, while the concept of democracy becomes decontested as the preservation and realization of justice: 'A Social Movement for Democracy: KCTU is committed to building a truly *democratic and just* society' (KCTU 2009, emphasis added).

A number of organizations linked the core concept of participatory democracy and the adjacent concepts of freedom/liberty and autonomy/sovereignty. For CUT, for example, democracy means having 'the liberty to organize yourself and to express yourself. And organize yourself with your own thinking!' (Steger 2010c). Hence, democracy becomes decontested as having freedom and autonomy of speech and association, also again linking democracy with rights.

While favoring participatory democracy over representative democracy, a number of organizations also recognized some drawbacks and disadvantages of participatory democracy. Lucien Royer, a member of the Canadian Labor Congress, noted that while it was important to have collective decision-making and participation in the development of policies, there also had to be effective leadership, so that coordinated action could be taken on the decisions and policies that had been formulated (Wilson 2011). FIAN members, too, were very aware that participatory democratic political processes can be more time-consuming than representative decision-making. At the same time, however, they firmly believed that participatory processes give more people ownership over the decisions made. As a result, they noted that the implementation of policy and change would be more effective in the long term because more people have involvement in the final decision (Wilson 2009d). Representatives from the World Council of Churches, Focus on the Global South, and the Transnational Institute echoed similar sentiments – participatory democracy may be more time-consuming and energy intensive – but ultimately they expressed their conviction that it produces decisions that are more just, more equal, and more inclusive (Wilson 2009e, 2009h, 2009i; Scerri 2011a).

The expressed preference for participatory democracy resonates well with the GJM's pervasive theme of multiplicity versus singularity. Most organizations we analyzed are reluctant to put forward one binding solution for all, but rather seek to include multiple voices in decision-making processes and develop multiple approaches to perceived problems. Their affinity for multiplicity was also expressed in their explicit endorsement of dual and multiple forms of citizenship. Indeed, we found clear evidence that 'citizenship' – both national and global – was widely used as an important adjacent concept to participatory democracy (Steger 2011a; Wilson 2009i).

Equality of Access to Resources and Opportunities

Nearly all of the 28 organizations that placed a high premium on equality decontested this core concept as *fairness* in terms of access to resources – economic, ecological, social – and access to opportunities. The latter is usually linked to demands for ending discrimination and marginalization as well as the recognition of rights of all people. Alessandro Bento from CUT put it this way:

> There is a big pre-occupation with the *inequality of access to justice as a right*. So all the powers of the judges, and the system, is *mostly against the poor, against the workers. It is to defend the rights of the rich people.* This juridical situation causes a lot of problems and it's hard work for the syndicates [unions]. For instance, if there is a conflict between a worker and the organization he's working in, and if you go to the court, most of the time the courts are pro for the owners. So it's very hard to get your rights defended in Brazil. (Steger 2010c, emphasis added)

Most of these organizations also linked equality to the idea of 'diversity' (Articulacion Feminista Marcosur (AFM) 2009; Ibase 2009). In our analysis, diversity, whilst not a dominant core concept, emerged as a strong adjacent concept that cuts across the seven core concepts we outline here. For most organizations, diversity is about valuing difference. In contrast to the uniformity of neoliberalism, these groups celebrate difference as a rich source of creativity and innovation. Indeed, diversity helps the GJM to develop alternative approaches to today's multiple global crises. The celebration of diversity we noticed includes differences related to gender, ethnicity, sexuality, religion, culture, age, and ability. These expressions of diversity also relate to how the 45 organizations understand and operationalize 'equality':

> Cultural, ethnic, religious and economic diversity are key to the vitality, resilience, and innovative capacity of any living system and must be respected. (International Forum on Globalization 2009)

> Our actions are based on the principles of horizontality and of collective group work, using essentially the dialogical and inclusive methodology, with *respect of diversity, differences and of similarities between cultures and peoples*. It is based on the encouragement of self-organization and self-determination. (Instituto Paulo Freire 2009, emphasis added)

> We want to be a society living in harmony with its ethnic and cultural diversity, which can offer equal opportunities for all Brazilians, with economic, social, political and cultural democracy. (Movimento dos Trabalhadores Rurais Sem-Terra (MST) 2009)

It is important to note that the commitment to diversity and its link to equality has become enshrined in the Charter of Principles of the World Social Forum:

> The World Social Forum is a plural, diversified, non-confessional, non-governmental and non-party context that, in a decentralized fashion, interrelates organizations and movements engaged in concrete action at levels from the local to the international to build another world. (World Social Forum 2002)

This discursive link between these two concepts of equality and diversity serves primarily as a tool to promote the social, political, and economic inclusion of traditionally marginalized peoples – women, migrants, indigenous groups, people with disabilities, the young, and the aged. Most organizations especially emphasize the connection between diversity and gender/economic equality: 'The principal objective of La Via Campesina is to develop solidarity and unity among small farmer organizations in order to promote *gender parity* and social justice in *fair* economic relations' (La Via Campesina 2007, emphasis added). With regard to geographical scales, 'equality' was utilized both nationally (among national citizens) and globally (transnational equality), especially as a key value for bridging the North–South divide.

Finally, many organizations linked equality explicitly to democracy, rights, and justice. Equality decontested as access to resources and opportunity is broadly seen as an indispensible precondition for the realization of a democratic and just society.

> All human beings and peoples are equal in all domains and all societies. They have equal access to wealth, to land, decent employment, means of production, adequate housing, a quality education, occupational training, justice, a healthy, nutritious and sufficient diet, physical and mental health services, old age security, a healthy environment, property, political and decision-making functions, energy, drinking water, clean air, means of transportation, technical knowledge and skills, information, means of communication, recreation, culture, rest, technology, and the fruit of scientific progress. (World March of Women 2004)

Indeed, the connection between 'equality' and 'justice' sometimes becomes so strong that these concepts simply collapse into each other. One example of this conceptual merger is the way the organization Coordenadora de Centrais Sindicais do Cone Sul (CCSCS) defines equality/justice in both inter- and intra-generational terms:

> To accomplish our objective of attaining a sustainable society, we believe it is fundamental to ensure that *inter- and intra-generational equality* and climate and socio-environmental *justice* be promoted, and, as a part of this effort, that issues linked to climate change be considered transversal topics. (CCSCS 2009, emphasis added)

Jubilee South provides a similar decontestation of justice as equality (Jubilee South 2008). At times, interviewees consciously addressed the fact that the strong interconnections between equality and justice challenges the GJM to educate the public about the precise meanings associated with each concept (Wilson 2011). Moreover, seasoned GJM leaders like Candido Grabowsky from Ibase pointed to the significance of cultural and linguistic contexts in distinguishing between equality and justice: 'The cultural content of justice is different in Brazil than in English-speaking countries. The struggle for equality has the same significance here in Brazil as justice. Justice is more related to law and the legal system' (Steger 2010b).

The fact that the concept of social justice carries the same meanings as equality in some other languages explains not only why the two concepts frequently bleed into each other, but also why some GJM organizations utilize more procedural and juridical understandings of justice than others.

Social Justice

Processes of globalization have heightened the sense of interdependence across the globe and raised questions about justice not confined within state borders nor limited to political and juridical issues of justice (Schweiker 2004: 18). Systemic injustices that contribute to poverty are also being more closely scrutinized as a

result of the economic interconnections generated through processes of globalization (Kokaz 2007). Nowhere are these trends more noticeable than within the
discourse of the GJM. Many organizations are driven by a cosmopolitan approach
to justice – an approach that understands justice as resting on universal principles,
especially human rights (Erskine 2002: 458; Nagel 2005: 119; Archibugi 2008).

We found that our selected WSF-connected organizations often link their
understandings of social justice to a number of reasons why so many individuals
and communities around the world exist in conditions of economic, political,
and social disadvantage. Dominant notions of justice among these organizations
thus focus on restoration for past wrongs and accepting responsibility for past
forms of injustice such as colonialism and imperialism. This also explains their
frequent use of 'justice' with regard to transnational corporations, governments
and international economic institutions that are seen as responsible for pushing
'neoliberal' and 'neo-imperialist' Washington Consensus on the global South,
trapping large segments of the population in unending cycles of extreme poverty
(Wilson 2009e). Other groups decontested 'justice' in explicit ecological terms as
'climate justice', which implies that prosperous countries in the global North
have a special responsibility for the mitigation of the effects of climate change
in poorer regions:

> In consequence and in view of the pressures that the most *developed countries should*
> *assume the responsibility that is theirs in the international search for sustainable devel-*
> *opment, in the transfer of environmentally friendly technologies and in the provision of*
> *the financial resources necessary to combat the consequences of climate change* indus-
> trialized societies exercise and exert on the world's environment. (CCSCS 2009,
> emphasis added)

In short, rich countries are encouraged to address past wrongs committed against
poor countries through reparations and technology transfers. Both CCSCS and
OneWorld provide clear examples of this view. At the same time, however, these
countries in the global South are encouraged to take responsibility for their own
contributions to global justice.

Social understandings of justice tend to highlight the need for international
justice involving different communities and societies. Procedural understandings of justice are often formulated to apply to individuals. Several organizations
project an understanding of justice that focuses on both its social and procedural
dimensions (Goodman 2010c; Steger 2011b). Eighteen organizations decontest
justice in social terms while only four organizations rely on an explicitly legal-
procedural conception of the idea. Those organizations foregrounding the social
dimensions and implications of justice privilege its restorative force as promoting reconciliation and rebuilding relationships.

Social justice is clearly linked with other core concepts such as democracy, sustainability, universal rights, and equality (Wilson 2009e, 2009f; Goodman 2010a).
An emphasis on rights often informs an organization's view of justice and how it

should be pursued or realized in practice. Justice may even be understood as the recognition and realization of rights – human, political, civil, economic, social and cultural, workers' rights, and so on. The implied universalism of justice as rights is consistent with cosmopolitan perspectives, which posit human rights as the basis for global justice (Erskine 2002: 458; Nagel 2005: 119).

As noted in relation to equality, 17 organizations either explicitly link or merge equality and justice. 'Justice has a number of components ... it really is about equality. It is certainly not about uniformity. It's also about diversity, embracing diversity, celebrating diversity ... So if you think about justice, it is that all are valued. None are valued less than the other, and justice is about the balance of that. If you think about the scales of justice, scales are about balance' (Wilson 2009h). This comment from the WCC representative also highlights that GJM notions of justice include an emphasis on multiplicity and diversity, rather than a singular conception of what justice is, who it is for and how it is applied.

Other organizations highlight inequality in wealth and resource distribution as a form of injustice (Steger 2010c, 2011b; Wilson 2009f). Consequently, it is possible to think of justice and equality as mutually dependent and reinforcing, as representatives from Focus on the Global South suggest:

> [O]ne of the core things that runs through the theme of justice that is important to Focus is recognizing that *there are really social inequities and inequalities in the world at different levels. Going at the root of that problem in terms of how people are oppressed or exploited is really important for us.* And to a certain extent it informs the basis of how we do campaigns, or how we plan for our work. It is a logical conclusion for us to have a vote for the marginalized in many of our work because we recognize that kind of social and cultural inequality that are present in the world. That's the kind of thing that we are trying to combat, or change when we talk about what kind of world that we want, or the big ambition, or the big things that we want to happen. (Wilson 2009e)

A critical theme in GJM discussions on justice and equality is the redefinition and redistribution of power in contemporary global politics. A small number of organizations explicitly mention power in their texts, particularly with reference to relationships between workers and corporations, populations, and their governments and in the context of control over and access to resources and opportunities, suggesting that power is related to equality. The General Union of Oil Employees in Basra (2010), for example, seeks to address power imbalances between workers and corporations, while other organizations such as the Transnational Institute, WCC, and ATTAC are concerned with redistribution of power at a global level. For these GJM organizations, power is about having the ability to make decisions about your own life, the resources you have, your environment, working conditions, and so on. At present, such power is seen as located in the hands of a powerful few who impose their decisions on the many, top-down. The GJM seeks to radically invert this model and decentralize power, with local communities and populations having the power to make the decisions that will affect them. Rights are a central component of this understanding of power, primarily as a means to regain power that has been taken away. Food First International Action Network (FIAN), for example, implies in its slogan that the concept of rights is a 'weapon' that can be used to 'fight' against hunger. FIAN works to educate populations about the rights that they have so that these communities can then claim their rights and thus claim power over decisions that affect them (Wilson 2009d).

Thus, considerations of existing power relations lie at the heart of questions of justice and equality. When organizations make a claim for justice or equality, often they advocate a redistribution of power, be it economic power or political influence. Occasionally, organizations may even propose alternative *conceptions* of power, recognizing that power does not simply come from money or military might or influence over international political and financial institutions. For the GJM, power exists also in other areas and other forms, such as popular social movements – 'people power' conceptualized around various notions of 'rights' (Central de Trabajadoes Argentinos (CTA), 2009a).

Universal Rights

As we have seen above, the concept of rights is intimately tied to notions of justice within the GJM. 'Rights' encompasses all types of rights – workers' rights, human rights, women's rights, migrants' rights, rights of nation-states, especially nation-states in the Global South, and even environmental rights, which suggest that the planet and the environment have rights within a justice globalism worldview. Jubilee South (2008) in particular employs this understanding:

> South governments in particular must promote alternatives that place *the needs and rights of peoples and the planet* first … That would include total and unconditional cancellation of the illegitimate debt claims against South countries and recognizing the sovereign right and obligation of governments to take unilateral action to stop payment or repudiate debts in order to *insure the preservation, protection and promotion of fundamental human and environmental rights.* (Jubilee South 2008, emphasis added)

Economic, social, and cultural rights clearly constitute the discursive center of gravity for twelve organizations and seven more also highlight civil and political rights. All organizations agree that these multiple dimensions of rights should be respected, defended, protected, and promoted. This suggests that rights are seen as fragile yet capable of carrying authority. Rights are depicted as natural and indivisible, something people are entitled to rather than a privilege or a fleeting construction for political purposes (Goodman 2010b). Our selected GJM organizations' understanding of rights is explicitly linked to international human rights instruments such as the Universal Declaration of Human Rights, the Convention on the Rights of the Child, the International Covenant on Economic, Social and Cultural Rights, and the International Labor Organization's Labor Standards.

The 2003 Declaration on the Full Realization of Human Rights in the United States issued by the Poor People's Economic Human Rights Campaign (PPEHRC) exemplifies the GJM perspective on universal rights:

> *Human rights are universal and indivisible.* Their realization requires guarantees for all persons – regardless of race, gender, class, age, sexual orientation, disability, immigration, language or other status – of the complete set of rights: *civil, political, economic, social, and cultural* ...

> *Human rights have become the cornerstone of the international political and moral order,* and are *embodied in a wide array of institutions and practices,* which seek the collective betterment of humankind, the equitable distribution of the fruits of progress, and the peaceful resolution of conflicts. (PPEHRC 2003, emphasis added)

In addition to its close association with concepts of justice, the idea of rights connects to other core concepts – especially equality and democracy – as well as to the adjacent concepts of diversity, autonomy, and freedom:

> We [FIAN] strive for *the right to food, the human right to food,* but particularly *for people to get access to* productive *resources in order to feed themselves* [linking to equality of access to resources]. This is important for us that they are not just given food, but that they have the ability to get the tools and the resources to feed themselves, to do it in dignity. That's very important ...

> We always use a human rights approach to present our work because we are a humanitarian organization. So we avoid to use very political terms or to do very political criticism and we go really to a human rights analysis to look into the situations but also to analyze. So always looking to the different levels of publications under the right to food and also to the principles – *transparency, accountability, human dignity participation, non-discrimination, empowerment and rule of law.* And I would also say indivisibility of rights now because we are working for the right to food group. (Wilson 2009d, emphasis added)

> [For TNI, justice is] about people having rights to determine how they want to live. What's healthiest for the community. It's about having rights and freedom to make those decisions. With climate justice, for me, it is that but it carries on into resources and having the rights to land resources. And when things are taken away, and the community resists, and are still not heard, and these decisions are placed on top of them, then that would be injustice. (Wilson 2009i)

Both FIAN and TNI emphasize that rights are central to GJM notions of justice and their political agenda. Further, however, they indicate that rights feature prominently in collective efforts to change decision-making structures and correct asymmetrical power relations. Recognizing the rights and freedoms of individuals and communities to make their own decisions about resources and social arrangements, our chosen WSF-connected groups expressed a strong desire to change top-down decision-making processes, which they see as inherently unjust. For them, the recognition and implementation of universal rights must go hand in hand with a fundamental shift to bottom-up decision-making. The vehemence and persistence of this demand confirms the accuracy of earlier characterizations of the GJM as a strong advocate for a 'globalization-from-below' challenging market globalism's vision of 'globalization-from-above' (Falk 1999).

Global Solidarity

Most of our selected organizations utilize 'solidarity' as a dynamic, fluid, vibrant concept that goes beyond simply supporting similar global civil society groups in their combined struggle against market globalism. For them, 'solidarity' is about entering into a long-term relationship with oppressed and marginalized people to fulfill the promise of social justice. Solidarity involves cooperation, unity, support, joint action with and for those disadvantaged communities across geographic, economic, political, cultural, ethnic, racial, gender, age, and disability divides. Such decontestations of solidarity are reminiscent of what the main advocates of Liberation Theology in the 1960s and 1970s called 'a preferential option for the poor' (Gutierrez 1988).

But in the more recent GJM discourse, 'solidarity' has become globalized and linked to concrete global problems and crises. Local campaigns take on global significance and global concerns intersect with local problems. For example, local campaigns concerning food rights and land tenure – such as those engaged with by La Via Campesina and FIAN – are tied into global campaigns around food governance and sovereignty. Consequently, solidarity networks emerge amongst groups operating at these distinct yet overlapping geographic levels. Indeed, such conceptions of 'practices of solidarity' most clearly reveal the reconfiguration of the local and national around the rising global imaginary:

> Solidarity is an intrinsic value of the trade unions. And solidarity is not just solidarity for Brazil, it is solidarity on a global scale … . If a company is on strike in Chile, there is solidarity in the same company in Brazil. Valle is a big Brazilian company. There was a strike in Canada and people working for Valle in Rio de Janeiro demonstrated their solidarity. It's fragile, and is not easy to organize, but … it's a very important thing to do and to invest in, and they [CUT] will be doing it more in the future. (Steger 2010c)

Perhaps more than any of the other core concepts we have identified in this chapter, 'solidarity' highlights the significance of the 'multiplicity versus singularity' theme within the GJM. Routinely decontested as rich and varied networks of reciprocity, solidarity contributes to the articulation of mutual political goals and aspirations that include realization of rights, ending poverty, and opposition to neoliberal economics. Multiple forms of solidarity manifest themselves in both symbolic ways and activist modes. For example, participants in the Palestinian Grassroots Anti-Apartheid Wall Campaign have held concurrent protests in various locations around the world while at the same time issuing joint statements, performing plays, and singing songs that express their solidarity for local people thousands of miles away (PGAAWC 2008). La Via Campesina (2007) sees solidarity as the act of building lasting relationships with those who are oppressed around the world. As a statement issued by the World March of Women (2003) puts it, 'We believe in the globalization of solidarity. We are diverse women and we work together to "build another world".' Thus solidarity becomes linked to other core concepts, especially social justice, democracy, and equality: 'The concept behind [GPF's goals] is solidarity, it is social justice, it is equity, it is peace and security. So the values that are strongly behind are the feelings and the thinking of the left' (Wilson 2009c).

For the GJM, solidarity reflects a multiplicity of causes, ideas, people, moral issues, social contexts, and political campaigns. Our selected organizations showed less concern for conventional working-class values that cast solidarity in a rather singular conceptual framework than for 'intersecting' visions of solidarity in which labor represented but one node in a network of multiple voices. This new conception of solidarity as a flexible network of mutuality also corresponds to a similar understanding of 'universalism' as a global and dynamic web of multiplicity rather than the monolithic predominance of a 'correct' view. As Cindy Wiesner, a member of Grassroots Global Justice, observes:

> Yes solidarity, but I think solidarity and the notion of much more of a joint struggle mutual interest perspective. So not just 'we support what is happening in Honduras'. But it's like we actually understand as people who have members in Honduras but also understand the role of the US and the dictatorship that is happening, and in the silence of it, and that we understand that that's ultimately about the US trying to regain control in the region. So that's what solidarity is for us. So *it's not just that we support what is happening there but that we understand the dialectical relationship there.* And that's just one example. *The other issue is for us being able to understand the crisis of capitalism, and the whole ecological and climate fiasco and crisis that we are in.* For us obviously the terms neo-liberalism, capitalism, imperialism, we use the system-of-oppression frame which we talk about, homophobia, heterosexism, patriarchy, white supremacy. And so I think that for a lot of the organizations on the ground and a lot of us really use that frame of the intersectionality of those forms of oppression and exploitation and their intersections. (Steger 2010a)

This passage conveys the widely shared view in the GJM that solidarity relates not merely to supporting common acts of resistance against oppressive forces and systems, but also in the sharing of resources, insights, and strategies for challenging and rethinking dominant market ideology. Thus, for the organizations under consideration, 'solidarity' is both an intellectual and practical enterprise that links local issues to global problems while safeguarding the living diversity of perspectives, contexts, backgrounds, and experiences.

Sustainability

Sustainability is a very important new concept, which initially became part of the ideological vocabulary of the GJM and then was quickly appropriated by the dominant market globalist discourse. In the last few years, 'sustainability' has turned into a central conceptual battle zone between market and justice globalists. Since this formidable decontestation struggle remains in full swing, it is still too early to determine which meanings will eventually achieve discursive hegemony.

This struggle over the meaning of sustainability involves more fundamentally the future trajectory of globalization and the tension between dominant forms of economic development and ecological concerns. Although the GJM first introduced the term to the broader public debates about 'globalization', market globalists have been working hard to pull the term into their meaning orbit. Thus, corporate elites have developed market-friendly definitions that posit a perfect compatibility between corporate interests and popular demands for a more sustainable environment (Dunphy et al. 2007). In their view, the growing legitimacy of market-based mechanisms to address climate change – such as carbon taxes and emissions trading schemes – show that environmental sustainability requires the establishment of globally integrated markets. The increasing emphasis on corporate social responsibility provides another example of the ways in which market globalists are attempting to dominate the debate over what sort of meanings should be associated with sustainability. Their ideological bottom-line has stayed fairly constant: as long as corporations remain committed to social responsibility, environmental sustainability and the free market are both compatible and necessary (Schwab 2008).

Justice globalists, however, claim that the sustainability of the market and the environment are fundamentally opposed to one another. Their ideological bottom-line is that our planet has finite resources and capacity. It cannot be sustained in the context of an unfettered market that requires infinite resources. Profit-oriented market relations must give way to people-oriented forms of ecological and social sustainability. The Council of Canadians, headed by Maude Barlow, succinctly outline this commitment in the second of their three main political goals:

> To work with Canadians and people around the world to reclaim the global and local commons which are the shared heritage of humanity and of the earth.

There exist common heritage resources that constitute a collective birthright of the whole species to be shared equitably among all. These include the ecological commons – land, air, forests, water and fisheries; the cultural commons – the shared knowledge and art that are the collective creations of our species; and the modern social commons – including health care, education, and social security. All of these commons are under threat as corporations seek to privatize and commodify them. Our vision and commitment must be to reclaim these commons from private interests. We recognize that this entails a moral obligation on the part of all peoples to ecological stewardship. We also recognize that it is impossible – and wrong – to fight for our commons birthright in Canada without securing such rights for all the peoples of the world. (Council of Canadians 2003)

Grassroots Global Justice also provide insight into how sustainability is defined by the GJM, and its connections with the core concept of equality:

Equitable sharing of this new 'green wealth' must be part of any definition of sustainability. A transition in which the majority of the world's people remain in poverty and lack basic human needs is not stable, secure, or, in the long run, sustainable. As long as the costs of environmental degradation (so-called 'externalities') remain hidden and fall disproportionately on historically marginalized communities, existing profit models will allow for the continuance of 'business as usual'. (Grassroots Global Justice 2009)

Our 45 chosen organizations decontested sustainability primarily in ecological terms that emphasized the intergenerational use of natural resources and the long-term preservation of the environment. Secondarily, sustainability was utilized in socioeconomic contexts such as food production and development problems in the global South: 'Africa's response to the global crises requires … the adoption of proactive policies in the areas of trade, finance, and production to re-position their economies and put them on the path of sustainable development' (Africa Trade Network 2009). WSF-linked organizations place specific emphasis on securing adequate resources for future generations (World Fair Trade Organization 2009). Sustainability is also linked to democracy, justice, equality, rights, and peace (CBJP n.d.). In particular, the texts suggest that sustainability must be based on equality.

Finally, we found that the GJM approaches the concept of sustainability in a much more holistic manner than market globalists. For the latter, sustainability means continued viable growth, to enable expansion of free markets, the preservation of corporate profits and high levels of consumer demand. For GJM organizations, sustainability involves the fulfillment of basic human needs regardless of buying power and the protection of the global environment. This holistic vision is anchored in universal rights that should be extended to certain nonhuman forms of life to assure the health of our planet.

Conclusion

Utilizing MDA, this chapter identified, mapped, and analyzed seven core concepts – transformative change, participatory democracy, equality of access to resources, opportunities and outcomes, social justice, universal rights, global solidarity, and sustainability – and a number of adjacent ideas. All of these emerged from our examination of key texts generated by 45 GJM organizations linked to the WSF. The adoption of new core concepts such as paradigmatic change and sustainability as well as the formation of distinct meanings associated with these core concepts – for example, participatory rather than representative democracy or social rather than procedural justice – points to the existence of a coherent and unique ideological structure we call 'justice globalism'. This conceptual distinctiveness corresponds to the first of Freeden's (1996, 2003) three criteria for determining an ideational cluster's degree of ideological maturity. The ideational richness of justice globalism is further evidenced in its successful differentiation from market globalism through sophisticated formations of meanings associated with its seven core concepts. Although the findings presented in this chapter provide initial evidence that the political vision of the GJM cannot be reduced to simplistic and incoherent 'anti-globalization' rhetoric, we need to engage in further analysis to gauge the ability of justice globalism to produce effective decontestation chains in the form of central ideological claims.

3

JUSTICE GLOBALISM: CORE IDEOLOGICAL CLAIMS

Introduction

Having identified the core ideological concepts of our chosen GJM organizations, our next task is to explore how they link these concepts together in effective claims that produce particular meanings. As we noted in the previous chapters, we seek to determine the ability of justice globalism to 'lock in' meanings in the form of 'decontestation chains' that assert and normalize what counts as 'correct' and 'real' in the global political environment. The surfeit or lack of evidence for such successful decontestation efforts constitutes one of Michael Freeden's (1996, 2003) three criteria for assessing an ideational cluster's degree of coherence and maturity.

In this chapter, we show that each of the examined GJM organizations did, indeed, formulate a number of such central ideological claims. These decontestation chains address both the alleged causes of current global problems and the meanings of core concepts by linking them together in simple and reiterated phrases and slogans. Our selected organizations managed to embed these assertions so deeply within their discursive practices that they considered them taken-for-granted 'truths'. Relying on our methodological framework of MDA, we mapped these claims by first compiling a list of core claims from each organization around textual samples typically related to neoliberalism, development, globalization, climate change, justice, human rights, the state, power, civil society, global citizenship, the local-global nexus, and other relevant themes. At that point, our analysis revealed the existence of a number of obvious intersections and overlapping meanings that connected these seemingly disparate themes. We then proceeded to compress these identified meaning structures into five core ideological claims.

It is important to bear in mind that these ideological claims represent compressed composites of discourses that were most common and most often repeated across the 45 WSF-connected organizations included in this study. While rarely appearing verbatim in the texts, these claims nonetheless constitute realistic composites that project meanings derived from the linked core and adjacent concepts assembled by each organization. To be sure, no single text or interview transcript contains all of the decontestation chains identified and discussed below. But almost all of the textual samples we analyzed contain at least one of the following five central claims of justice globalism:

Claim #1: Neoliberalism produces global crises.
Claim #2: Market-driven globalization has increased worldwide disparities in wealth and wellbeing.
Claim #3: Democratic participation is essential for solving global problems.
Claim #4: Another world is possible and urgently needed.
Claim #5: People power, not corporate power!

Underlying each of these five central claims there is an assumed interconnection among previously identified core concepts such as universal rights, equality of access to resources and opportunities, and social justice. According to our selected GJM organizations, the present global condition is one of profound injustice and inequality, in which serious and multiple violations of human rights occur on a daily basis. The organizations' very use of the word 'crisis' provides a striking example of this interconnection. While market globalists employ this term primarily in reference to the global financial crisis or serious natural disasters like the devastating 2011 earthquake in Japan, justice globalists extend the meaning of 'crisis' to events less covered by the mainstream corporate media such as the global food emergencies or the changing climate. Thus, for justice globalists, the notion of 'global crisis' is inextricably linked to gross examples of unsustainability as well as all large-scale violation of rights and systemic forms of inequality and injustice – particularly those affecting communities in the global South. The five claims we identified not only contain implicit political imperatives emerging from these conceptual links, but also suggest how the GJM might protect and reassert these values by developing and implementing alternatives to the dominant market globalist model. Discussing each claim in turn, we show below how the conceptual building blocks (core concepts) are linked together and how these claims intersect with each other.

Claim #1: Neoliberalism Produces Global Crises

Identifying the economic doctrine of neoliberalism as the basic cause of contemporary global crises underlies the other claims of justice globalism. As we discussed in Chapter 1, the GJM developed originally as both a reaction against and a critique of neoliberalism. Hence, it should not be surprising that the political ideology of the GJM relies on a foundational claim that blames neoliberalism for producing global crises. But in what, precisely, lies the failure of neoliberalism? The textual samples of our chosen organizations point unmistakably to both ethical shortcomings and biased economic practices. For the GJM, neoliberalism has failed ethically because it has put the needs of markets and corporations ahead of the needs of individuals, families, communities, and nation-states. It has come up short economically because the flawed policies of privatization, deregulation, and liberalization have neither benefited ordinary people nor lifted the populations of developing countries out of poverty. Instead, the GJM argument goes, poverty has become more entrenched and social inequalities have dramatically increased around the world. Indeed, the claim that neoliberal measures at the heart of market globalism must be held responsible for global crises emerged as the most common and consistent allegation across all 45 organizations. The following quotations provide clear examples for their articulation of this foundational claim:

> The global financial system is unraveling at great speed. This is happening in the midst of a multiplicity of crises in relation to food, climate and energy. It severely weakens the power of the US and the EU, and the global institutions they dominate, particularly the International Monetary Fund, the World Bank and the World Trade Organization. Not only is the legitimacy of the neoliberal paradigm in question, but the very future of capitalism itself. (Focus on the Global South 2008)

> The unprecedented global economic crises, which have afflicted the whole world over the past two years, have their origins in the advanced industrial economies of the West. They are rooted in the neoliberal capitalist model aggressively promoted by corporate forces and allies over the past decades. (Africa Trade Network 2009)

> COSATU regrets that the G20 meeting did not clearly acknowledge that the global economic crisis has been caused by the policies of the Washington Consensus, which propagated a 'one-size-fits-all' economic model based on withdrawal of the state from the economy, emphasis on market fundamentalism, deregulation, privatization, trade liberalization, cuts in government spending, and high interest rates, implemented through lending conditions attached to IMF and World Bank loans for poor countries. (COSATU 2009)

The organizations' rationales for claim #1 are usually based on the forging of semantic linkages between the core concepts of equality, participatory democracy, universal rights, and social justice. The contextual narrative binding these building blocks together often suggests that decisions made by powerful corporate elites that have had a directly detrimental impact on a majority of the people on the planet. Had decision-making processes been more bottom-up and participatory, our organizations imply, such global crises might have never materialized. In addition, they frequently criticize the conceptual singularity ('one-size-fits-all') of neoliberalism's 'free market' approach and the Eurocentric arrogance underlying its assumption of universal applicability. Our chosen organizations contrast this neoliberal position unfavorably with their preferred justice-globalist vision of more democratic economic approaches that empower citizens to regulate markets in various ways in their quest for a more equitable generation and distribution of wealth. Constant repetitions of claim #1 in its countless mutations turn the allegation of neoliberalism's failure into a taken-for-granted 'truth'. This ideological foundation of justice globalism then serves as the conceptual fertilizer for its other ideological claims while at the same time supporting a vigorous campaign for finding political alternatives.

Claim #2: Market-driven Globalization has Increased Worldwide Disparities in Wealth and Wellbeing

Extending beyond the statement that neoliberalism has caused global crises, claim #2 makes more specific assertions with regard to the social impact of market globalism. It is not difficult to see the semantic link between the condemnation of market globalism and the core concepts of equality and social justice. The latter, with its imperatives of restoration, reconciliation, and redistribution, implies a concern for individual and community wellbeing and the recognition of human rights. Thus containing a far broader meaning range than merely pointing out material inequalities, claim #2 reflects the GJM's conviction that existing disparities of wealth and wellbeing are fundamentally unjust because they violate universal norms of fairness. A number of our organizations also assert that market-driven globalization is unsustainable because it creates acute discrepancies not only in the social world but also severe imbalances in our planet's natural environment.

We also noted that this claim's emphasis on fundamental disparities implied the importance of 'solidarity' with the disadvantaged:

> The poor and workers have paid, and it is clear who benefits. The wealth of the world's 587 billionaires is greater than the combined incomes of the poorest half of humanity. CEO salaries in the US are over 300 times the salaries of workers. Government controls on the financial system have been decimated. Greed and avarice have been allowed to run wild in the world economy since the Reagan era. This must end. (Guerrero 2008)

> Neoliberal economics and its by-products, such as damage to the environment, grossly lowered production, especially of some nations' agricultural production, unemployment, and the dramatic increase in migration, have created the cultural and socio-economic conditions that through factors like poor nutrition and psychological stress cause disease in affected populations. Additionally, health care system reforms imposed by the World Bank and the International Monetary Fund with their emphasis on privatization and decentralization of health care services have destroyed the already deficient hospital care infrastructure and the existing systems of control of diseases like malaria and tuberculosis and have eliminated access to medical services for those most in need of such services. (Allianza Social Continental n.d.)

As these passages show, claim #2 carries an important emotional charge designed to confront the reader with the real-life devastation caused by the vigorous application of neoliberal doctrine during the last three decades. Like all ideologies, justice globalism generates claims designed to connect the rational and emotional aspects of human perception on the basis of concrete examples and illustrations that can be readily grasped by everyone. Invoking the specter of losing basic medical services, for example, creates strong anxieties for most people that easily cut across class lines or ethnic divisions.

Finally, some organizations noted a paradox: while disparities in wealth and wellbeing produce disempowered and disenfranchised human beings, they also heighten people's awareness that alternatives must be found. As expressed in the next claim, both the formulation and application of such alternatives require broad democratic participation.

Claim #3: Democratic Participation is Essential for Solving Global Problems

Privileging the core concept of participatory democracy, this claim implies that the rectification of the substantial disparities created by market globalism can only be achieved through bottom-up decision-making processes that consciously address the multiple global crises of our time. Most of our chosen organizations expected social disparities and ecological imbalances to worsen in the future and thus called for collective action against the major institutions of market globalism. Once again, the core concept of participatory democracy assumes a central position in moving these GJM groups from mere rhetoric – the diagnosis of shortcomings and the blaming of market globalism – to concrete political action tackling such recalcitrant global problems as poverty, irregular migration, poor health care, and environmental degradation.

Indeed, the call for multiple models of participatory democracy on a local-global scale represents a crucial conceptual bridge that connects social activists residing in the richer countries of the northern hemisphere to the principal victims of distributive injustice in the global South. Our WSF-connected organizations recognize that democratic resistance is not guaranteed to weaken, yet nevertheless facilitates the articulation of alternatives to the dominant discourse:

> The false solutions to climate change – such as carbon offsetting, carbon trading for forests, agro-fuels, trade liberalization and privatization pushed by governments, financial institutions, and multinational corporations – have been exposed. Affected communities, indigenous peoples, women and peasant farmers have long called for real solutions to the climate crisis, solutions which have failed to capture the attention of political leaders. (Focus on the Global South 2007)

In many cases, our selected organizations couched their imperative for democratic participation in urgent calls to national governments to reassert the common good against the narrow interests of corporations. As we noted in Chapter 2, governments do have an important role to play in the GJM's preferred vision of a more equitable global order. But in order to uphold human rights and protect vulnerable communities from the excesses of the market, governments must be transparent and held accountable by their citizens:

> Central to [avoiding a return to the politics of greed] is restoring the role of government in regulating the private sector, and ensuring public provision to meet fundamental social needs. (ITUC 2008)

> The state must play a role to prevent that the production and distribution of food are exclusively subjects of the desires of the market, thus risking the violation of the human right to adequate food and health. (Ibase 2009)

In addition to 'participatory democracy', then, claim #3 also puts into operation the concept of transformative change by calling for a fundamental shift away from contemporary forms of representative democracy mired in 'politics-as-usual'. Indeed, the GJM's recognition of the global reach of today's social problems leads to its explicit commitment to paradigmatic change by means of nonviolent mass action aimed at redistributing power from global corporate elites to ordinary people at the grassroots.

Claim #4: Another World is Possible and Urgently Needed

This claim – a variation of the official WSF slogan – represents perhaps the most well-known and widely recognized demand of the GJM. At its heart lies the 'concrete utopia' (Bloch 1995) of an alternative global order based on the core concepts of justice globalism we discussed in Chapter 2. In particular, claim #4 combines the GJM's appeal for transformative change with an almost visceral sense of urgency. In the view of many WSF organizations, we have reached a critical moment in the history of humanity. If we fail to bring about a paradigmatic shift in the basic values that drive global politics and economics within the next few decades, we have crossed the point of no return – especially with regard to the environment. It is this sense of urgency that weaves together the core concepts of transformative change, social justice, sustainability, and equality. Claim #4 also builds on and extends the three previous claims: since neoliberalism has failed both economically and ethically, humanity faces the vital task of finding alternatives as soon as possible through common action in the spirit of solidarity:

> We believe by working together – Another World is Possible, a world based on the principles of international solidarity, justice, peace, dignity, equality, human rights, sustainability and democracy! (Grassroots Global Justice Mission Statement n.d.)

We believe that Another World is Possible:

- A Healthy World is Possible

- Health for All Now is Possible. (People's Health Movement 2004)

The World March of Women illustrates the resolve of citizens of the world to build a peaceful world, free of exploitation and oppression – a world in which people enjoy full human rights, social justice, democracy, and gender equality. A world in which women's work, both productive and reproductive, and their contribution to society, are properly recognized. A world in which cultural diversity and pluralism are respected, and a world in which the environment is protected. We consider it is urgent to assert and defend our sexual and reproductive rights, including the right to informed choice, in particular by free access to health care and free and safe measures of contraception and abortion. In short, we believe that together we can and must build another world. (World March of Women 2003)

Each of these passages points to the kind of world our GJM organizations seek to create. But most the 45 organizations we analyzed agreed that the establishment of 'another world' must be more than a mildly reformed version of the existing status quo. They expressed a strong commitment to insert their own core values into the political, economic, and ecological dynamics that globalize the world of the 21st century.

Claim #5: People Power, not Corporate Power!

In order for 'another world' to become a reality, our chosen organizations demanded that existing power relations must be fundamentally revised. In our analysis, we frequently came across this people/corporate binary, usually couched in terminology that sought to expose the undemocratic concentrations of power that dominate the supposedly 'democratic' societies in the global North. However, our GJM organizations directed their critique of 'power elites' not only toward the corporate world, but also condemned democratically elected representatives for bending all too easily to the will of moneyed interests. For many justice globalists, politics and business have formed a permanent symbiotic relationship designed to monopolize power in the name of democracy. Moreover, they accuse such power elites of using crises of their own making as a pretense to keep ordinary people in line: 'Today it is clear that power groups are trying to use the economic crisis to halt the progress in the advancement in popular power that was seen in recent years in Latin America' (Central de Trabajadoes Argentinos 2009a).

Once again, the nature and pace of the required social changes stand at the center of the 'power debate' within the WSF. Our WSF-connected organizations usually start their quest for 'people power' by calling for deep reforms in existing democratic governments and to establish democracy where there presently is none. Once again, the key to such reforms lies in greater civil society participation in political and economic decision-making (Wilson 2009d, 2009e, 2009h, 2009i). In addition, our chosen organizations seek to reclaim 'people power' by raising awareness of rights and encouraging ordinary citizens to confront governments that commit human rights violations (Wilson 2009d).

Moreover, justice globalists consistently demand greater corporate and government transparency and accountability (Corpwatch 2002). Core concepts such as global solidarity, participatory democracy and universal rights are linked together to specify the main features of 'people power'. Some organizations made clear that they are not trying to usurp the power of the state. Rather, they introduce themselves as civil society partners to national governments willing to question their dependency on corporate power and express their desire to serve the common good (ITUC 2008). Finally, the GJM's understanding of 'people power' extending beyond existing national borders in claim #5 once again demonstrates the GJM's belief that global solidarity is an indispensible force in their ongoing efforts to bring about profound social change.

> What is needed, *in the interest of the large majority of the people*, are *real changes toward another paradigm*, where finance is forced to contribute to *social justice*, economic stability and *sustainable* development … . The crisis is not the result of some unfortunate circumstances, nor can it be reduced to the failure of regulation, rating agencies or misbehavior of single actors. It *has systemic roots, and hence the structure and the mechanisms of the system, in general, are at stake*. New international agreements must put other goals – like *financial stability, tax justice, or social justice and sustainability* – over the free flow of capital, goods and services. (ATTAC 2009, emphasis added)

Let us end this section by considering an extended passage taken from a statement issued by Focus on the Global South. It provides evidence for the invocation of all five central claims of justice globalism identified in this chapter:

> We are entering uncharted terrain with this conjuncture of profound crises – *the fall-out from the financial crisis will be severe. People are being thrown into a deep sense of insecurity; misery and hardship will increase for many poorer people everywhere.*
>
> *Powerful movements against neo-liberalism have been built over many decades.* This will grow as critical coverage of the crisis enlightens more people, who are *already angry at public funds being diverted to pay for problems they are not responsible for creating*, and already concerned about *the ecological crisis and rising prices – especially of food and energy.*
>
> There is a new openness to alternatives. To capture people's attention and support, they must be practical and immediately feasible. *We have convincing alternatives that are already underway, and we have many other good ideas attempted in the past, but defeated. Our alternatives put the wellbeing of people and the planet at their center. For this, democratic control over financial and economic institutions* are [sic] required. (Focus on the Global South 2008, emphasis added)

The high levels of frequency, consistency, and clarity with which these claims were deployed by the 45 organizations (see Table 3.1) provide ample evidence

Table 3.1   Distribution of Core Claims across Organizations

	Claim 1	Claim 2	Claim 3	Claim 4	Claim 5
ACTU	•			•	
AFL-CIO	•		•		
AFM		•	•	•	
AIDC	•		•		•
ARCI			•	•	•
ATN	•	•			•
ATTAC	•			•	•
CBJP			•	•	
CCSCS	•		•	•	
CES/ETUC	•	•	•	•	
CLACSO		•			
CLC	•		•		
CoC	•		•	•	•
Corpwatch	•		•	•	•
COSATU	•		•		•
CTA	•	•			•
CUT		•	•		•
ENDA				•	
FIAN	•		•		•
FIDH		•	•	•	
Focus	•	•	•		•
Friends		•			
General Union		•			•
GGJ		•	•	•	•
GPF		•		•	•
HAS	•	•			•
Ibase		•	•	•	
IFG	•	•	•	•	•
IPAO		•	•		
IPF		•		•	
ITUC	•		•	•	
Jubilee South	•	•	•		•
KCTU		•	•		
MST		•	•		
OneWorld	•	•		•	•
PGAAWC		•	•		
PHM	•	•	•	•	•
PPEHRC			•	•	•
TDH			•	•	•
TNI	•		•		•
TWN	•	•	•		•
Via Campesina	•	•	•	•	•
WCC	•	•			•
WFTO	•				
WMW	•	•	•		•
Totals	26	27	31	22	26

for their ability to engage in effective conceptual decontestation – one of Freeden's three criteria for gauging the coherence and maturity of ideational constellations. The discursive prominence of these five central claims adds further weight to our findings in Chapter 2 regarding the ideational richness of justice globalism.

Thus, the combined findings presented in Chapters 2 and 3 (core concepts and central claims) allow us to respond in the affirmative to one of the main research questions posed in this book: Does the GJM offer a coherent ideological alternative to market globalism? Our assembled evidence confirms the existence of a maturing ideology, which meets at least two out of three criteria introduced by Freeden (1996, 2003): its effective conceptual decontestation of core concepts and claims; and its distinctiveness in relation to other political ideologies (specifically market globalism). Our findings thus far also point to the applicability of the third criterion – justice globalism's context-bound responsiveness to a broad range of political issues. Still, we will address this criterion in more detail in the remaining chapters dedicated to policy issues related to three global crises.

With regard to the criterion of distinctiveness, let us note that some of the core concepts of conventional ideologies – especially liberalism and socialism – also appear in justice globalism. Yet, these key ideas are articulated in much revised and hybridized ways and often linked to new core concepts such as 'sustainability'. Most importantly, as confirmed in our quantitative analysis below, the unique ideological morphology of justice globalism is no longer bound to a largely *national* framework. Rather, we are witnessing the birth of a new ideological configuration linked to the rising *global* imaginary.

Insights from Quantitative Analysis

Our quantitative analysis provides further evidence for the formation of justice globalism as a coherent political ideology. Extending MDA methodology pioneered by Freeden (1996) and Steger (2009), we introduced basic quantitative content analysis as an additional instrument for gauging justice globalism's ideological coherence and maturity. Our qualitative MDA allowed us to analyze and interpret concepts generated and utilized by our chosen GJM organizations. Our quantitative content analysis opened up an additional dimension by determining how frequently these core concepts appear throughout our textual samples and interview transcripts.

We processed a total of 135 texts for word frequency counts using Nvivo, specialized data analysis software developed to analyze complex and unstructured non-numerical data. We settled on Nvivo because of its integrated programming, which enabled analysis of multiple documents of various origin and formats (pdf, doc, and html files) as well as searches of terms across multiple documents. This analysis was conducted only for English-language sources.

Materials from websites not in English (French, Italian, Spanish, and Portuguese) were professionally translated before the analysis was run. We then used Word and Excel software to produce tables and charts that allowed a visual representation of the results.

Initially, we conducted separate, individual word frequency counts for each organization. We gave specific emphasis to words that were value-laden (justice, rights, equality, and so on) as well as words that highlighted particular focus issues (for example, economy, trade, social, environment, democracy). In addition, we included words that indicated a geographic focus for the organization's activities (local, regional, national, global). Words contained in the organization's name were excluded, except in cases where the words were value-related or had significance for determining the overall ideological structure of the GJM. For example, for the word frequency count conducted on the organization Focus on the Global South, we excluded the words 'focus' and 'south', but retained 'global' for its significance in contexts other than the repeated mention of the organization's name. Words with the same root, but used in the plural ('worker' and 'workers'), in different tenses or with different spelling (for example, 'globalization' and 'globalisation') were merged in order to develop the most comprehensive overview of word usage across the texts.

The word frequency analysis for the individual organizations produced separate word frequency tables and graphs for all 45 organizations. Once this was complete, we merged these results to produce findings regarding frequency of word usage for the organizations as a whole. The top ten most frequently used words across all 45 organizations are presented in Figure 3.1.

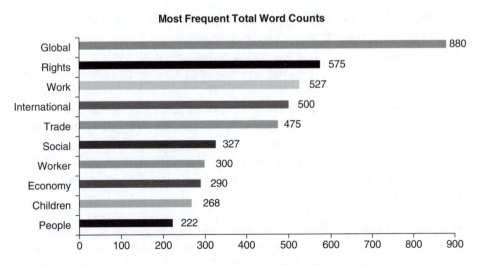

Most Frequent Total Word Counts

Word	Count
Global	880
Rights	575
Work	527
International	500
Trade	475
Social	327
Worker	300
Economy	290
Children	268
People	222

Figure 3.1   Most Frequent Word Counts across all 45 Organizations

A) The Rising Global Imaginary

Figure 3.1 clearly shows that there is an overwhelming usage of 'global' in the texts produced by our select GJM organizations. Indeed, we found nearly 900 references to 'global' across the 135 texts. This term yielded 300 more appearances than the next most frequently used word – 'rights'. This, of course, is one of our core concepts identified in the morphological discourse analysis. Alongside this overwhelming word count of 'global', there were an additional 500 references to the related word 'international'.

The remarkable frequency of these two concepts in the texts produced by our GJM organizations, coupled with the fact that the parallel term 'national' does not even feature in the top ten word count, clearly indicates the magnitude of the shift from the national to the global imaginary reflected in the political ideological landscape of the 21st century. Complementing the qualitative findings of the MDA, these quantitative results suggest not only that justice globalism is a maturing political ideology, but also that it is a *global* political ideology. In other words, the core ideas and concepts of political ideologies increasingly translate the largely prereflexive global imaginary into concrete political programs and agendas (Steger 2008). The following textual passage represents a typical example of the increasing ability of the 'global' to bind the 'national' to its meaning orbit:

> We [Focus on the Global South] believe that national contexts have their own set of specificities which might not only be a translation of globalization, or the impact of global forces, but that it's much more complex. But at the same time we try to see what are the relationships between what is happening at the global level and at the national level, and vice versa. (Wilson 2009e)

This statement not only makes clear that the global and the national are interconnected, but also suggests that the 'national' becomes increasingly mediated by the 'global'. Up to the postwar era, this relationship was the other way around, with the 'national' dominating the 'international' (the term 'global' was hardly used before World War II). Thus, in order to effectively challenge the dominance of market globalism, the GJM faces the formidable task of recognizing the importance of projecting its ideological claims to a worldwide audience without losing its local constituencies. As our findings show, the principal codifiers of justice globalism have so far done an excellent job in meeting this challenge. Keenly aware of this 'global' challenge facing his organization, Rafaele Salineri's comment nicely illustrates this point:

> We are not local, and we are not global. We are a glocal organization, in the sense that we still have and we share a global vision because the world is so small and the big issues are so common – environment, energy, bio-diversity, human rights, global challenge – that we must articulate those global challenges at local level, because more and more people are attached to their daily life. We must understand how it is possible to

change the global through the local. That means we must be able to propose daily changes to daily style, daily laws, daily small tools that are also workable by any single citizen in order to change the reality. *So we try to keep the balance between the global and the local.* (Steger 2011b, emphasis added)

Indeed, this passage reveals Salineri's awareness of the changing nature of the relationship among all geographical scales, not just between the national and the global. Moreover, the complexity of global relationships between increasingly overlapping levels of political and economic decision-making also shapes the perspectives of our WSF-affiliated organizations, such as the WCC:

I think *the global community is becoming more conscious* and is looking for ways to do this. Our job as churches is to proclaim the gospel; to proclaim the 'good news', which is what 'gospel' means. And what is good news in this context, in 2009 or 2010, on the brink of an agreement at Copenhagen that may or may not be fair enough, ambitious enough, and binding? I think 'good news' is that *the people are waking up, that old systems are being challenged for the unjust oppressive impacts that they've had on people, and on nature, on all of life.* I think the good news is that people can't look backwards now; that *change, social transformation is afoot – you can see it.* (Wilson 2009h)

Confirming the findings of our quantitative content analysis, this passage suggests the GJM's growing recognition of the increasing political and social significance of the rising global imaginary and its complex dynamics that bind the 'national' and the 'local' to the 'global' in new and unfamiliar ways. Given the increasing significance of global consciousness, one would expect the ideological contest between justice globalism and market globalism to focus even more on 'global problems'.

B) Socioeconomic Focus

Indeed, our quantitative findings also yield insights into a number of policy-related issues that will test justice globalism's capacity to meet Freeden's third criterion – its ability to respond effectively to contemporary political issues. The high frequency of 'rights', 'trade', 'economy', and 'work' in the quantitative data reveals that GJM organizations remain primarily focused on socioeconomic issues. On the one hand, this focus on material aspects is quite surprising, given the cultural focus of many of the organizations we examined, such as the World Council of Churches, ARCI, Alternative Information Development Network, OneWorld, and the Instituto Paulo Freire. On the other hand, it would stand to reason that even these cultural organizations should use socioeconomic language in a discursive environment dominated by market globalism and its economistic core doctrine of neoliberalism. In short, at this stage of their struggle, most GJM organizations seem to prefer countering in kind the socioeconomic claims of market globalism.

Equally important, the GJM's primary target is corporate-driven globalization, not conventional national governments. This is supported by additional qualitative data, with a number of organizations affirming the importance of national governments in the process of building more equitable institutions of global governance. In this context, we need to remember that claim #3 of justice globalism implies the need for democratic governments to act against corporate interest that routinely violate the rights and undermine the wellbeing of citizens.

Our quantitative data also highlights an obvious distinction between justice globalism and market globalism with regard to their engagement with socioeconomic issues. The presence of 'social' in our list of top ten words clearly indicates that the values and focus of justice globalism are quite different from those of market globalism. This data intersects with our qualitative finding that makes 'social justice' the most prominent core value of the 45 organizations we analyzed. Steger's previous analysis of market globalism (2009) suggests that its elite codifiers rarely talk about 'social justice' or 'wellbeing', but instead concern themselves with 'economic growth', 'material benefits', 'liberalization of trade', and 'integration of markets'. Once again, this suggests that justice globalism's socioeconomic claims are primarily concerned with the social and ecological consequences of economic policy, not merely whether such policies produce economic growth.

C) Recessive Themes

Finally, our quantitative content analysis reveals a number of recessive themes, that is, topics that do not feature prominently in the narratives of our select GJM organizations. Most notable is the relative paucity of textual references to race and racism, and, to a lesser extent, gender and sexism. One possible reason for the low profile of these potent 'identity concepts' might be their potential to divide or at least undermine the unity of the GJM as a whole. Race, in particular, has the proven capacity to fracture social networks built on values of equality and solidarity. It could be that the present focus on socioeconomic dimensions also serves to keep potentially explosive identity politics in check.

While the main ideological thrust of the GJM has been to challenge the dominance of market globalism primarily with regard to economic and political issues at the expense of cultural themes, we also found strong discursive dynamics involving environmental issues, especially global climate change. Moreover, the global media coverage afforded to recent ecological disaster events such as the 2011 earthquake in Japan and the related Fukushima nuclear meltdown or the 2010 BP oil spill in the Gulf of Mexico points to the growing prominence of environmental themes in public discourse. GJM organizations might increasingly take advantage of this opening by further balancing their current socioeconomic focus with even greater socioecological engagement. The shift toward socioecological language allows a strong re-embedding in both environment and cultural contexts, beyond potentially divisive identity politics. Indeed, several organizations suggested that engagement with the cultural and ecological contexts of specific localities holds the key for a successful evolution of the movement. Many organizations report that they are devoting more time and effort to developing and advocating for socially just and sustainable practices for local livelihood and living environments. In the current shift toward the socioecological domain, we see a process of re-localization, re-embedding, and re-positioning concrete forms of social engagement vis-à-vis the dominant forces of market globalism. These efforts contrast with market globalism's attempts to camouflage 'business as usual' with strident claims for 'sustainable business'.

Conclusion

Our morphological discourse analysis in Chapter 2 identified seven distinct core concepts and a number of adjacent concepts that mutually reinforce each other. While sharing some conceptual similarities with liberalism and socialism, these seven key ideas form the conceptual skeleton of 'justice globalism' – a distinct ideational constellation that articulates the rising global imaginary in concrete political programs and agendas.

Building on the core concepts discussed in Chapter 2, the key focus of this chapter has been to examine the ability of justice globalism to produce effective decontestation chains. Ultimately, we identified five central ideological claims, which reappear with great frequency in the textual samples drawn from the 45 organizations analyzed for this project. The discursive prominence of these claims provides additional evidence that justice globalism arranges its core concepts in unique ways to assemble a distinct conceptual map of global politics in the early 21st century.

While our analysis points to a broad agreement within the GJM about these concepts and ideological claims, we emphasize that such agreements are always provisional, unsettled, and open-ended. That is, the process of establishing and negotiating core concepts and central claims reoccurs on a daily basis. However, this process of conceptual evolution applies not merely to the GJM organizations examined in this study, but to all social movements engaged in the codification of political ideas. As a part of the perpetual contest within and among competing political ideologies, there must always be constant dialogue, conversation, and debate about what

(Continued)

(Continued)

the core concepts or values are, how they are to be understood, and how they combine to provide ways of making sense of a political universe. Thus, we recognize that the concepts and claims we mapped and analyzed actually evolved over a prolonged period in which GJM activists have sought to articulate what they stand for, not simply what they oppose. This process will undoubtedly continue as both justice globalism and market globalism change and evolve in response to each other and an altered global environment.

Our qualitative and quantitative findings suggest that, contrary to the assertions made by prominent market globalists, the GJM cannot be characterized as an unimaginative collection of disparate 'anti' groups – or an instrumental alliance of single-issue movements. There might have been some truth to this 'anti' charge when the GJM first emerged in the 1990s. But in the ensuing decades, the movement and its political ideology have grown and matured to the point where such a criticism simply ignores contrary evidence. The GJM organizations we examined articulate a mature and coherent political ideology that provides clear conceptual alternatives to the dominant worldview of market globalism. We also found evidence for widespread recognition across the GJM that the articulation of such constructive alternatives is indispensable in the struggle against neoliberalism (Wilson 2009e; Goodman 2010c; Participants in 'Responding to Crisis' Workshop, 1 July 2011).

Finally, the quantitative content analysis employed in this chapter clearly establishes the centrality of 'the global' in GJM discourse. While political ideologies in the 19th and 20th centuries expressed the national imaginary, justice globalism, like market globalism, rearranges the 'local' and 'national' around concepts and images of 'globality'. A distinguishing feature of these new global political ideologies is their recognition of the global interconnections cutting across nation-states, localities, and regions. The rise of these 'globalisms' in the 21st century is bound to radically reshape the study of political ideologies (Steger 2008).

In the next chapter, we shift our analytic spotlight from matters of ideology to applied politics by exploring crucial processes around the generation of policy proposals within our chosen GJM organizations. In particular, we examine how the core concepts and central claims of justice globalism outlined in Chapter 2 and 3 enable both particular critiques of global politics and practical responses to global crises.

4

RESPONDING TO GLOBAL CRISES: FROM CORE CONCEPTS TO POLICY ALTERNATIVES

Introduction

Our findings presented in Chapters 2 and 3 clearly established that justice globalism should be considered a coherent political belief system according to at least two of Michael Freeden's three criteria for ideological maturity. On the first criterion of distinctiveness, its articulation of the global imaginary and its central ideological claims demonstrate that justice globalism can be distinguished from both the conventional national ideologies such as liberalism, conservatism, socialism, and so on, and competing globalisms such as market globalism. Furthermore, justice globalism's five central ideological claims highlight its ability to meet Freeden's second criterion, namely, the ability to produce effective conceptual decontestations that help people orient themselves in their complex political environments.

We now turn to an assessment of how well justice globalism meets Freeden's third criterion – an ideational cluster's context-bound responsiveness to a broad range of political issues. Gauging justice globalism's capacity for generating such responses is an extremely important task because it allows us to ascertain the veracity of the key criticism made by opponents of the GJM that 'anti-globalization' activists are utopian dreamers incapable of generating concrete policy alternatives. Indeed, if the GJM amounts to more than a disparate group of anti-globalization protestors, it will need to produce a variety of policy alternatives to the pressing political challenges of the global age. Delving into the crucial specifics of the GJM's responses to three major global crises, Chapters 5 to 7 will examine in much detail the political responsiveness of justice globalism.

Before commencing this task, however, this chapter scrutinizes some of the basic processes by which GJM activists generate these alternative responses. We look specifically at the interactions between the core concepts and claims identified in Chapters 2 and 3 and the generative processes of GJM elites developing agenda-setting campaigns with clear policy alternatives. Ultimately, we argue that these generative processes are crucial catalysts through which the core concepts and claims of justice globalists acquire meaning to gain normative traction. In turn, this normative traction can then be used to reorient the political agenda. We also emphasize that the relationship between ideology and policy is not linear. Rather, the concepts that form the heart of justice globalist ideology interact with the alternatives the movement generates, mutually influencing and constituting one another.

We identify three stages in the GJM process of generating alternatives. The first is opposition and refusal – refusal to accept the dominant analysis and policy prescriptions of market globalism. Part of this opposition and refusal stage also includes a mutual recognition of like-minded others and the development of networks – who else is refusing market globalist analyses and why? What are the shared issues and values that enable different groups to work together?

The second stage, which is perhaps the lengthiest and most complicated, is agenda setting. Having established their networks of opposition to market globalism, organizations then outline their political agenda. We highlight three categories or types of agenda setting – framing, dialogue, and reflexivity. These are not exclusive categories but overlap and complement one another. The final stage is tactical mobilization – strategies for mobilizing others around the identified agenda in order to maximize political impact. Again, it is important to stress that these stages are not necessarily linear. Global justice activists move between these three different stages depending on the issues and campaigns that they are focused on. Often these processes overlap and influence each other.

We concentrate our analysis on the insights of GJM elites into the process of realizing strategic leverage, articulated in the 24 qualitative interviews with leading players in our organizational sample. These leaders of the GJM identify and produce the key generative issues that shape the agenda of the movement. Clearly there are other sites, which may come into play at different moments in the process of contestation, such as social media and grassroots community organizing (which are often the starting point for GJM articulations of the key issues). Nonetheless, the population for our sample is the set of organizations that initiated and maintain the WSF, members of its International Council and the Liaison Group within that Council. Consequently, this chapter explores how this elite group, and through them, the GJM, translates its core values and claims into practical alternatives, in the process reorienting public issues, mobilizing grassroots and realizing agency.

Thematic Background

Two of the additional themes we identified in Chapter 1 are critical for understanding the generative processes of the GJM – multiplicity and power. Multiplicity arises out of the sheer diversity of groups and perspectives within the movement. The agendas and strategies that the movement develops must reflect this multiplicity if they are to gain widespread support. The question of power is also central. The capacity to reconfigure the debates in the public sphere hinges on politicizing the exercise of power, and creating public issues out of otherwise normalized and accepted abuses of power. The ability to transform a set of depoliticized practices into a contested public issue is central to any social movement: collective action only becomes possible when the public issue or issues generate wider public concern.

'Generative issues' thus perform the role of spawning public engagement, exposing the exercise of power and polarizing the public sphere. The resulting controversy offers a means for people to deliberate over and contest dominant norms and values, and the ways in which these norms and values manifest in public policy. Our analysis is informed by a rich lineage of social thinkers engaged with questions of praxis and dialogue in movement leadership, where the 'generative' component expresses both the dynamism of the social field and the contingent process of realizing agency. Paolo Freire's work on 'generative themes' is especially instructive. Freire utilizes the term 'generative themes' to refer to tools of popular education, ways of reframing social and political issues that enable an embedded transformation in political consciousness to realize revolutionary agency (Johnston and Goodman 2006). In other words, Freire argues that generative themes, or certain specific sites of social and political contestation, are necessary to enable people to understand the social forces that dominate our lives, and thereby to act on them. For our purposes, we utilize the notion of 'generative issues' to refer to the process of action, where the public contestation is deliberately instigated to enact movement values and pursue its claims. As a movement ideology, justice globalism rests on the capacity to produce emancipatory values and claims, but also to engage in strategic action to generate public issues.

Opposition and Refusal

Opposition and refusal is a central feature of GJM generative processes, since in its early days the GJM was essentially an oppositional movement against the ascendency of market globalism. As market globalism unfolded across the globe from the 1980s onwards, it presented a series of naturalized and supposedly inevitable policy prescriptions (Steger 2009). By the early 1990s these policy prescriptions had acquired the character of a global constitutional framework, expressed in the universalist reach of the neoliberal governance arrangements (Gill 2002). The framework made visible power relations on a global scale, and swiftly came under challenge from emergent movements for global justice that similarly began to assume and assert global constitutive power. In the context of unfolding global crises that highlight profound systemic flaws, this constitutive challenge from justice globalists has gained some traction.

Unlike the process of defining and elaborating market globalism, orchestrated 'from above', justice globalism sought to embed itself in a participatory and democratic process of dialogic engagement, even in the early stages of opposition and refusal. The various justice globalist counter-conferences organized to coincide precisely with neoliberal summits provide a clear example of this tendency. These alternate meetings are specifically designed to contest the dominance of neoliberal policies. One example is 'The Other Europe Summit' (TOES) which began meeting in parallel session with the European Council from 1990. Another is the counter-APEC conference, held from 1993. As protests sought to block the streets, alternative conferences sought to capture the political agenda. The WSF itself demonstrates the process, moving from counter demonstrations and conferences at the WEF in Davos from 1996, to Paris in 1999, to the WSF in Porto Alegre in 2001, and across other continents from 2003. In this respect, the WSF itself is a strategic intervention, deliberately designed to spatially counter Northern WEF agenda-setting with a Southern counterpart.

Thus, the formation of the WSF was a critical oppositional moment for the GJM. It deliberately countered North with South and exclusivity with inclusivity. Its establishment announced to the world that the GJM did not accept the market globalist TINA mantra ('There Is No Alternative'). Instead, through the WSF, the GJM declared their own mantra – TAMA (There Are Many Alternatives), that in fact 'another world is possible'.

Yet, as we shall see, a number of the organizations we spoke with are concerned that the WSF has not met expectations. They suggest the WSF may have remained in the opposition and refusal stage, either unable or unwilling to move on to agenda setting and tactical mobilization, or doing so in only very limited ways. There is a sense that the WSF and perhaps the movement as a whole has tended to revert to oppositionalism, giving grounds for the market globalist critique that the movement had little to offer in the way of alternatives (Wilson 2009b, 2011; Steger 2010b; Responding to Crisis 2011).

The WSF was conceived as an ideal speech community, where alternatives would emerge dialogically, from the engagement of different counter-globalist perspectives. In part this reflects a strong rejection of market globalism's ideological claims, as the exercise of elite power. Struggles and campaigns would themselves generate alternative perspectives from the process of contestation: the WSF was constructed as an 'open space' for the interaction between these perspectives, not a programmatic site to generate a single global justice imaginary. Partly reflecting the diverse confluence of social forces within the ambit of justice globalism, the movement disavowed 'one worldism' in favor of 'a world where many worlds fit' (EZLN 1997, cited in Waterman 2009), embracing pluralities against the singularity of market globalism.

A key question for the GJM is how to translate this assertion of plurality into mobilizing strategies that give traction to ideological claims. Strategizing does not produce a single program, but rather a common orientation, reflected in movement networks and shared perspectives. As such, constructing strategy directly engages the singularity-multiplicity theme, and the approaches outlined here highlight how that narrow pathway is negotiated. There is multiplicity in institutional orientation, from organizations seeking 'insider' status with governments and inter-governmental processes, to those jealously guarding their organizational autonomy. There is also multiplicity in organizational form, from membership-based movement organizations to self-selected expert groups. Across these groups the key aim is to generate critiques and alternatives that open up political space for movements to contest market globalism. In several respects, we see organizations self-consciously seeking to set the agenda, and thereby play a constitutive role in transforming social relations.

A central role for any social movement is to politicize the exercise of power: unless normalized power is exposed and contested there is no common social foundation for the movement. Through the process of opposition comes the mutual recognition of like-minded others, and the possibility for collective contestation. Once exposed, the shift in consciousness transforms the meaning of power structures and, as the WCC put it, we 'can't look backwards', suggesting that exposure itself can produce a remarkable mind shift.

The power of opposition should not be underestimated. It represents a democratic moment where all possibilities are on the table for overcoming power structures. As such, refusal prefigures more proactive strategies: opposition raises the question of 'what next?', and offers the platform for alternatives.

Clearly, though, the move to a more proactive position, of putting forward alternatives, narrows the field of possibility and, as discussed here, always involves the exercise of power, albeit counter-power. The organizations interviewed for this project broadly argued that oppositional power had to produce counter-power if it was to gain leverage: opposition to market globalism needed to point to alternatives (Responding to Crisis Workshop 2011). Indeed, as we discuss in Chapter 5, the limits of reactive oppositionalism became clear when the GJM was confronted by the Global Financial Crisis and failed to offer an alternative program in its immediate aftermath that could gain political traction.

Some organizations defined the failure to provide adequate responses as a problem for the WSF, rather than for themselves. They expressed frustration with what they saw as the overly oppositional stance of the Social Forum, despite its emphasis on generating dialogue for alternatives. The OneWorld representative was especially concerned at the events at the third European Social Forum, held in the UK in 2004. In her view, it demonstrated the 'danger of becoming like what you oppose ... within the same paradigm'. Breaking with the dominant paradigm, meant not lending it legitimacy by exclusively focusing on it: 'I want something that is more different than just being oppositional' (Wilson 2009f). The FIDH representative was more concerned at the weakness of the alternatives. 'The WSF hasn't been able, in my opinion so far, to come up and really be a counter balance ... and have good proposals' (Goodman 2010b).

The ETUC saw the WSF as a place 'to represent the workers in the new alternative movements', and was useful for this reason, although in broad terms the WSF 'didn't really confirm the hope that it would become a really big alternative to the World Economic Forum' (Wilson 2009b).

Frustrations with the WSF reflect a wider series of dilemmas around strategizing, and perhaps suggest a problem of misrecognition. For Ibase the key purpose of the Social Forum was to construct an 'ethical' consensus, to correlate perspectives against 'the few who own the earth, ten banks, the big multinationals, some media groups' (Steger 2010b). The great achievement of the WSF was to create a 'common sense' that this process was necessary, and to enable the emergence of a set of values that 'eighty per cent will interpret in the same sense' (Steger 2010b). How to act on the basis of this consensus was and remained the key point of contention. This question of action, and the strategic questions it raises, are played out amongst global justice organizations, both within and beyond the context of the WSF.

Agenda Setting

We identified three broad categories of agenda-setting methods amongst the organizations analyzed: framing, dialogue, and reflexivity. Framing is a primarily interpretive process, where the organization defines how to approach, interpret, and respond to key issues. As such, it is most directly related to movement leadership. Through dialogue, these frames are developed and adjusted within the organization and the wider movement. Reflexivity encompasses solidarity relations, especially North–South, and the process of engaging with movements, especially in terms of openness to challenge and critique. While distinct in their content and process, these different categories of agenda-setting overlap and complement one another. Together they provide the organizational foundation for translating ideational values and claims into ideological agendas, which have the capacity to generate public issues. We discuss each of these categories in turn.

(i) Framing

To achieve leverage GJM organizations define an interpretative lens, a way of seeing the world and its crises differently. There are a wide range of framing lenses amongst the 45 organizations we analyzed. Many of the frames draw on the core concepts of justice globalism ideology we identified in Chapter 2. Using the core concepts enables justice globalists to pinpoint specifically what the problems are with contemporary political arrangements and articulate what these arrangements should be, in a sense shifting from the real to the ideal. The process of framing then serves the purpose of casting a political vision that is specific to the contemporary context. The key frames that we identify are crisis as opportunity, deglobalization, universal rights, system of oppression, social justice, bio-liberalism, participatory democracy, and social economy (as opposed to market economy).

Crisis as opportunity is perhaps the key shared frame for justice globalists. Where crises are interpreted as the product of market globalism, they are seen as indicators of its failings and as such point to possibilities beyond it. This is a frame shared across the organizations analyzed for this project, illustrating the extent to which leverage hinges on the more oppositional task of exposing the failures of market globalism. Importantly, though, the key task of justice globalists is to transform market globalism's crises into justice globalism's opportunity. As OneWorld points out, 'It's only an opportunity if you make it an opportunity' (Wilson 2009f). How to 'make it an opportunity' is the key strategic question for justice globalists. For the organizations analyzed here, this is centrally a question of agency.

'Deglobalization' is the principal 'frame word that guides the work of Focus on the Global South', informing programs on alternative regionalism, the commons, climate and justice, peace and security (Wilson 2009e). As articulated by Focus, deglobalization 'describes the transformation of the global economy from one centered around the needs of transnational corporations to one that focuses on the needs of people, communities and nations and in which the capacities of local and national economies are strengthened' (Focus on the Global South n.d.). Walden Bello, a senior analyst for Focus and highly respected global justice intellectual, has been influential in the development and deployment of deglobalization as an interpretive frame (Bello 2005).

For the FIDH, the core concept of universal rights and the international human rights regime constitute their key conceptual frame, as an indivisible universal claim for economic and social rights across North and South (Goodman 2010b). Grassroots Global Justice makes use of an interpretive frame that also draws heavily on the notion of rights, alongside equality and social justice. They refer to this as the 'system of oppression frame', which they use to make sense of 'the crisis of capitalism, and the whole ecological and climate fiasco and crisis that we are in' (Steger 2010a). This frame lays special stress on the intersection between capitalist exploitation and different forms of oppression, 'homophobia, heterosexism, patriarchy, white supremacy' (Steger 2010a).

The WCC also make use of the core concept of social justice as a framing device, defined in terms of material surpluses and debts. For example, in the context of the climate crisis, they self-consciously asked 'how can you frame the climate issue so that the focus is on how to deliver justice?' They had begun asking 'who is the creditor and who is the debtor?', developing the concept of climate debt as a framing metaphor for understanding North–South relations and endeavoring to recast core issues in the climate negotiations (Wilson 2009h). Terre Des Hommes (TDH), in contrast, focuses on the impact of market globalism on individual circumstances, which are then defined as having a universal resonance. 'We call the vision bio-liberalism. This is our vision. The liberalism which is attached directly to the bodies of human beings. They would like to make profit from the bodies; the worst form of liberalism' (Steger 2011b). For TDH the most pernicious aspect is the impact of bio-liberalism on children: its priority as an organization then, is to highlight and contest these impacts. This translates into a strategic framing process for contesting market globalism through the figure of the child:

> We are fighting for child rights, so let's bear in mind those children. Don't look very far … . My child, my son, I am working for him, because he is all children. So now, if we take this particular child who represents all children, and we try to figure out a comprehensive picture of what's going on in the world concerning the violation of child rights, which are the priorities? (Steger 2011b)

Trade unions utilize the core concepts of universal rights and participatory democracy as interpretive frames for key issues around work. For the AFL-CIO, the right to a say in the workplace, to workplace democracy, is the foundation of all other rights:

> That's the most fundamental of all. Recognition and rights under the laws and government of a country to say that trade unions are part of that society, they have a fundamental economic right and legal rights to be in those workplaces, and the workers have a democratic right to have a voice … from this flows dignity and justice, and through unions, access to the ability to realize economic rights. (Wilson 2009g)

Ibase, too, utilizes participatory democracy as its interpretive frame, arguing that democracy must be central to the process of development. Ibase is focused on creating 'an alternative to development' that is grounded in sufficiency, environmental justice, and sustainable livelihood. For Ibase, these agendas are at the core of a new 'wave' of democratization, that democratizes development itself, and Ibase is deliberately focused on making struggles around these issues politically 'visible' (Steger 2010b).

The ETUC frames its demands in terms of the social economy, defined against neo-liberalism's free market economy. In the current climate this puts the ETUC 'on the defensive, so 99% of their work is to defend workers, against the attacks against the social model. So it is more difficult today than before' (Wilson 2009b). The CLC uses a similar frame, focusing on educating its members and the wider public about the constraints of market globalism. 'The more that people understand the connection between decision-making at the international level and how that affects the political and economic climate here, then it is a lot easier to actually proceed with an agenda' (Wilson 2011).

(ii) Dialogue

The second agenda-setting category we note is dialogue. Dialogue is widely used across the GJM to generate agendas, reflecting the GJM's emphasis on participatory democracy, equality, and social justice. For the GJM, identifying political issues and setting agendas should not be an exercise for the elite but should involve as many voices as possible. In this way, dialogue is one of the key mechanisms the GJM uses to challenge the top-down power dynamics that have become socially embedded through market globalism. Through dialogue, organizations identify specific issues, events, and flashpoints, such as trade agreements, human rights abuses and humanitarian crises, by which they can extend their agenda and maximize their political influence. They also further develop relationships with partners and networks that can participate in their agenda setting. This means that organizations must have a strong degree of flexibility and adaptability built into their strategizing. Dialogue occurs across a variety of different sectors and groups – internally within organizations, across networks with other organizations, with communities at the grassroots, counterparts in other countries and occasionally (depending on the context and the issues) even with governments and corporations.

For TNI, dialogue is a deliberate process of anticipatory strategizing, of identifying the political ground, conducting investigations and campaign plans to open up issues for intervention, to expose the exercise of power and enable mobilization. In this respect, TNI has both followed and defined trends: its work on market globalism began with the WTO in the early 1990s, moved on to alternative regionalisms and a focus on the WTO's General Agreement on Trade in Services (GATS), and then shifted to defining water and energy commons against privatization. By the mid-2000s, TNI had moved to focus on carbon trading as a result of their work on energy. The sequence is not pre-planned or internally driven, but rather arises from intensive engagement and dialogue with others in the GJM, over the issues as they emerge (Goodman 2010c).

The CLC works with counterparts in other countries to contest neoliberal proposals as they are coming on to the table. The primary target of this kind of dialogue is free trade agreements. The goal is to influence outcomes as the agreements are being negotiated, not simply articulate opposition and dissatisfaction after the event, when it is too late to change the specifics. This type of dialogue also requires some engagement with governments in order to know what is on the negotiating agenda, as well as to anticipate what the key issues of the negotiations and the agreement will be (Wilson 2011).

Indeed, many organizations deliberately establish a process of network brainstorming to predict future issues and keep ahead of the market globalist agenda. TDH for instance had developed its focus on child trafficking in the 1980s through a process of internal discussion. This early development enabled TDH to have a significant impact on international child-trafficking debates. At the time we interviewed them, however, they were seeking to reorient their focus to connect the rights of the child to environmental contexts, and were doing this through debate amongst its wider networks.

In contrast, the Global Progressive Forum (GPF) develops external dialogue with other actors from various different sectors. It works across six themes with the emphasis depending on the political agenda: in 2009 the focus was finance and climate rather than migration, trade, governance, or working conditions. To assist in setting its strategic direction, the GPF deliberately established a network of senior politicians, civil servants and advisors, from international organizations as well as governments, dubbed 'the Geneva Group', meeting twice a year. In addition the GPF links into broader networks: it has a formal link with social democratic political parties in the Socialist International and works closely with peak NGOs, such as Solidar (representing more than sixty European NGOs, the ITUC, and the ETUC), and with the Foundation for European Progressive Studies. These links are used to construct common campaigns, such as the GPF's 'Europeans for Financial Reform' campaign.

Member-based movement organizations have strong internal structures for decision-making and strategizing. Trade union confederations such as the CLC have a formalized structure of internal democracy and accountability, although the executive has the power to initiate programs and campaigns. CUT strategizing occurs more locally, through works councils, organized sector by sector. The ETUC clarifies that some trade unions will range more widely than others, depending on their vision:

> There are trade unions with shorter vision so they are more to defend the workers, to defend employment, and to improve the wages, and there are others with long-term visions and they want to change the society. But before all, trade unions are workers associations which defend workers. (Wilson 2009b)

The union federations make use of dialogue in an effort to construct consensus across differences, in a way that accommodates all players. The ITUC stresses the politics of this, which contrasts dramatically with that of, for instance, an expert-based NGO. There are over 300 trade union organizations affiliated with the ITUC, so frequently the positions and policies voiced are the result of lengthy negotiation and compromise. This process has both strengths and weaknesses. Its strength is that, because it is based on consensus, few, if any, disagree. Conversely, however, its weakness is that no one is completely happy with the final outcome. Nonetheless, the ITUC believe there is tacit agreement amongst all its members that this is how the organization works. Gaining consensus from over 300 organizations from culturally diverse backgrounds is no small task (Wilson 2009a).

WCC dialogue structures, both within its membership and beyond it, have a global reach and engage in extended collaborative research. In the case of its program on 'Alternative Globalization Addressing People and Earth' (AGAPE), for instance, the process began in 1999 and ended in 2006. The follow-up, from 2006 to 2013, focused on the relationship between wealth, poverty, and ecology with a program of engagement across five continents, including at the grass-roots level of local congregations and related communities. One of the aims of its current research period is to establish a 'greed line' to correlate with the poverty and 'green' lines – to define an ethical limit on personal wealth and income. In an era of widening global inequalities the WCC was targeting the super-rich as by definition living beyond ethical social and ecological limits, directly driving global poverty and environmental degradation.

For several organizations their strategizing was part of movement building. ARCI for instance seeks to build movements by translating its values into social practices as well as producing proposals for government. Paolo Beni from ARCI argued as follows:

> We do not only think that citizens must demand that public institutions implement policies that reflect our ideas and values, but we believe that it is also necessary for citizens to act and to put in place practices of self-organization and self-management that can in practice implement our ideas ... our objective is that of linking these social practices against discrimination, racism, inequality and so forth with public policies. And also in that sense influencing public policies via the spreading out of practices of active citizenship ... which actually builds these policies via the capacity of citizens doing things on their own. (Steger 2011a)

Grassroots Global Justice (GGJ) also defines itself as a 'movement-building' organization, an alliance of locally-based or issue-specific networks. Their focus is on organizing people for participatory global justice, thereby initiating a grounded 'new internationalism ... not just around solidarity, but also how do we understand a joint struggle model' (Steger 2010a). Such an identity necessarily requires dialogue across a vast number of different groups and organizations. FIAN likewise was committed to the networking model of strategic engagement for movement building, arguing that:

> People are really taking up these issues as their own ones, and can distribute them in their own networks, that has a real multiplying effect ... the aim in the end is that people mobilize themselves and that NGOs like ourselves are just superfluous because everybody can claim it for themselves so it's of utmost importance to just get as many people as possible on board. (Wilson 2009d)

Other organizations will sometimes position themselves more as facilitators than as strategists. Ibase stresses the role of movement engagement through the WSF, arguing that strategy arises from the process of engaging across different perspectives, green, feminist, queer, and gay liberation, Marxist, communist, social democratic, 'to create a collective intelligence ... a University of Citizenship all over the world' (Steger 2010b).

OneWorld, too, sees itself as a facilitator of dialogue. It works 'catalytically' to enhance the positive sum process of networking and information sharing. It thus seeks to create knowledge hubs for interactive diversity that can strengthen movement capacity. OneWorld states it does not 'have policies for other people ... we are a values driven group', a communications organization focused on 'making voices heard' (Wilson 2009f). This facilitative role, where organizations do not necessarily claim responsibility for political interventions, but enable them to occur, is a feature of a number of the organizations. TNI for instance will often not claim responsibility for activities it has generated so as not to 'own' the issue or perspective, and instead catalyze engagement. This unwillingness to be seen as the owner or driver of a particular initiative or campaign highlights the justice globalist desire to redistribute power from the North to the South, from the center to the margins, reflecting its core value of transformative change.

Focus on the Global South also reflects this drive to redistribute power. It has a 'core principle' of not speaking for movements, but instead responding to their requests and supporting movement mobilizations. The research they undertake is thus movement-led:

> We have determined from the very start, that when we develop our position on land, or on water, or on trade, this should reflect in large part what our partners on the ground want. It's not the other way around. It's independent research and we will try to educate our partners on this. Of course there is an element of that, but if there is a conflict, the preference is that you reflect what the grass-roots partners want. (Wilson 2009e)

The balance is seen to be central, if difficult: 'We try as much as possible to be self-reflective as well in terms of whether we are really speaking on behalf or whether it's in collaboration with. We are kind of sensitive with those issues. Even if, for example, it's on the issue of land, we don't say that we are from the farmers movement, [we say] we work with the farmers movement' (Wilson 2009e).

As network facilitators, organizations become more open to issue formation as a fluid process that is less deliberate, and has no fixed or anticipated outcomes. It is the dialogue itself that matters. Through dialogue, the core issues will naturally surface and become part of the strategic political agenda. Without dialogue, it is difficult for the core issues to even be identified in the first place.

(iii) Reflexivity

The third main category of agenda-setting processes is reflexivity. This category entails a high degree of critical self-analysis, assessing the problems and the potential of certain perspectives, strategies and engagements. It encompasses a strong degree of openness, with organizations and elites willingly and readily acknowledging that they do not have all the answers, do not know the most effective ways for campaigning or the best solutions for which to campaign. Hence, it also overlaps with dialogue, which ensures that multiple perspectives are heard.

For all GJM organizations the process of envisioning global justice must be pursued in a North-South context. Northern NGOs constantly need to assess their own biases and assumptions that stem from their position in the privileged North. TDH goes further and argues that the Northern perspective is increasingly ossified in contrast with much more engaged and creative Southern perspectives. Coming from an established Northern NGO, Rafaele Salineri, the director of TDH, is concerned that 'more and more we are part of the problem not part of the solution'. He argues that Northern global justice organizations need to reflect on their role in the world and shed the assumption 'that there is something to develop with our tools and instruments, that we are the birth and witness to democracy and human rights, that we are the interpreters of global justice. Which is not true at all, not any more' (Steger 2011b). This insistence that standards of justice not be interpreted according to Northern precepts is particularly apposite.

For Salineri, the solution is to campaign for global justice in the first instance in Northern societies, in partnership with Southern organizations, rather than imposing Northern assumptions on the South:

> More and more organizations like ours, but coming from the southern part of the world like Asia and Latin America, are really growing and taking our place. So at a certain moment we must make a choice. We must more and more decide, as we are doing, to fight for child rights and human rights and the environment here, that means in our environment, in our nations, trying to change the lifestyle here, and not just go abroad and export something ... . And that means establishing more and more networks between Northern and Southern NGOs. (Steger 2011b)

The approach requires greater capacity to engage in genuine North–South alliance building and is consistent with the 'glocal' approach adopted by the TDH, that 'we must understand how it's possible to change the global through the local'.

Other global justice organizations have themselves emerged from this process of North–South reflexivity. The Brazilian trade union federation, CUT, was founded by trade union support from the US and Europe, and hence is grounded in international solidarity. CUT is now developing this international solidarity further, creating closer coordination with other national trade union confederations across South America through a joint council 'on challenges they have in common' founded on member autonomy (Steger 2010c). Ibase was similarly born out of international exchange and played a key role in both the development of democracy in Brazil and in wider international mobilization through the WSF.

The group 'Grassroots Global Justice' (GGJ), began as a US delegation to the World Social Forum in 2004, and soon itself became a US-based campaigning organization. Their representative outlines how:

We began to meet with our counterparts internationally, the conversation came up, 'It's great that you are coming here as a delegation, but where is it that you do work to challenge your own government policies? Economic policies, policies of war?' And so the challenge came out of those conversations to actually begin to make an alignment of organizations. (Steger 2010a)

Other Northern organizations have become Southern dominated. FIDH for instance is an international human rights network composed mainly of Southern members, but still is 'labeled' Northern, as its offices are in Europe and it has a European history.

Across these different ways of engaging in agenda setting – framing, dialogue, and reflexivity – we can see global justice organizations self-consciously seeking to construct the strategic agency required to produce generative issues. The process is, by definition, internally contradictory, as it necessarily involves at one stage or another the assertion of leadership over the movement. The key insight from these accounts is that these organizations – which have formed the elite of the global justice movement – recognize the necessity to act and to intervene in the political process, but also the inherent tensions involved in doing this. Another critical observation is the significance of the core concepts identified in Chapter 2 for the movement's agenda setting. Social justice, universal rights, participatory democracy, solidarity, and transformative change all play a critical component in the interpretive frames used by the organizations, and inform processes of dialogue and reflexivity, enabling organizations to cast alternative visions of how politics and society should be organized.

Tactical Approaches

Movement strategy and agenda-setting can enable the construction of public issues but it is the tactical mobilization for these issues that generates political traction. As with all movements, GJM tactics are developed in conjunction with its values and claims: tactics must adequately express the ideological message, not contradict it. Social movements produce tactical innovations that symbolically express, through action, the movement's values. Tactics literally enact the movement, bringing it into being as a political force. As such, movement tactics are a central aspect of the ideological responsiveness of the GJM. The tactical innovations of the GJM have centered most clearly on oppositional tactics, with the global days of action targeting market globalist institutions, various modes of 'monkey-wrenching' efforts to stall market globalism by playing states off against one another, arguments to 'fix or nix' institutions, or to 'derail' them, or simply the cry 'Ya Basta!' (Enough is Enough). All these are familiar oppositional global justice tactics. What we focus on here are more proactive tactics, not simply undermining existing policy approaches, but aiming to re-set the agenda and propose and implement alternatives.

The movement's tactics vary depending on the issue, the type of organization and who their main targets are for engagement and action. We note that these tactical approaches exist along a continuum that ranges from partnership with established powers to complete disengagement and autonomy. Most organizations in our analysis opted for a kind of 'conditional engagement'. The various tactics employed include negotiation and engagement with governments and corporations; protest in various forms (marches, demonstrations, alternative meetings); research and critique through publishing briefing papers, holding seminars and public education sessions; and symbolism, making use of art, theatre, and music.

Organizations seeking to directly engage are forced to adopt a stance of tactical ambivalence. The FIDH for instance does not in principle oppose free trade agreements, or other neoliberal instruments, but rather asserts 'the primacy of human rights', so that 'human rights are at the core rather than the other way round' (Goodman 2010b). If agreements or policies are found to be failing this test, the FIDH will critique or reject policy instruments, but only on the basis of evidence, and on the prospects for achieving change. This presents a series of dilemmas across fields of neoliberal policymaking:

> What's a constant challenge is trying to match the expectations and the needs of our member organizations with policy opportunities that arise. So we've been trying to push for the least worst, to at least include some of the safeguards, but without necessarily saying whether we are in favor of trade liberalization or not. It's difficult. (Goodman 2010b)

Others see no necessary conflict. The ETUC for instance uses established consultative channels, presenting its proposed agenda to governments and to the EU, and often finds governments receptive to dialogue over their proposals. The ITUC is directly represented in some institutions – notably the International Labor Organization, and also the UN's Global Compact. Here they play a representative role in promoting social dialogue that involves workers' unions. In other contexts the ITUC oversees international framework agreements between global union federations and TNCs.

Other organizations are less institutionalized, but still define engagement instrumentally. Focus on the Global South will engage, provided there are results. The key point for them is that 'you always push forward':

> We will always work for something that will bring results for our partners. We will not go into something just to stalemate the entire thing. But we also know when to disengage, when to just dis-continue the resistance, when the process will not go anywhere … or when to say we have to change the menu … . But there is always a component of a movement behind that. I mean it won't only be Focus. (Wilson 2009e)

Several organizations bring representatives of affected peoples to put their case to policy-makers. The WCC for instance is involved in hosting affected peoples to engage international financial institutions, what it calls 'talking to power', where the WCC is 'available as a space for enabling the common voice of those who suffer from these policies to speak for themselves' (Goodman 2010a). In 2001 the WCC produced a guide to effective engagement with the IMF, titled 'Lead us not into temptation' (WCC 2001). The aim of the booklet was 'to alert the church that these guys are not part of your agenda, they have their own agenda, and they just want to use you because they know faith-based organizations are much closer to communities' (Goodman 2010a). The IMF reacted by seeking a meeting with the WCC to have the booklet withdrawn. The WCC refused but instead entered into a three-year 'encounter', leading to a document in October 2004 that summarized the main disagreements. The key point of difference, as the document put it, was that 'the WCC does not believe that market-based economies are necessary to improve human welfare' (WCC 2004). Looking back on this encounter, in light of the financial crisis, the WCC representative summarized that the IMF were simply 'talking about wealth creation, which leads into poverty creation' (Goodman 2010a).

Conditional engagement of this sort is common amongst the organizations. CUT actively seeks conversations with power-holders, including transnational corporations, insisting engagement 'is a two-sided thing', that it's 'not only to say "Yes Sir"' (Steger 2010c). Ibase had campaigned for ethical corporate practices, for private banks especially, but had withdrawn from engagement when corporates were involved in arms production or tobacco production (Steger 2010b). FIAN engages with elites by appealing to enlightened self-interest in food rights: 'you are really having to show to the people who now have the lands or the resources that it is also good for their security, their freedom, for the good functioning of the state, not having people hungry' (Wilson 2009d).

For some organizations engagement merges with broad-based coalition building, where otherwise rival organizations are brought together for common causes. Coalitions are a central tool for the AFL-CIO, which usually acts through coalitions, seeking to define the issue and then assembling a constituency on the basis of a power analysis. The aim is often to create unusual alliances, for instance the Fair Currency Coalition which included domestic manufacturers in the USA, and the Coalition for a Prosperous America, which worked with farming groups:

> We find this over and over again on different issues, where your mix of alliances of who you are working with can range from consumer groups, environmentalists, to health care advocates and professionals. It just depends. There isn't much we go it alone on. You have to work with others of like interests. That's how you get things done. (Wilson 2009g)

The ITUC similarly argued that challenging globalization requires working in alliances with partner organizations that share the same values. This includes

NGOs, social movements, and from time to time even political parties (Wilson 2009a). The CLC representative was more skeptical of coalitions, arguing they would fall apart when the constituent organizations, including trade unions, felt the coalition had become too powerful. For the trade union movement, the CLC argued, the key is achieving a greater maturity in seeing the wider picture, rather than using coalitions to pursue separate interests (Wilson 2011).

To be successful, engagement can require a great deal of dexterity. The FIDH for instance may be taking legal action against a corporation to impose account-ability, while at the same time entering into a partnership with another corpora-tion to encourage human rights observance. For FIDH this combination of sticks and carrots creates a 'very fine line' between partnership and campaign-ing, with global social compliance programs requiring the corporation not to market the relationship, and to allow full access to worksites to monitor adher-ence to standards (Goodman 2010b).

Other organizations regularly shift across institutional levels, or work at mul-tiple levels to achieve their aims. Sometimes organizations will try to establish an inter-state commitment, and campaign to have this implemented at sub-state levels. An example of this is the Reality of Aid Network that helped to set relatively rigorous international commitments through the OECD's 'aid effec-tiveness' agenda, and then pursued these with government agencies and civil society players. In doing so they embarked on a deliberate country-by-country process that began with public awareness raising, moved to NGO engagement, and then put pressure on government departments to implement what had been agreed (Scerri 2011a). This grounded process mobilizes new constituencies and then feeds into the development of new common agendas on aid and development to be pursued at the international level (Scerri 2011a).

Likewise, FIAN aims to implement international food rights at the national level. As a result they maintain a critical but respectful relationship with govern-ments and inter-governmental organizations. For FIAN, 'this is one of our most important tasks, to look to the realities in the places, at the field level, and bring these realities to the international law so that international law can answer to the needs of the people and not just be a good exercise of theoretical standards' (Wilson 2009d). Reflecting this, FIAN produces a handbook on how to apply indicators for the realization of food rights, at the national level, and has devel-oped a methodology for the purpose, linked to twenty-five criteria as required under the UNESCO rights reporting process. Importantly, for FIAN, they see their role as principally to ensure that what is already agreed by governments, in terms of food rights, will be implemented on the ground. In this way, they do not see themselves as a particularly radical, oppositional or political organi-zation. States have already agreed to these values and principles. FIAN simply seeks to ensure that states are meeting their responsibilities (Wilson 2009d).

For most organizations, though, local-level solidarities and mobilizations are forged out of the process of contesting international agreements, not from seeking to implement them. For the CLC for instance, the process of challenging free trade agreements (FTAs) has opened up new relationships and created new allies. With Canada signing more than 36 FTAs, the CLC states: 'country-by-country we end up engaging with the national trade union body that we wouldn't have otherwise ... the fact that we have so many trade agreements with other countries just requires you to have more interaction with the trade union movements in those countries' (Wilson 2011).

Within this context, organizations engage in the tactical use of information power. This is especially important for expert-based organizations that do not have a strong membership base in the wider populace, and thus do not necessarily have access to wider forms of mobilizing power. FIAN for example does not confront governments but offers expertise, practical solutions, and evidence, to help them resolve technical implementation issues. For them, the key is to provide authoritative research and solutions that address the practical problem of food rights: 'if you do a good work, a serious work, putting arguments then you have legitimation that makes you credible' (Wilson 2009d).

Finally, organizations engage in a wide range of symbolic actions designed to heighten the dramatic power of their claims. Through these symbolic actions, organizations seek to generate an affective response, for instance in focusing on the figure of the child in the case of TDH. In another case, the WCC helped produce symbols of global warming, such as bleached coral and rocks retrieved from a melted Greenland glacier, both to speak of despair and to offer signs of hope for restoration (Wilson 2009h). Around the time of the COP15 in Copenhagen, the WCC also coordinated a global day of bell ringing for climate justice on 13 December 2009. The timing of these symbolic actions is crucial, as organizations attempt to expose the exercise of power and create outrage in anticipation of proposals in order to force them off the agenda, or transform them.

Conclusions

The analytical model pursued in this book has disaggregated three components of justice globalism – concepts, claims, and alternatives. For the purposes of analysis, we have separated these components out and examined them in a particular order. We stress, however, that the processes of ideological contestation are anything but static and linear. Values may produce tactics but also, tactical innovations have the capacity to force a reassessment and reconfiguration of ideological values. This more dynamic understanding of the relationship between the aspects of justice globalism is borne out in this chapter, where the process of strategic engagement brings to the fore key principles of justice globalism, especially questions of participatory democracy and solidarity. In many respects, we may argue, these values both generate and are generated by the kinds of mechanisms discussed here, not solely in the abstract imagination of movement elites.

Overall, we can observe that global justice organizations seek to express the diverse grounds in which they flourish. The organic intellectuals engaged in constructing justice globalism are embedded in the contention between radically different perspectives. Their role, often, has been to congeal alternative visions from the cut and thrust of contradicting perspectives, whilst endeavoring to gain traction in a political process still largely dominated by market globalism. It is important thereby to convey the engagements that produce the policy perspectives of justice globalism: they are not set in stone, and are tested against their own internal critics. As a consequence, they are generative, in producing new perspectives and visions, and programs, to address the social field. In large part this reflects the logic of any social movement, as a dialogic engagement for paradigmatic social change. The resulting debates are necessarily fluid: they wax and wane with the political climate, but as such are more organic than programmatic.

These conditions may render the task of identifying and weighing up the policy proposals of justice globalism almost impossible, a task that we attempt in the next three chapters. Such a task, it may be argued, contradicts the participative and democratic ethic of the movement, and is itself an exercise in exerting power over the movement rather than realizing power with it. The dilemma arises for any engagement-at-a-distance, academic or otherwise – who are we to exercise our power as would-be intellectuals, divorced from the frontlines of contestation, from the intimate experience of 'personal troubles'? While this is a valid concern, we suggest in response that the exercise of reflection, of Mills' (1959) 'sociological imagination', is a necessary responsibility if there is to be any possibility of apprehending and meaningfully engaging the power structures that pattern social life. Failing to translate values and visions into possibilities that have real political traction, as antidotes (rather than palliatives) to the deepening crises of market globalism, is clearly not an option. Yet, the proviso remains, the responsiveness of justice globalism is not uniform. Just as with any ideology, 'smooth' justice globalism is a myth. If it is a field at all, it is rough-hewn, with chasms and edges. This is one of the key features of ideologies – to present a coherent unified whole, whilst downplaying internal contradictions. As scholars of political ideologies, it is necessary that we acknowledge these dynamics of coherence and contradiction as we attempt to explore the nuances of justice globalism.

(Continued)

(Continued)

In this spirit the alternatives we present in the next three chapters are contingent responses. They are patterned by the 'new constitutionalisms' of market globalism, and by the ensuing constitutional crises and cognitive dissonances on display by elites in the context of policy failure. They are also patterned by their own plurality. For the purposes of analysis we stress three broad strands: first, a reform tendency, seeking a deepened social globality through regulation; second, a 'delinking to relink' tendency, of asserting the autonomy of an alternative globality against existing institutional formations; and third, a transformative tendency, that seeks to construct horizons beyond current definitions of 'the political'.

Building on our insights here regarding how values, claims, and alternatives interact, our objective throughout the next three chapters is to arrive at some account of the overall 'responsiveness' of justice globalism to prevailing crises. The policy fields – in finance, food, and climate – are chosen as sites of crisis in constitutionalist market globalism that have contributed to the ideological development of justice globalism, and its historical narrative. More broadly they are sites that have the capacity to force systemic collapse and widespread social upheaval. This remains the case: the global bail-out and stimulus, amounting to a fifth of global income, deepened rather than resolved the financial crisis; the food crisis that followed the financial 'correction' appears to have entered an escalating positive feedback loop, now recurring as the 'norm'; climate crisis, meanwhile, has become the universal 'final' crisis, challenging comprehension, let alone official policy. Centrally, if justice globalists are to have the capacity to overcome market globalism, then it is here, in these systemic crises, that they must gain traction.

5

JUSTICE GLOBALISM AND
THE GLOBAL FINANCIAL CRISIS

Introduction

The Global Financial Crisis of 2008–09 (GFC) represents one of the most cataclysmic events of our time. Spilling over into the devastating EU Debt Crisis in 2011, the GFC has assumed the form of a worldwide economic malaise of unknown duration. Just as a reminder, our examination of major 'global crises' that follows in the next three chapters directly relates to Freeden's (1996) third criteria for gauging the maturity of an ideational cluster. In our case, we examine how well *justice globalism* responds to pressing political issues. The contemporary financial system and its underlying ideology of market globalism have been the primary focus of critique for the GJM since its genesis. In many ways, perceptions of growing inequality and disparities in wealth and wellbeing served as the main catalyst for the formation of the movement and its political ideology. Indeed, examining justice globalism's capacity to generate concrete *policy alternatives* in response to the GFC reveals much about its ideological coherence and maturity.

Historically, finance capital has been a central globalizing force because it enables commensurability of different use values. The process of putting a price on a product that can be used in specific ways turns it into an abstract commodity that can be exchanged more easily on the market. Indeed, its price expresses an abstract measure of 'exchange value', which makes qualitative distinctions between products secondary to the quantitative feature they hold at the point of sale. Capital's search for new sources of profitable return always involves this process of commodification. In the age of globalization, the commensurability of commodities in terms of exchange value becomes extended across the world, thus affecting our planet in all its social and ecological dimensions.

Fixated on quantitative measures of value, finance capital does not distinguish between 'good' and 'bad' products. Its exchange value alone designates whether a product is economically viable. Ethical ends of social and ecological wellbeing are secondary, considered only as part of rational-legal frameworks developed in capitalist societies. After all, it is the abstraction of exchange value from a product's usefulness or moral quality that renders a sword, a ploughshare, or labor power 'commensurable' indicated by a price expressed in quantities of money. This 'violence of abstraction' (Sayer 1989) presents a major problem not just for the quality of social interactions, but also for apparently 'impersonal' finance markets. The viability of many financial products – such as the famous 'derivatives' or 'securities' that pushed global markets into chaos during the GFC – ultimately depends on the accumulation of capital through arbitrage or speculation. Societies that excessively 'financialize' their assets choose the path of speculation in order to escape the falling rate of profit that affects more conventional forms of capitalist production. The remarkable expansion of finance capital in the last two decades reflects speculative dynamics whose spectacular short-term 'successes' ultimately cannibalized the global economy.

Critical economists have pointed to an endemic tension between the 'nominal' economy and the 'real' economy, which corresponds to the conflict between the exchange value of commodities and their use value to society (Harvey 2005). This problematic relationship between these two forms of value periodically escalates into a systemic crisis of capitalism. In short, the key problem linked to the most recent phase of corporate-led economic globalization – and the wave of asset financialization that has accompanied it – is the growing disjuncture between exchange value increasingly lodged in esoteric financial instruments such as global hedge funds, and the 'real' use value of products. As the nominal economy becomes more and more abstracted from everyday contexts in the 'real world', finance capital gains more autonomy and imposes its logic on the larger economy.

Market globalists, however, consider the resulting periods of financial instability merely a temporary aberration. They expect that largely unrestricted market forces will always ensure the approximation of exchange value to use value, and thereby advance economic efficiency in terms of resource allocation. Real-world deviations from this assumption are usually treated as indicators of the extent to which market principles need to be more forcefully applied in terms of lessening remaining forms of social control and regulation. For global justice advocates like the World Council of Churches, the economic tensions rendered visible in the GFC correspond to the growing disjuncture between what they call 'planet finance' and the 'ordinary planet' (Goodman 2010a). We found that many of our select GJM organizations expressed a strong desire to 're-embed' finance capital within larger qualitative social relations rooted in a global ethic of justice, solidarity, and sustainability. Consequently, their policy responses to the GFC are part of their overall effort to promote an alternative form of globalization.

This chapter starts with a discussion of the growing power of the global financial regime facilitated by transnational elites who are seen by the GJM as a key social force in the codification and dissemination of market globalism. After our ensuing detailed consideration of the GFC, we first present and then place the specific policy responses offered by our 45 WSF-connected organizations into three analytically distinct thematic categories: reregulation for the common good; delinking to relink; and re-democratization ('transformation via democracy'). As we shall see in Chapters 6 and 7, these three thematic categories also apply to the GJM policy alternatives in response to the global food crisis and global climate crisis.

The Global Financial Regime

There is little doubt that finance capital led the charge in market globalism's triumphant march around the world. Indeed, the globalization of financial markets, the financialization of assets, the growth of global financial speculation, and the related growth of financial houses are often taken as key measures of economic globalization (Harvey 2010; Stiglitz 2010; Rodrik 2011). An important feature of the rise of market globalism has been the attempt to assert principles of 'market access', especially for finance capital, and to embed those principles in law and institutional power. By institutionalizing neoliberal disciplines, new horizons for 'creative' financial product innovation have been legitimized and extended.

Since the 1980s, the institutionalization in the global finance regime has leached across public and private spheres. States and other public authorities increasingly act directly for the powerful finance sector. As Stephen Gill (2002) defines it, this 'new constitutionalism' is transnational in scope and serves to enforce financial disciplines across national contexts. One of the world's most influential neoliberal advocates, Thomas Friedman (2000), famously called this the 'golden straitjacket' that kept politicians out of the finance market, and maximized returns for the financial sector. Many governments in the North voluntarily donned the neoliberal straitjacket – others in the South had to be 'persuaded'. With the breaking of a major international debt crisis in the 1980s, the IMF discovered a new role for itself, requiring debtor countries to sign up to neoliberal structural adjustment programs (under the 'Washington Consensus') as a non-negotiable prerequisite of debt rescheduling. Since the 1980s, its emphasis has been on creating institutional structures that would prevent the reversal of neoliberal prescriptions (Stiglitz 2003). Ironically, with the emergence of the GFC in 2008, this architecture has facilitated massive government bailouts for the financial sector.

The financial sector as a whole has grown 'too big to fail' because of its enhanced capacity to call on the state to insure it against the risks that it generates, notwithstanding the ensuing 'moral hazard'. The result is a peculiar institutionalization of crisis tendencies. Neoliberal doctrine is belied by an ever-growing government role in facilitating finance markets: politicians have handed regulatory power to technocratic elites who regulate for the finance industry, not for the general public. The rise of central bank governors is one significant measure of this dynamic. At the national level, governors have gained independence and have been granted more power, ostensibly to insulate financial regulation from national politics. At the interstate level, central bank strategy has become increasingly coordinated with the Group of 20 Finance Ministers and Central Bank Governors, formed in the aftermath of the 1998–99 East Asian Financial Crisis. It is remarkable that the G8 Heads of State meetings are now increasingly overshadowed by what are seen to be more representative G20 meetings whose agenda is in large part driven by the concerns of technocratic bank governors.

To further institutionalize these dominant policies – and insulate them from national regime change – the Organisation for Economic Cooperation and Development (OECD) made an effort in 1996 to construct a new market-globalist constitution for finance through the 'Multilateral Agreement on Investment' (MAI). Renato Ruggiero, then Director-General of the World Trade Organisation (WTO), proudly described it as 'the constitution of a single global economy'. The MAI was never implemented, partly because of opposition from the fledgling GJM, which established a network of campaigns against it across the OECD, successfully pitting national negotiators against each other in a tactic later characterized as 'monkey-wrenching' (Goodman and Ranald (eds) 2000).

With the MAI shelved, investment 'liberalization' was pursued through a change in the IMF Articles of Agreement that would allow it to enforce investor 'freedoms' (Chossudovsky 1998). In the event, and again partly due to pressure from the emerging GJM, the IMF only gained enhanced 'surveillance' over investment policies. A similar stand-off emerged in the WTO: efforts to extend its authority into promoting market access for investment were, from 1996 on, repeatedly stalled by Southern negotiators lobbied by GJM groups. Ambitious calls for a new 'global financial architecture' were followed by more modest incremental measures rooted in neoliberal ideology.

With an overarching global agreement in abeyance, bilateral and regional arrangements were instead used to institutionalize financial 'freedoms'. Most significant amongst the regional agreements was the North American Free Trade Agreement (NAFTA), which extended 'national treatment' to investors, giving them the right to sue signatory governments should they believe they had been discriminated against. The NAFTA model resurfaced in the MAI, IMF, and WTO proposals, and has been written into the US 'model text' used as the basis for its negotiations on Free Trade Agreements (FTAs). Subsequently it surfaced in other regional FTAs, in the Caribbean and Central America, Asia-Pacific, as well as in a wide variety of US bilateral FTAs. Claims under these provisions relate to public health, transport, agricultural, and environmental policies and in 2011 amounted to US$12 billion (Public Citizen 2011).

Investor protection commitments and rights to arbitration for corporates were also written into a growing proliferation of bilateral investment agreements. There were 385 such agreements in 1990, but by 2010, this number had grown to 2807. In terms of coverage, bilateral investment treaties and investor provisions under free trade agreements are together estimated to account for two-thirds of world investment (UNCTAD 2011). Increasingly, corporations have used these rules to litigate against national governments. In 2006, there were 255 cases pending against seventy countries involving corporations claiming lost earnings as a result of actions of governments, in several cases leading to large payouts (UNCTAD 2005, 2006).

With public authority institutionalizing the private power of financial institutions, government economic policy has become increasingly aimed at attracting 'footloose finance capital' based in 'offshore' financial centers. Initially based in extra-legal 'tax havens' designed to evade national regulatory structures, offshore finance has now become the norm, surpassing the 50% mark of all financial flows as early as 2000 (Palan 2003). Credit-ratings agencies are one of the more visible manifestations of this shift in the global financial architecture, especially as they mediate between private finance houses and public financial institutions, across reserve banks, to the Bank for International Settlements, G20, and IMF/World Bank. At the governmental level three global credit ratings agencies – Standard and Poor's, Fitch, and Moody's – now co-shape the framework for national policymaking. Governments pay these agencies large sums to provide a 'sovereign' rating that determines access to international finance. In 1975, Standard and Poor's conducted ratings for only three countries; in 2004 it produced assessments for more than one hundred (Klein 2007).

Despite its rapid growth and broad acceptance by a large proportion of governments worldwide, the theoretical basis for the dominant neoliberal global financial architecture is not supported by strong empirical evidence (Crotty 2009: 564). Furthermore, rather than reducing the need for government bailouts – as claimed by market globalists before the GFC – the global financial regime and its devastating wave of mass deregulation has actually increased government intervention. Indeed, the inherent weaknesses of financialization have made large-scale economic crises more frequent and more severe (Crotty 2009: 565; Patomaki 2009: 21).

The Crisis of 2008

As public regulation of financial products gave way to self-regulation by private agencies, the conflicts of interest deepened, and ultimately triggered crisis. The 2008 sub-prime crisis is widely attributed to credit rating agencies that stood to gain from the booming business in 'securitized' bad loans. The final report of the US Financial Crisis Commission (USFCC), released in January 2011, is damning: 'The three credit rating agencies were key enablers of the financial meltdown. The mortgage-related securities at the heart of the crisis could not have been marketed and sold without their seal of approval … . This crisis could not have happened without the rating agencies' (USFCC 2011: xxv).

The Commission detailed Moody's as a key player, approving $337 billion in securitized products in 2006 alone, earning it $887 million. Close to half of this business was with just two clients, Merrill and Citigroup, both of which were hit by the crisis, and bailed out with public funds (Bank of America bought Merrill in 2008, and was bailed out at $138 billion; Citigroup was bailed out at $306 billion; USFCC 2011: 149). Remarkably, Moody's continues to operate much as before the crisis, declaring on its website, without evident irony, that it is 'empowering risk professionals' (Moody's Analytics 2012), helping captial markets respond 'with confidence' and contributing to financial market transparency (Moody's Corporation 2012).

The Crisis Commission suggests that the events of 2008 can be interpreted as a case study in systemic mispricing. More fundamentally, however, the origins lie in the decades of financialization that preceded it. Market globalism was a key player insofar as marketization enabled appropriation, or as Harvey (2005) calls it, 'accumulation by dispossession', which produced a financial bubble of unprecedented proportions. Much of the world has been forced to live with the phenomenon of footloose speculative capital since at least the mid-1980s, when Susan Strange diagnosed these dynamics as a case of 'Casino Capitalism' (1997). These trends have been strengthened considerably in the intervening years. In 1980, total international private lending stood at about a tenth of global income; in 2006 it was nearly half of global income (McGuire and Tarashev 2006). With financialization came concentration as finance houses ascended the corporate league tables: in 1989 none of the world's 50 largest corporations were rooted in the finance sector; in 2003 there were 14 such companies on the list (UNCTAD 2005: 19).

The key question for these corporations has been how to maximize returns in the context of overall falling profit rates (Brenner 2006; McNally 2011). One key response has been to compete to create new financial products in the form of derivatives. In terms of value, in 1995 total derivatives turnover stood at $9.2 trillion, in 2003 $874 trillion, in 2007 $2,288 trillion, equivalent to 40 times world annual income (BIS 1996, 2004, 2008, Statistical Annex, Table 23). As such, derivatives effectively acquired the status of a parallel currency, traded according to self-fulfilling prophecies (Bryan and Rafferty 2006). When the US housing bubble burst in 2008, these faux currencies posed such a threat to the value of 'real' money that they had to be honored in those terms – through government bailouts. By 2010 $3.6 trillion worldwide had been allocated to bailout funds, equivalent to 5.7% of global GDP. A further $9.4 trillion was spent on the economic stimuli of various sorts, which amounts to 15.3% of global GDP (Harvard Business Review, January 2010: 30–1). These bailouts were followed merely by a series of minor amendments to the rules of the game for financial markets. The causes of the crisis, in terms of the ongoing process of financialization, and the absence of meaningful regulation of financial 'innovation', remain in place.

One measure of this ongoing dynamic is the swift return to profit in the sector, and the resumption of derivatives trading. Another measure is the increasing spillover of speculative flows into other commodities, including into food futures, and carbon markets (as discussed in the chapters that follow). A third measure is the rise and rise of algorithmic investment strategies, now expressed in so-called 'high frequency trading' where financial decision-making is outsourced to supercomputers, which operate on split-second margins. By 2010, high frequency trading had overwhelmed equities markets, and was prompting new debates about regulation (Tregillis 2011). Moreover, the magnitude of speculative flows has rebounded since 2008. Global hedge funds passed the 2007 high-water mark in April 2011, and continue to grow at an unprecedented rate (Jones 2011). Remarkably, the value of derivatives turnover only fell marginally between 2008 and 2009, and was recovering by 2010, just as the real economy began to feel the effects of the crisis (BIS 2010, Statistical Annex, Table 23). Simultaneously, the reach of finance capital has been extending still further as can be seen in the ongoing commodification of greenhouse gases and the expansion of the genetic bio-economy.

Despite finance capital's apparent return to normalcy, there is much to suggest that a deeper reassessment of the current global financial architecture is required. Although the GFC was the most spectacular economic calamity in decades, smaller crises of the global neoliberal model have occurred intermittently since the late 1970s and early 1980s (McMichael 2004: 231–2; Patomäki 2009: 4). The problem of unregulated markets was widely believed to be the cause of the only other financial crisis to rival the most recent GFC in severity – the Great Depression of the late 1920s/early 1930s (Crotty 2009: 563). Indeed, the 'inner circles' of global financial management remain worried about the 'fragility of a deregulated world monetary system' (McMichael 2004: 195). Even previous staunch supporters of the neoliberal agenda such as Alan Greenspan and Martin Wolf have recently called for profound systemic change (Soros 2008; Crotty 2009: 575; Wolf 2009).

Justice Globalism Responds

How has the GJM responded to the GFC and its aftermath? The question of global finance was central to the development of the movement and its associated political ideology. While many economists and government policy makers have only recently begun to perceive the inherent flaws in the global financial architecture, the GJM has pointed to the dangers of this system for some time.

The Transnational Institute was one of the earliest critics of global financial inequalities and neoliberal policies in the 1970s and 1980s (George 1976; TNI n.d.). Other GJM groups such as the International Forum on Globalization were formed in the mid-1990s as the detrimental impacts of neoliberal economic principles became more apparent. As we noted, the OECD's MAI negotiations marked a key moment in the genesis and mobilization of the global justice movement, in terms of its advocacy for alternative financial policies and structures.

Some of the major criticisms of the current global financial system relate directly to the underpinning values of the GJM as outlined in Chapters 2 and 3, especially its critique of neoliberalism's assumption of a 'level playing field'. For many GJM organizations, marketization deepens social class divisions and exacerbates pre-existing inequalities or power imbalances. At the same time, the high degree of volatility generated by financial speculation is seen as profoundly destabilizing. Notwithstanding market globalism's ideological claim of a rising tide (eventually) lifting all boats, the economic crises brought on by casino capitalism exemplify the dictum that surpluses must be privatized and costs must be socialized. Many GJM organizations note that neoliberal crises affect the least powerful the most as markets displace the burden of adjustment 'downwards'.

A further GJM critique is that the principles of the free market have been implemented unevenly. While countries in the global South have been forced to reduce tariffs and duties on imports as part of structural adjustment programs and poverty reduction strategies in return for financial aid from the IMF and World Bank, the North continues to impose tariffs on imports from the South. Moreover, the global North subsidizes its agricultural production and allows its products to flood markets in the global South (Chossudovsky 1998: 104–6). For some organizations within the GJM, the priority is to correct these double standards through the introduction of market controls. Others argue outright that the possibility of market-based human development is a fallacy.

In addition, GJM policy analysts have emphasized the negative impacts of privatizing previously state-owned utilities such as electricity and water, arguing that the neoliberal policy prescription has enriched the private sector while increasing the costs for consumers, particularly in the global South where private fee-for-service has quickly replaced public service provision. The market-based structural adjustment model, required by the IMF for many debtor countries as a condition of further financing, is seen as having dramatically failed in its stated goal of facilitating 'development' in the world's poorest countries. Frequently cited evidence of this failure includes the IMF's growing list of 'Heavily-Indebted Poor Countries' deserving of limited (highly conditional) debt relief and the World Bank's re-badging of SAPs as 'Poverty Reduction Strategy Programs' (World Bank 2000a, 2000b; Haselip 2005: 82; Haselip et al. 2005: 2–3; Castro 2008: 65).

Other major GJM criticisms of the global financial regime relate to issues of transparency and accountability. Global financial flows are not subject to the transparency required of other asset types, yet their social impacts are severe. Public authorities devolve power to the industry, to regulate itself, and to financial technocrats that are only in the loosest sense accountable to elected politicians, despite the system-wide significance of decisions that they make. Until the most recent GFC, the G7/8 and the OECD countries determined the rules governing global finance (Tan 2007). Global financial procedures and rules are characterized by a lack of transparency and a lack of democratic procedure (ATTAC 2009). After the GFC many of the decisions about global finance have shifted from the G8 to the G20 and for many GJM observers, this amounts to a 'shell game' of simply institutionalizing financial technocracy and relegitimizing G8 dominance. Meanwhile, as many WSF-connected groups insist, inequality is rising across global North and South. For concrete examples, see Table 5.1.

Table 5.1 The Global South: a Fate Worse than Debt (cited in Steger 2009b: 44–5)

Original debt of developing countries in 1980	US$618 billion
Total external debt of developing countries in 2007	US$3.3 trillion
Cost of the war in Iraq to the USA (2003–08)	US$3.3 trillion
Total amount paid by developing countries in debt servicing 1980–2006	US$7.7 trillion
Amount of money spent by Western industrialized nations on weapons and soldiers every year	US$747.5 billion
Amount of debt that the G8 promised to write off	$100 billion
Amount of debt actually written off so far	$46 billion
Number of countries eligible for the international Heavily Indebted Poor Countries initiative (HIPC)	42
Proportion of bilateral debt that the G8 countries have promised to cancel for the 42 HIPCs	100%
Proportion of multilateral debt that the World Bank and International Monetary Fund will eventually cancel for the 42 HIPCs	65% (approx)
Total amount of multilateral debt owed by the 42 HIPCs that is NOT eligible for cancellation	US$93 billion
Amount of money the world's poorest countries spend on debt servicing each year	US$37.5 billion
Profits made by ExxonMobil 2007	US$39.5 billion
Amount of money the United Nations estimates is needed annually to curb the AIDS epidemic in Africa through education, prevention, and care by 2010	US$20–23 billion
Amount of money African nations pay to service their debts each year	$21 billion
Amount of money wealthy countries spend on defence every year	US$625 billion
Amount of money African countries have paid in debt servicing 1980–2006	US$675 billion

(Continued)

Table 5.1   (Continued)

Amount of money the world's poorest countries spend on debt servicing every 12 days	US$1.25 billion (0.2% of what the rich world spends on defence each year)
Amount of money Kenya owes in external debt (2005)	US$7 billion
Amount of money Kenya allocated to health, water, roads, agriculture, transport and finance in 2005	US$7 billion
Profits made by Wal-Mart in 2007	US$11.3 billion

Sources: World Bank, *World Development Report 2006: Equity and Development* (World Bank, Washington DC, 2005); Nakatani and Herera (2007) 'The South has already paid its external debt to the North' *The Monthly Review* 59: 2. http://www.monthlyreview.org/0607pnrh.html (accessed 18 March 2008); Joseph Stiglitz, cited in 'Under the cloud of War' by Daniel Flitton, *Insight The Age Newspaper*, 15 March 2008, p. 4. http://www.theage.com.au/news/in-depth/under-the-cloud-of-war/2008/03/4/1205472076737.html; Earth Trends: *The Environmental Information Portal*, World Resources Institute. http://earthtrends.wri.org (accessed 15 March 2008); Jubilee Debt Campaign UK, June 2006, 'HIV/AIDS in Africa 2007–2010: Major Challenges Ahead'. http://www.worldpress.org/Africa/ 2602.cfm; *Fortune* magazine top 500 companies http://money.cnn.com/magazines/fortune/fortune500/2007/full_list/index.html> (accessed 18 March 2008)
© Manfred B. Steger (2003), pp.44–45. Table 5.1: The Global South: A fate worse than debt, from Globalization: *A Very Short Introduction* by Steger, Manfred (2003). By permission of Oxford University Press.

Another problem our selected GJM organizations highlight is that the attempt to attract foreign direct investment at any price leads to a lowering of labor and environmental standards, especially in the global South. It is often pointed out that trade and finance rules are enforced above environmental, social or cultural values, and that the neoliberal financial architecture extends rights to corporations, giving them a legal personality under international arbitration law that is not available to individuals. The consequent 'race to the bottom' places highest priority on financial accumulation and private wealth, over the economic, social and cultural rights of populations around the world, at the expense of the common good (ATTAC 2009).

Other WSF-linked groups are strongly critical of the pervasive consumerism and greed that is embedded in the current global economic system (Grassroots Global Justice 2009; World Council of Churches 2009a). They argue that neoliberal economics disregard the immediate or long-term social consequences for the majority of people in the world while paying close attention to the immediate financial consequences for TNCs and global investors. Consequently, the global economy becomes abstracted from local contexts and real-life situations. In part an extension of this problem of abstraction, feminist critiques of market globalism highlight its patriarchal bias; its failure to recognize and acknowledge the value of the 'hidden economy'; the private work of many women in homes, child-rearing, housekeeping, and caring for sick and elderly relatives. Finally, many justice globalists are critical of the deterministic language of neoliberalism, which posits neoliberal globalization as inevitable, irreversible, and natural, thus profoundly discouraging the creation of viable alternatives to policies of deregulation, privatization, and liberalization (George 2001; Steger 2009).

Opportunity and Alternatives

Several observers from within the GJM now look upon the GFC as a lost opportunity to really change international finance and move away from neoliberalism (Wilson 2009c; Goodman 2010b, 2010c; Steger 2010c). CUT stated that the movement had 'lost a big opportunity during the financial crisis' in terms of 'the opportunity to show more unified statements' (Steger 2010c). For FIDH the financial crisis was also a missed chance. However, FIDH did not stake out a specific position on financialization and speculation, stating rather that human rights needed to be taken into consideration in any regulatory proposals: respect for human rights would set a boundary on financial markets. Still, FIDH insisted that organizations 'needed more input from the WSF for alternative proposals … I think we all – and I include us in that – missed an important opportunity. For years we've been saying in the WSF that the system as it is doesn't work, and there was big, big proof, evidence, and we were not there to react' (Goodman 2010b).

The TNI representative agreed with these self-criticisms, outlining how the so-called 'Beijing Declaration' of the Asia-Europe People's Forum was not taken up by the movement. Issued in October 2008 at a meeting of 500 GJM representatives from 70 organizations, this Declaration constituted an effort to put forward a plan of 'grand regulation', which contrasted sharply with the mere 'tinkering' of the G20 reform proposals:

> There was a call for a reconstituted global economic order. Which is this global vision thing again, the kind of quite grand-scale cosmopolitan vision, within which all these things – corporate codes, labor standards – would be embedded. So it was almost like a call for a new economic order, that kind of scale, if not bigger actually. And UN-centered, and an attempt to ensure the real economy was subservient to finance. I just found that an interesting response to the financial crisis. But quite grand if you know what I mean, obviously saying the G20 was tinkering, but this is grand regulation. It wasn't saying things like we've got to de-globalize the banks, we've got to dismantle the speculative system, so much as impose a range of codes and regulations. (Goodman 2010c)

The wording of the Declaration offers an important insight into the combination of themes constituting this immediate GJM policy response. The Statement marked the historic moment with the following preamble:

> What is currently being presented as a 'financial crisis' is in reality the latest in a series of interlinked crises – food, energy, climate, human security and environmental degradation – that are already devastating the lives, and compounding the poverty and exclusion faced on a daily basis by billions of women, men and children.

> There is a strong consensus across Asia and Europe that the dominant approach over the last decades – based around deregulation of markets, increasing power of multinational corporations, unaccountable multilateral institutions and trade liberalization – has failed in its aims to meet the needs and rights of all citizens.

We need to go beyond an analysis and response that focuses solely on short-term measures benefiting a few financial institutions.

Our governments and the citizens of Asia and Europe have a unique and historic opportunity to transform our social, economic and political futures so that all can live in peace, security and dignity. We all need to take responsibilities to work together to create and implement the radical and creative solutions needed for people-centered recovery, change and a harmonious world – we will not have this opportunity again. (TNI 2010)

The Statement demonstrates how the core claims of the GJM organizations outlined in Chapter 3 are linked to an alternative policy response to the global financial crisis. The Peoples' Forum Statement put a series of demands to the Asia-Europe Meeting of heads of state from the EU and Asia, held in Beijing. They related their demand for regulation and accountability directly to the GFC:

Use the opportunity of the current financial and political crisis to put in place an alternative financial architecture and infrastructure that will promote and enable a more equitable, carbon neutral and just global economic system, reclaiming national development policy rights and empowering working people. Financial institutions and financial decision-making must become truly accountable and transparent. (TNI 2010)

While the TNI representative stressed the significance and policy potential of the Beijing Statement, she also observed that there was no concrete follow-up action by GJM groups:

The Beijing Declaration was put together by probably seventy or eighty organizations represented in the room from Asia and Europe. And all of us were probably involved again in our home areas in other networks whose members were also talking about the financial crisis, out of which also other declarations emerged. But in no case did we try to build on what we had. Because the Beijing Declaration was the first written response, so one would think there would be a basis and you would refer back to it and see how you could develop. But people just don't work like that somehow. In these crisis moments it's somehow telling. (Goodman 2010c)

This lapse of a potential grand policy vision into diverse proposals for regulatory design suggests a failure of movement strategy. According to the TNI there was a failure to create opportunities and inadequate follow-through. The Stiglitz Commission at the UN, in particular, is cited as offering an important opportunity not taken up by the movement, despite the fact that there were a 'lot of our people there' (Goodman 2010c). After all, the spectacular bank bailouts around the world had temporarily socialized large segments of finance capital, offering a real possibility of demanding they therefore should be publically owned on a permanent basis. However, as TNI observed, the GJM blinked, suggesting 'some psychology of crisis' at work in the movement (Goodman 2010c).

But a different perspective demonstrates the broad range of policy positions within the GJM. The GPF, for example, argued the official G20 response to the crisis actually offered real possibilities for reform.

> When you have a huge crisis you have a huge opportunity for transformational change for the generations to come … . So we are trying to exploit the bad aspects of what happened to actually push forward a fairer model and a more sustainable model. Would it be a different ideology? I think so, because at the end of the day, if you look at the economic and financial policies, at the micro-economic level, you've got different ideologies, and the neo-liberal one is challenged by many others. (Wilson 2009c)

The GPF outlined the range of policy debates in terms of the public–private divide:

> The main issue, without going into the different schemes, is the level of state intervention … . So we hope that people now realize that maybe we shouldn't leave everything in the private sector. After all, the financial crisis is about 160 people in a few buildings around the world who made the crisis happen through speculation. We hope we can counter-balance this with transparency and more regulation, and more regulation means state intervention … (Wilson 2009c)

GPF was positive about the gains being made, in terms of the dramatic legitimacy crisis for finance markets as well as the encouraging alternative policy debates that had emerged over how to regulate the sector. There was also debate about the appropriate forum for public debate beyond the G20, which, it argued, 'should not be seen as the real legitimate power in the global age' (Wilson 2009c). Finally, GJM organizations discussed the form financial regulation should take:

> I think there is space for change. The progressive change that has taken place in the United States with the change of government is important. So that is a positive change. The same will happen in Japan. The crisis gives hope. Whether we will be successful or not is another question, but I think we are in a much better position today to try and push our goals than we were two years ago. Two years ago, talking about private equity and hedge funds was absolute nonsense, but maybe today it starts making sense. I think the situation is a lot better now. (Wilson 2009c)

Some voices in the GJM had predicted a major financial crisis for some time, but these warnings had failed to generate sustained debate until the GFC. On the upside, however, these warnings had provided the movement with a language that addressed what was increasingly recognized as the cause of crisis: neoliberal financialization. In this respect, Focus on the Global South echoed some of the more positive views expressed by GPF:

> I think you will remember that Focus had been talking about the kind of financialization that was happening in the world a year before the financial crisis hit the US. No one would believe us back then. But when the financial crisis hit the US, now you even get economists taking up our analysis – but, of course, with their own spin. But at least now we are being heard, I suppose we're being read. (Wilson 2009e)

Setting aside the question of the immediate effectiveness of GJM critiques in the aftermath of the 2008–09 GFC, there is no doubt that justice globalist critiques of the financial sector have translated into a clear set of policy proposals. These alternatives address what our WSF-affiliated organizations regard as the primary flaws of the current global financial regime that generate the recurring patterns of global financial crisis. Indeed, global justice organizations highlight three main problems with the current global financial system, which, they argue, are the underlying causes of recurring crisis:

- Deregulation
- The separation or abstraction of finance from local contexts (in other words, the 'nominal' economy or financial world versus the 'real' money economy)
- The authoritarian tendencies of global finance capital.

Intimately linked to these three causes of contemporary global financial crises, most of the policy proposals put forward by GJM groups can be placed in the following three thematic categories: reregulation, relinking, and re-democratization ('transformation via democracy').

Reregulation for the Public Good

As GJM organizations have argued that neoliberal deregulation prepared the ground for the GFC, it makes sense for them to suggest as remedy a process of reregulating finance for the public good rather than private gain. One of justice globalism's key players, ATTAC (Association for Taxation of Financial Transaction to Aid Citizens) was created in the aftermath of the East-Asian Financial Crisis of 1998–99 and thus was well equipped to spearhead the critique of deregulation within the GJM. Their proposals to reregulate global finance through a variety of mechanisms, including the famous 'Tobin Tax' on transnational speculative financial transactions, have gained considerable ground in recent years. The European Parliament has voted in favor of a proposal to introduce a tax of up to 0.05% on financial transactions undertaken by EU-based banks (Aldrick 2011). Related proposals for a 'Financial Transactions Tax', or more popularly, a 'Robin Hood Tax' are designed to generate sufficient funds to meet basic social needs as well as mitigate climate change impacts. Support for such a tax is exceptionally strong in the GJM, among organizations like ATTAC, Focus on the Global South, the Transnational Institute, and Jubilee South. But, as noted, this tax campaign led by the GJM is also increasingly backed by mainstream voices. One thousand of the world's top economists – including Jeffrey Sachs and Giancarlo Gandolfo – urged leaders at a 2011 meeting of G20 finance ministers to introduce a Tobin Tax (Stewart 2011).

Related to the Tobin Tax proposal, GJM organizations including the ACTU, COSATU, Focus on the Global South, the Global Progressive Forum, Jubilee South, the Transnational Institute, and the World Council of Churches, have developed a broad range of policy measures designed to reregulate and further stabilize the global financial system. These proposals also include the closure of all tax havens as part of a broader effort to minimize global tax evasion by individuals and corporations. Putting an end to tax evasion worldwide would generate a large pool of public funds that could then be used to address other social and environmental problems, including funding climate change adaptation technologies and providing the means to develop public health and education systems in the global South (Focus on the Global South 2008; ACTU 2009: 7; GPF 2009a; WCC 2009b).

Closing tax evasion loopholes would also help to offset the 'race to the bottom' since it would prevent countries from lowering labor and environmental standards in order to attract foreign direct investment. Consequently, such a strategy would assist in preserving the rights of populations in poor regions, as well as strengthening the decision-making powers of governments in the global South. This, in turn, could contribute to improving local and national governance structures in the South. A number of GJM organizations have made the prevention of tax evasion part of a broader effort to develop a global tax system that targets speculative short-term financial transactions and environmental pollution in order to generate funds for public goods (Focus on the Global South 2008; WCC 2009c). A related policy proposal involves 'setting limits on excess compensation of top level management of financial institutions [executive bonuses] and the elimination of forms of incentive compensation that reward excessively risky behavior' (George et al. 2008; see also ACTU 2009: 7). Other related policy proposals focus less on the financial sector and more on the 'real economy', particularly the provision of basic social services. Both the People's Health Movement (2004: 3) and the Poor People's Economic Human Rights Campaign (Normand 2003) argue that there should be stronger regulatory mechanisms around the involvement of the corporate sector in the delivery of social services such as health, education, electricity, water, and transport. PPEHRC, in particular, insists that privatization and deregulation should be prohibited when it risks depriving a majority of the public from access to basic services (Normand 2003).

Underlying these reregulation proposals one can find justice globalism's ideological core concepts of participatory democracy and universal rights. Many GJM organizations consider the current deregulated and deliberately opaque nature of global finance as undemocratic and inextricably linked to persistent human rights abuses, particularly with regard to people's economic, social, and cultural rights (ATTAC 2009; Corpwatch 2009). Hence, justice globalists are confident that reregulating the financial sector will increase accountability and transparency, enabling greater democratic control and oversight of financial services and decision-making as well as safeguarding human rights. Thus, they embrace reregulation not as an end in itself, but rather, as an alternative way of organizing the economy that opens up new possibilities for the realization of social justice. ITUC, for example, interprets workplace inequality as the central issue that creates financial accumulation and produces the need for regulation (Wilson 2009a).

Likewise, GPF sees regulation as a necessary first step on the path to social justice that was finally gaining ground in the wake of the GFC:

> To give you an idea until last year the European Commissioner… said these financial actors were beneficial for the markets. This is not the case today. In the United States, a similar line has taken place … we have been in legislative terms quite fast in bringing about change. The other questions are a lot bigger, and bit-by-bit, it doesn't happen overnight.

> Financial markets? Here we have several dimensions again. You've got the global governance issue, so the reform of the Bretton Woods institutions, which also brings the issue of democratic representation. Then we've got the issue of regulation. Then we've got the issue of trying to put a cap on the bonuses, which is a very popular public feeling at the moment. Then you've got the issue of making the link between what happens, and therefore the banks, and the political choice behind it. That is, people haven't really managed to make the link between the banks themselves and the political system behind it … . Then you've got the issue of tax havens and effective tax systems. Then the issue of speculation, and we could continue for a long time. (Wilson 2009c)

The overall policy approach articulated by our selected GJM organizations is essentially to build a more stringent and effective regulatory regime that benefits ordinary people around the world. Even those groups that accept the capitalist system as the world's dominant economic framework for the foreseeable future reject the neoliberal utopia of 'self-regulating markets'. Hence, they demand stronger political control over central banks and the institution of new redistributive tax systems (Wilson 2009b). WCC echoes these concerns: 'I do think you can change globalization. But it shouldn't be like this. It should be much more regulated, it should be much more rights-based, much more respectful of human rights. But we are not calling for stopping globalization or the integration of markets. Our position is to make it fairer' (Goodman 2010a).

Delinking to Relink

A second set of policy proposals advocates the gradual process of delinking from the global financial regime and relinking to local contexts. GJM groups backing this vision consider the impact of neoliberal financial dynamics on unprotected localities as a major contributing factor to the outbreak of recurring economic crises. Consequently, these proposals focus on ways to delink the local (and sometimes national) economy from the global economy in order to insulate localities from global economic shocks. Some of these delinking proposals gained great popularity in Asia with the unexpected emergence of the regional financial crisis of 1997–98. Decoupling efforts also found traction in Latin

America in the context of continent-wide revival of left-progressive projects for the regional delinking from global finance and commodity flows through the institution of independent regional financial regimes.

Moreover, autonomous South-to-South development financing has a number of supporters across the GJM. Part of this idea involves a shift in global flows of lending and borrowing. Instead of borrowing from the global North and its affiliated international financial institutions, organizations like the Alternative Information Development Centre (AIDC), the World Council of Churches (WCC), and the Allianza Social Continental (ASC) promote the development of regional banks and financial institutions that are situated in the Global South and focused on local issues. They also argue that countries in the global South should create mutual-aid-and-trade networks and efficient lending and borrowing schemes (Dembele 2009).

The desire for regional and local arrangements to respond to specific needs corresponds to the justice globalist conviction that the global financial system has little incentive to respond to regional needs. The aim is to embed finance in local contexts, not to exaggerate forces for capital flight. Similar proposals emerged from various 'Bolivarian' movements in Latin America. In fact, the eight-country Bolivarian Alliance for the Peoples of Our America created its own regional currency in 2010. Again, autonomy from global flows, and in this case from the US dollar, is portrayed as the principal means of enabling the realization of global justice.

Focus on the Global South is one of the main GJM organizations that has championed policies of delinking as part of its broader frame of 'deglobalization', discussed in Chapter 4. It provides the following rationale for this position:

> We are looking at regions, both the formally organized regions like ASEAN, the south, as well as the idea of regions itself … they are not perfect organizations. I mean at the worse they replicate the worst disease, or the worst short-comings of the many other inter-governmental mechanisms … . But if you look at the possibilities, it's a lot. Like if regions, and different regional members and individuals are not so encumbered by their dependence on the US, their dependence on global trade, their dependence on the dollar, then there are more options for them to consider. (Wilson 2009e)

Proposals that encourage delinking from current global financial mechanisms include the regulation of trade in derivatives and speculative investments in food staples. Some organizations propose a complete ban on speculative trading schemes (Focus on the Global South 2008; Jubilee South 2009; World Council of Churches 2009b). Imposing limits on finance, they argue, would open up space for local communities and cooperatives to regain control over the pricing and distribution of locally produced commodities and would facilitate a closer relationship between the 'real' money economy and the world of finance – largely by reducing the size and scope of the nominal economy.

Many organizations also promote the development of local 'popular' markets insulated from global financial markets. Such proposals are particularly strong amongst organizations in Africa (Dembele 2009; ENDA n.d) and Latin America

(WMW 2004; CTA 2009; La Via Campesina 2009b). According to these schemes, local markets would deal only in goods and services produced locally for specific communities, thereby reintegrating the economy within its corresponding socio-ecological framework while at the same time delinking it from global macroeconomic structures. Allianza Social Continental (2008), for example, suggests that the central focus of regional and national economies should be to produce what is consumed nationally and regionally, thus lessening the need to export goods that are urgently needed at home.

Related proposals include taxes on goods that are not locally produced. Focus on the Global South (2008) advocates for a levy on goods that have been transported more than 1000 kilometers; on luxury items (for example, cars, televisions, designer clothing); and on imported goods that are already produced locally. These measures would ensure that local producers have fair access to local markets, rather than being excluded as a result of tariffs and subsidies required as part of Poverty Reduction Strategies enforced by International Financial Institutions (IFIs) or due to binding articles in bilateral free trade agreements. Ultimately, proposals to delink local and national economies from the global economy are meant to facilitate local ownership and control over production and consumption. Once again, these policy proposals project justice globalism's core concepts of universal rights, equality and sustainability:

> A society's economy should serve the women and men composing that society. It should be based on the production and exchange of socially useful wealth distributed among all people, the priority of satisfying the collective needs, eliminating poverty and ensuring the balance of collective and individual interests. (World March of Women 2004)

For Focus on the Global South, the key to relinking is region-level institution-building. Focus draw on the concept of subsidiarity, an idea deployed by the European Union in the 1980s, that decision-making must be devolved to the lowest level where it can still be effective. This means financial regulation should occur at the 'macro-regional' level:

> In the spirit of subsidiarity and democracy we believe that for the world to be truly democratic we should be able to develop different centers of influence and power ... looking at the realities on the ground, and the logic of shared histories and shared concerns, the region can actually be an important arena to confront common issues as well as to serve as alternatives. (Wilson 2009e)

Several GJM organizations argue that East Asia, for example, is already interconnected in terms of finance, trade, and migration. As an economic bloc, it has the capacity to create social stability by deploying financial reserves or through common mechanisms dealing with human rights issues, migration, or foreign policy. An 'East Asian Model' could draw on similar proposals currently underway for the development of a Peoples Union of South Asia.

This idea of 'people's regionalism' has emerged as an alternative to market globalism at the international level. GJM groups like TNI stress regionalization as a form of political resistance:

> The only chance the southern countries had, given what the WTO was trying to set up, which was clearly the new global trade regime, was to get themselves together regionally, because only by strengthening themselves could they either contest or engage. And then the idea came up that that was fine at a geo-strategic level, but what about people's region? What is our vision of a people's-centered regional development, and how could coming together regionally, economies of scale if you like, help make that an easier project? (Goodman 2010c)

It is crucial to note that GJM organizations in favor of delinking are *not* promoting 'anti-globalization'. The proposed delinking mechanisms aim at overcoming historic and contemporary inequalities that are engrained in the globally-integrated market as a result of colonial exploitation and long-term discriminatory trade practices. As Focus puts it:

> [W]hat we really mean by deglobalization is not anti-globalization, but we say that there's another way that globalization as a process can move forward. Especially for us, we recognize that there are positive things in how globalization is moving forward … . Economists would say there are winners and losers, but what do you do with the losers? … [O]ur preference is to help the losers … . It's a preference for the marginalized. (Wilson 2009e)

This careful explanation of deglobalization also suggests that solidarity – both within and across regions – is an important core concept animating GJM proposals to delink local and national economies from global financial markets and relink with alternative networks. Focus on the Global South sees deglobalization as a precondition for this process of relinking that then can produce needs-based alternatives:

> Deglobalization would mean you have achieved some kind of justice … . You have what's called sovereignty; you have equitable access, and sustainable stewardship of resources like water and land. You are able to function in an effective democracy where different groups have equal representation or effective representation and ample voice and a political space in the process. (Wilson 2009e)

Re-democratization (Transformation via Democratization)

A third set of alternative proposals seeks to transform global finance by putting it under democratic political control. Rather than regulating private finance, or delinking societies from the impacts of financial decision-making, this approach emphasizes that private finance has public impacts and, therefore, must be brought under public control. The argument mobilizes justice globalist principles of accountability and transparency for transformation, arguing that those affected by private finance should enjoy greater access to relevant knowledge and be more involved in the decisions that so crucially shape their lives. Although there are clear overlaps with the reregulation approach, re-democratization centers on the process of decision-making and favors a more thorough 'socialization' of financial decisions.

Arguments for democratization have been greatly boosted with the onset of the GFC that made transparent how finance capital ultimately depends on the public purse. Taxpayers' money was used to save the finance sector, while ordinary citizens were left to fend for themselves. GJM organizations have exploited the ensuing credibility gap to promote alternative models for financial management as crucial means for 'deepening' democracy. Frequently citing the power of finance capital in the global economy as a major cause for systemic instability, they have drawn up policy prescriptions that take as their point of departure the deliberately obscure speculative transactions of 'casino capitalism'. A number of organizations, including Focus propose establishing public citizens' boards for the oversight and regulation of credit rating agencies. The WCC goes further, arguing that finance should be treated 'as a public service', not as a sector that is separate from and of little relevance to the lived experiences of people around the world (WCC 2009c).

Such policy proposals express the GJM's aspiration to utterly transform the rules governing the global financial regime. A WCC representative, for example, suggested that accumulated wealth is a contradiction in terms: 'It is not wealth if it is just accumulated wealth. It is wealth when it starts to be shared with the community … it's not for accumulation, it's for use' (Goodman 2010a). This simple injunction provides the overarching rationale for the establishment of a more just financial system. Such a system would require new institutions that prevent accumulation, so that, 'Before you create wealth you have to create conditions for sharing that wealth already during its generation, and sharing among people and sharing it with the Earth' (Goodman 2010a).

Obviously, the required institutional transformations would be wide-ranging. As we noted in previous chapters, some of our WSF-connected groups believe that existing global financial institutions can be reformed, while the majority favors a complete dismantling of the World Bank, the IMF, and other 'neoliberal' development banks such as the Asian Development Bank. Many GJM organizations, like Focus, reject the argument for reform of international financial institutions on pragmatic grounds: given their existing voting structure, efforts at reforming the World Bank or IMF would be highly unlikely (Wilson 2009e). Instead, several organizations suggest that global financial decision-making should rest with the UN, through institutions established by the UN General Assembly. As such, the UN offers a place where those affected by international financial institutions can have at least *some* influence over financial decision-making. The WCC, for example, calls for the creation of a UN-based Global Economic Council, which would carry the same weight as the UN Security

Council. The aim would be to establish a 'whole different social contract around financial institutions', with 'regulatory frameworks that would actually hold institutions to account' (Wilson 2009h). The ultimate result of such an arrangement, according to the WCC, would be 'transformational change ... around everything, from investment practices to corporate activity like mining'. Other organizations endorsing this shift in global financial arrangements include the Transnational Institute, ATTAC, Focus on the Global South, ASC, Ibase, and Jubilee South. To some extent, the UN itself has advanced such a proposal, primarily as an effort to promote the effective integration of Global South countries into international financial debates and decision-making processes (United Nations Department of Economic and Social Affairs, Population Division 2009).

Additional proposals relating to the democratization of finance include a requirement for full public disclosure of all activities and strategies of banks, regulatory agencies, investment funds and financial institutions to protect against risky investment behavior.

The underlying assumption expressed in these GJM proposals is that democratization extends well beyond limited regulatory frameworks to more radical measures such as returning banks to public ownership by communities and governments, instead of private ownership by shareholders and financial corporations. There are also various strong proposals for the involvement of workers and the general public in regulatory and supervisory bodies. More broadly, GJM organizations are advocating for the reintroduction of national control over tariffs, subsidies and other policies related to regulation and development strategies, primarily in contexts where decision-making on these issues has been taken out of the hands of state governments and handed to IFIs, such as the G20 and IMF, as part of Poverty Reduction Strategies.

The desire for greater control over global financial decision-making, and also for greater national and community autonomy, relates also to spiraling debt. Many of the GJM organizations that advocate for greater transparency and national autonomy in financial decision-making also argue that the long-term debt of developing countries should be cancelled, since this is a key mechanism through which global financial institutions have maintained power inequalities between the global North and South. These groups insist that debt institutionalizes historical inequalities and hands control over key policies to international financiers (Focus on the Global South 2008; World Council of Churches 2008; Jubilee South 2009).

The call for debt cancellation without any preconditions expresses justice globalist values of participatory democracy, including local and national autonomy, and social justice. It is aimed at taking structural pressure off the global poor. In addition, several GJM organizations have proposed new limitations on the 'global rich'. The WCC, for example, calls for a global 'greed line' intended as a counterpart to a global 'poverty line'. The greed line is based on 'values of sufficiency and solidarity as opposed to the winner-takes-all attitude', linking social justice and ecological impacts by relating 'limits to growth [with] limits to acquisition' (Wilson 2009h). Indeed, the idea of a 'greed line' suggests that more for the wealthy means less for the rest, and as such politicizes and personalizes overdevelopment, insisting on a values-based approach that addresses both social and ecological justice. As such it is clearly a provocation, but one that is highly productive, especially in the context of global bailouts. In 2011, similar political demands were at play in cities around the world in what became characterized as the 'Occupy Movement' that held the wealthiest '1%' of the global population responsible for the GFC at the cost of the remaining '99%'.

Conclusion

Critiques of the global financial regime coming from the GJM do not, as many of their market globalist detractors have argued, amount to unproductive oppositionalism (Friedman 2000, 2005; Stiglitz 2003; Wolf 2004; Bhagwati 2004; Greenwald and Kahn 2009; Wilson 2009e). The material presented in this book so far suggests that justice globalists hold coherent ideological commitments that allow them to produce constructive alternatives to global financial arrangements based on neoliberal principles of deregulation, privatization, and financialization.

This chapter provides a representative summary of some of the main policy proposals that our selected GJM organizations developed in response to the perceived flaws and shortcomings of the current global financial architecture. While progressive social forces have for many years sought viable alternatives to speculative finance, concrete policy proposals are now being developed in response to the most devastating financial crisis since the 1930s. In the wake of this GFC, prominent mainstream economists like George Soros, Joseph Stiglitz, Jeffrey Sachs, Dani Rodrik, and Paul Krugman have endorsed some of the proposals. Soros (2008) and Patomäki (2009), for example, have suggested that the economic 'boom and bust' cycle is becoming exponentially worse, with large booms being followed by even larger and deeper crises, occurring with increasing rapidity and severity. These observers warn that unless significant reforms occur in the global regulation of finance, the world will likely witness yet another crash in the late 2010s or early 2020s – a financial crisis that is even more devastating than the calamity we are presently emerging from.

We noted that several GJM organizations believe that their movement had not yet fully taken advantage of the political opportunities that emerged in the wake of the GFC. Arguing that their longstanding critique of neoliberalism has been vindicated, they concede that the more difficult next step is to shift the public policy agenda in the direction of social justice. At this point, they recognize that only the weakest of regulatory measures – mainly around capital adequacy – have been implemented, leaving the finance sector free to start yet another round of speculative accumulation. Following unprecedented bailouts and the first truly global stimulus package, governments in the North face a massive burden of debt, which they now seek to reduce at the expense of the general public. Government public spending is now figured as the problem, not private financial power. The quick succession of stimulus packages and severe austerity measures has deepened the GFC into a lingering economic crisis characterized by spiraling debt, falling tax revenue, and high levels of unemployment.

In large part, this second phase of the crisis, which has impacted the North as much as the South, has spawned new movements like 'Occupy' that are based on global justice values. Many of the GJM organizations we interviewed in 2009 and 2010 anticipated this scenario:

> Some argue that perhaps the financial crisis in some way and in the short-term has only had an impact on those who were already rich and had the money to invest in these toxic assets. But we will face, in a different timing, the effect on jobs. That's when people will realize what the real impact of the crisis is and will be on ordinary people. Only to a certain extent has the savings of people been affected by this crisis. But I think the unemployment crisis will be a lot more relevant for them and a lot more dramatic … . So I think the crisis has different timings, and soon we are going to go from the financial crises to the actual social and unemployment crisis. (Wilson 2009c)

Partly inspired by the Arab Spring and by the 'Indignants' movement in Spain, the Occupy movement is explicitly centered on the social injustices of the GFC and the resulting measures of public austerity. Occupy mobilized most clearly against the capture of public policy by corporate elites, contrasting 'corporate welfare' for the '1%' with austerity and misery for the '99%'. Many GJM organizations supported the Occupy movement as it surfaced in New York and then moved across several other countries, including Australia, the UK, Germany, and France. Remarkably, in December 2011 the question of whether to introduce a financial transactions tax rattled the EU. Several European governments, including Germany, supported the introduction of such a 'Tobin Tax' (Gladstone 2011). The UK government represented the opposite end of this controversy. Explicitly acting on behalf of the City of London, Prime Minister David Cameron declined to participate in the EU27 Stability Pact, thus precipitating a crisis in the UK Government that spilt over into the EU. It appears that GJM policy responses to the GFC have finally entered the mainstream public discourse on the changing nature of the global financial architecture. Meeting our third criteria for gauging the maturity of an ideational cluster, it seems that justice globalism responds well to pressing political issues.

6

JUSTICE GLOBALISM AND THE GLOBAL FOOD CRISIS

Introduction

The global food crisis offers another test of the responsiveness of justice globalism. Of the three crises we explore in this book, the global food crisis is by far the most immediate. Its impact is felt on a daily basis by vast segments of the world population. The United Nations Food and Agriculture Organisation (FAO) calculates that 925 million people – 13.6% of the total global population – are under-nourished (FAO 2010). In addition, there are further hundreds of millions of people – perhaps even more than a billion – who may have sufficient food yet exert little or no control over the type of food they can access and afford. Still others, including those in the global North belonging to a growing class of dispossessed and displaced, are increasingly unable to feed themselves (Magdoff 2008). Thus, the global food crisis is not only a global phenomenon but also a multi-layered problem, both in its causes and consequences.

Most importantly, the global food crisis reflects a fundamental disjuncture between food as a basic human right and food as a commodity. This tension exemplifies the different discursive dynamics governing justice globalism and market globalism. Various international human rights conventions have clearly established a 'right to food'. The International Covenant on Economic, Social and Cultural Rights, for example, entrenches the 'fundamental right to be free from hunger' and requires states 'to ensure an equitable distribution of world food supplies in relation to need' (Article 11). As a commodity, however, food is like any other product that can be bought and sold on local and world markets (Chand 2008; Magdoff 2008: 2). The price mechanism governs global agricultural trade and food distribution. Since food is allocated according to price, the lack of 'effective demand', that is, the inability to pay the relevant market price, produces global hunger (Magdoff 2008: 2). Food crises have occurred on all geographic scales throughout modern history revealing a structural conflict between market forces that shape the production and distribution of food and the normative human rights imperative to be 'free from hunger'.

Market globalists claim that global economic integration will increase overall productive efficiency, and thus 'raise all boats' (Steger 2009). The benefits of economic growth are said to eventually trickle down to everyone in the global community and therefore lift hundreds of millions out of poverty. The chief ideological codifiers of market globalism present 'free trade' as a positive win-win situation for all, notwithstanding the fact that empirical research shows that some win more than others (Stiglitz 2003). Still, this central market globalist claim that everyone benefits from increased market access drives much of mainstream trade policy-making. Indeed, the extension of neoliberal market rules into agriculture has been institutionalized at the international level in the form of the WTO.

As national regulations are rewritten in conformity with WTO rules, the question of how to reconcile global food markets and food rights has become a major preoccupation for government and non-government actors alike. As discussed in this chapter, justice globalists have been at the forefront of these efforts. Focusing on the conflict between food markets and food rights, they have argued that governments who are signatories to international human rights covenants are obligated to prevent, as far as possible, malnutrition and famine. As we shall see, the GJM organizations we examined for this study have articulated three distinct food policy proposals: i) more effective reregulation of food markets to secure 'food rights'; ii) models of delinking (and relinking) national food production from global markets in order to achieve 'food security'; and iii) the transformation of the dominant neoliberal paradigm in the direction of needs-based models of 'food sovereignty'.

We begin this chapter with a historical overview of the evolution of market-based approaches to food and the role of government in these developments. Following our examination of the particulars of the current dominant WTO-led regime and its implication in the global food crisis, we present the main features of the three justice-globalist alternatives to market-globalist food policies.

Free Trade Theory and Food Markets: A History of Food Crises

Historically governments have played a key role in food markets, in terms of the direct provision of food and the regulation of production, distribution and pricing. This active government involvement in food markets is based on the understanding that if left to private players, food markets would fail to meet basic food needs. Food markets are highly unstable, mainly due to the seasonal character of food production, which exaggerates supply volatility and price fluctuations. The need to guarantee a living income for cash-cropping small-scale farmers and at the same time maintain sufficient food stocks to meet people's needs has led to extensive government involvement in income maintenance and price stabilization.

This ongoing government involvement signals from the outset a sharp tension between the 'right to food' and market-based approaches to food that promote deregulation and minimal government intervention.

Problems with free trade theory and agriculture date back at least to the 'Great Hunger' – *an Gorta Mór* – in mid-nineteenth-century Ireland. One of the first food crises of the modern age, the Great Hunger is widely understood to be a product of the integration of Irish agriculture with the industrializing British economy (Woodham-Smith 1991). In these early days of free trade ideology, British-enforced property rights ensured that one million people in Ireland died of hunger while the country increased its agricultural exports to Britain. Following demands from the Irish people and their government that Britain recognize their food rights, the British provided highly limited food aid – inedible maize from the Americas, deliberately designed not to disrupt Ireland's agricultural trade with Britain. This response from the British state stands in direct contrast with the Irish Home Rule Parliament's response to an earlier famine in 1782, when they closed Ireland's ports and prevented the export of food staples (Kinealy 1995).

These two contrasting responses demonstrate the basic tension we highlighted in the introduction of this chapter: purely market-driven food distribution leads to hunger and famine, while government-regulated food distribution seeks to ensure that a population's food needs are met. The parallels with the contemporary global food crisis are telling. In 2008, facing a doubling in global food prices, 25 countries restricted the export of food staples in order to protect local food stocks. Indeed, many countries across the developing world are as a result revising their food policies to achieve self-sufficiency rather than rely on global food markets, thereby driving a 'paradigm change' from market reliance to state provision (Demeke et al. 2009: 24).

The pattern of market reliance, food crisis, and state intervention occurred throughout the 20th century as well. Governments developed proactive responses to defend food rights in the context of food shortages and price rises, directly contradicting *laissez faire* free trade theory. In response to the income insecurity of rural workers in the USA during the Great Depression, the Roosevelt administration introduced 'agricultural adjustment' as part of the New Deal. Agricultural adjustment managed food prices and outputs, while imposing strict limitations on speculation in food finance. In Europe, the Common Agricultural Policy of 1958 introduced Europe-wide price supports to stabilize agriculture. Meanwhile, in response to the famines that had occurred under British colonialism in India, especially in Bengal of 1943, the independent government of India established its own food pricing and distribution system. Many other postcolonial countries followed suit with programs to displace profiteering in food markets and to subsidize staples for the national populace.

Agricultural policy became more and more embedded in conceptions of 'national interest', highlighting the special significance of food security and production. Prior to the advent of the WTO in 1994/95, governments placed a high priority on maintaining their national policy space in the regulation of food markets. Food trade was not subject to the provisions of the General Agreement on Tariffs and Trade (GATT) and governments were free to provide whatever subsidies and tariffs they deemed necessary to enable national food access and protect national food production. International standard-setting for food trade, through CODEX Alimentarius from 1963, centered on establishing minimum standards for subsidies and tariffs: governments could exceed these standards as they saw fit, regardless of the impact on trade. As such, in the post-World War II era, agriculture was firmly positioned in the national domain of policymaking – a sphere to be regulated by the government, not by the market.

The WTO's 'Market Access' Regime

In the early 1990s, however, food and agricultural policies began to shift away from government regulation as the globally concentrated agri-industry gathered strength. The Uruguay Round of GATT (1988–92) transformed the international trading regime by linking it explicitly to the neoliberal tenets of market globalism. The ensuing WTO regime that ultimately replaced GATT in 1994/95 was both comprehensive and far-reaching in that it covered all sectors of the economy (including agriculture) and provided the disciplinary framework for key aspects of government policy. This represented a significant shift from government-regulated trade to market-driven commercial exchanges. Any government activity that gave advantage to domestic suppliers and disadvantaged international competitors was considered potentially discriminatory 'trade-distortion', subject to penalties. This new 'market access' regime, institutionalized at the WTO, was thus founded on the implicit assumption that global market forces were preferable to national government provisions. As a result, with the advent of the WTO, the central role of government in delivering national development was subsumed into a neoliberal regime of market development and global integration (McMichael 2004).

The WTO's new market-globalist order built on and expressed national-level policy imperatives starting in the late 1970s that had been introduced by national governments in response to corporate globalization or had been forced on governments by the IMF and World Bank through its neoliberal Structural Adjustment Programs (Stiglitz 2003). The WTO succeeded in concretizing a series of structures at the international level that made these marketization efforts permanent. Further, the WTO extended the market globalist agenda into new areas including agriculture, services, investment, intellectual property, and government procurement – domains that had previously been the sole purview of national governments.

Agricultural trade occupied a special place in this emergent regime. Low-income countries have historically enjoyed only limited access to the food markets of rich Northern countries. The WTO's 'Agreement on Agriculture' offered the prospect of reduced barriers to agricultural trade – both in terms of tariffs and subsidies – as a major concession to the Global South. The WTO claimed that the new 'Agreement on Agriculture' would make food trade fairer and enable market-led development. In return, developing countries were expected to agree to new provisions for 'market access' in services, trade-related investment and intellectual property rights, which chiefly benefitted high-income countries. To a large extent, then, the question of agriculture became central to the legitimacy of the WTO: if the WTO Agreement on Agriculture failed to open markets for Southern countries then the entire Uruguay package deal would unravel.

Exactly this scenario unfolded in the years following the launch of the WTO in 1994/95. The initial expectation amongst OECD countries was that the WTO would swiftly be extended into broader fields, including investment flows, government procurement, trade facilitation and competition policy. In contrast, non-OECD, low-income countries were more concerned that commitments under the Uruguay Round be implemented, especially the promise that OECD countries would open up their agricultural markets to imports from the global South, and that Southern countries would be able to maintain reasonable protections for food security. When it became clear that there were 'implementation issues' with regard to agricultural trade, developing countries voted against the 'Millennium Round' at the 1999 Seattle Ministerial Meeting, thus halting the WTO regime in its tracks.

In response, efforts by the North focused on winning back the active support of low-income countries through a new 'Development Round', launched at the Doha Ministerial in 2001. The key concession wrought at Doha affirmed the commitment to 'comprehensive negotiations' in agriculture aimed at 'substantial improvements in market access; reductions of, with a view to phasing out, all forms of export subsidies; and substantial reductions in trade-distorting domestic support'. Through this slightly revised framework, Doha also offered some limited policy space in terms of 'special and differential treatment for developing countries ... including food security and rural development' (WTO 2001: para 13).

Developed countries presented these agreements as major concessions that required a further *quid pro quo* on non-agricultural issues, such as investment flows, government procurement, trade facilitation, and competition policy. In practice, however, the agricultural concessions were constrained by Article 13 and Annex 2 of the Agreement on Agriculture, which affirms a very limited 'Basis for Exemption from the Reduction Commitments'. For example, government subsidy and price stabilization programs were acceptable for ensuring food security, but only at 'reasonable' levels and if set according to 'objective criteria'

(WTO 2004: paragraph 22). As such, regardless of Doha's recognition of food security and rural development needs, governments were still required to reduce their aggregate supports.

While developing countries were forced to reduce their agricultural supports after the Doha round, the same was not true for the US and the EU. The key loophole in the Agreement on Agriculture – the distinction between 'trade distorting' subsidies that needed to be reduced and 'non-trade distorting' subsidies that could be escalated – remained in place. Under Doha, the USA and the EU were committed to further reductions in 'trade-distorting subsidies', but governments quickly shifted this support into the non-trade-distorting category, so that overall agricultural subsidies could be maintained (Khor 2009). To be clear, non-trade distorting measures mainly involve forms of income support for farmers that are defined as being 'decoupled' from trade, as against 'trade-distorting' supports for production and price stabilization. Yet, the WTO's endorsement of these 'non-trade-distorting' subsidies actively discriminates against poorer countries that cannot afford to provide the same level of income support to their farmers. Indeed, income support systems are only available to 20% of the world's population (Hawkes and Plahe 2010).

Facing limited control over their own agricultural policy and only minimal access to markets in the global North, low-income countries became increasingly reluctant to sign up to further market access measures. Meanwhile WTO rules were creating a dire situation on the ground in developing countries. The lack of market access led to reduced food production for export. Conversely, production for domestic markets was undermined by the reduction of tariffs and the phasing out of price stabilization subsidies. Centrally important, developing countries severely curtailed government funding for agricultural development. From the 1980s public investment in agricultural research and development plummeted, especially in developing countries (OECD 2009: 66). The UN shows public annual expenditure on agriculture falling in developing countries from 11.2% in 1980 to 5.4% of total public expenditure in 1990, remaining at that level through to the 2000s (UN 2009: 48). This directly reduced the capacity for domestic production. The United Nations' 2009 World Economic Prospects report put it this way:

> The policy shift towards more confidence in price signals to stimulate production and less attention to government support for infrastructure investment and research and development for agricultural technology, together with lower official development assistance (ODA), has been most detrimental to agricultural productivity growth … productivity growth for major food crops has stalled, and there has been no significant increase in the use of cultivated land. Thus, production has fallen woefully short of growth in food demand. (UN 2009: 48)

Increased reliance on market-driven food production and distribution had broad impacts. Market power shifted dramatically away from producer countries to global agricultural industries (IFAD 2011: 96). These transnationally net-worked food distributors and suppliers have become increasingly concentrated. A mere 100 companies, predominantly based in the Global North, now control 40% of world grocery sales (ETC 2008). As IFAD notes, food markets are 'becoming more integrated and concentrated in their structure ... to exclude small-scale suppliers, a process that has intensified with the imposition of higher product and process standards by northern retailers' (IFAD 2011: 6).

One of the consequences is that low-income countries have become more vulnerable to import surges from high-income countries. These import surges have increased in frequency and intensity from the mid-1990s, with devastating results for local production (de Negris 2005). Today, this pattern has been well established. When there is an international glut, domestic markets are flooded with cheap imports, displacing local producers. When shortages ensue, domestic food production capacity no longer exists, and countries swiftly become net food importers. Within two decades, several developing countries, such as Mexico and the Philippines, went from being net food exporters to being net food importers (Bello 2008). The impacts are twofold: first, cash-cropping farmers are displaced from the land and usually forced into city slums; second, local food prices become increasingly determined by global food markets. The end result of this market-driven approach is increasing economic subordination for Southern producers to Northern TNCs, in the process exacerbating global disparities of food production and distribution.

The Global Food Crisis

The disenchantment of developing countries in the global South with WTO-led marketization turned into active hostility with the onset of the global food crisis. In 2008, the FAO index of 'average food prices' reached more than double the 2000 level. In a decade, an additional 180 million people became under-nourished, increasing the overall total to almost 1 billion (FAO 2010). With the onslaught of the GFC in 2008, world food prices fell by about 40%, raising hopes that the problem had been short-lived. Unfortunately, however, the slow recovery in financial markets led to the rise of food prices in 2010. By October 2010, the price index had risen above the 2008 high water mark, and by May 2011 it had surged further (FAO 2011a). In this second food crisis, the prices of all key commodities had risen (World Bank 2011: 5). Moreover, an inverse relationship between financial health and access to food had become visible: 'healthy', speculative 'bull' markets drive food prices up, increasing food inequality and undernourishment, while financial collapse and 'bear' markets pull them down, expanding access to food.

Market globalist agencies such as the IMF insisted the global food crisis was primarily caused by supply problems. Rising oil prices had driven up the cost of farm inputs. A depreciating US dollar had made commodities relatively more attractive. Growing prosperity in late-industrializing countries such as India and China had increased demand for meat, with grains being channeled into stock feed. An appreciable global shift to biofuels was also responsible for a decrease in grain supplies, as growing quantities of grain were siphoned off into low-emission fuels. Finally, as a result of impacts from global climate change, more harvests were failing and some global stocks came close to depletion (see Chand 2008; OECD 2010: 49–51).

Undoubtedly, all of these factors contributed to the 2007–11 global food crisis. WSF organizations like Food First International Action Network (FIAN), for example, highlighted the switch to 'agrofuels' (their preferred term to 'biofuels') as diverting food supplies and forcing up prices (Wilson 2009d). However, as the UN Special Rapporteur on the Right to Food has argued, none of these factors either alone or together are able to explain the very large swings in global food prices starting in 2007:

> [A] significant portion of the increases in price and volatility of essential food commodities can only be explained by the emergence of a speculative bubble. In particular, there is a reason to believe that a significant role was played by the entry into markets for derivatives based on food commodities of large, powerful institutional investors such as hedge funds, pension funds and investment banks, all of which are generally unconcerned with agricultural market fundamentals. Such entry was made possible because of deregulation in important commodity derivatives markets beginning in 2000. These factors have yet to be comprehensively addressed, and to that extent, are still capable of fuelling price rises beyond those levels which would be justified by movements in supply and demand fundamentals. Therefore, fundamental reform of the broader global financial sector is urgently required in order to avert another food price crisis. (Schutter 2010: 1)

As we noted, there is increasing evidence of a direct correlation between food prices and non-food financial risk, especially in the context of a second very rapid increase in food prices in 2010 and into 2011. This situation has fueled debate about the need to limit speculative activity in food. Some key players remain adamant there is no proven link between speculation and pricing. In June 2010 the OECD released its report on the issue, one week in advance of a key US Senate vote on regulating commodity markets. The OECD report argued that speculative activity had no role to play in the food crisis (Irwin and Sanders 2010). In May 2011 the World Bank stressed volatility is 'largely due to persistent uncertainty on the supply side against projected rising demand', although it did acknowledge the role of 'substantially higher commodity index investment flows' (World Bank 2011: 1, 8).

Others argue that market speculation is the main cause of food crisis. In 2011, research by the UN's Food and Agriculture Organization found that the market in food futures was providing a relatively secure, low-risk option for non-commercial traders seeking to offset higher-risk markets, thus creating a direct correlation between food prices and the non-food financial sector (FAO 2011). In 2000, the US government had lifted the ban on food speculation by introducing the 'Commodity Futures Modernization Act'. The consequences were immediate: between 2002 and 2008 futures contracts on food tripled, while 'over-the-counter' asset swaps rose fourteen-fold to US$14 trillion. The dramatic fall in total commodity derivatives trade in 2008, from US$13 trillion in the first half of 2008, to US$3 trillion, is directly mirrored in the falling price of food from mid-2008 on (Magdoff 2008). As Chand argued at the time:

> Several reports in the international media indicate that professional speculators and hedge funds are driving up the prices of basic commodities in commodity futures following the collapse of the financial derivatives markets. These dealers are reported to be shifting investments out of equities and mortgage bonds and ploughing them into food and raw materials. (Chand 2008: 119)

In its 2011 report on the global economic situation, the UN highlighted the 'financialization of commodity trading' and its role in raising commodity prices through 'self-reinforcing speculative bubbles'. The report welcomed 'political recognition of the problem, especially in the US and EU and the G20' but acknowledged that efforts to address the problem face 'strong opposition from vested interests in the industry' (UN 2011: 53–4). In November 2010, the G20 articulated a highly restrictive mandate for itself: 'to develop options for G20 consideration on how to better mitigate and manage the risks associated with the price volatility of food and other agriculture commodities, *without distorting market behavior,* ultimately to protect the most vulnerable' (FAO 2011: 3; emphasis added). In other words, the G20 sought to mitigate risks without 'distorting' the very 'market behavior' that tends to create those risks in the first place. Similar initiatives by American and EU regulators clearly demonstrate the significant barriers and opposition for any effort to re-impose limits on speculative activity in the global food trade.

Reflecting its origins, the G20 has remained hamstrung by its neoliberal commitments to 'market behavior'. The G20 Interagency Report on the global food crisis released in June 2011 expressed the lowest common denominator in policy consensus between bodies such as the OECD, IMF, FAO, and UNCTAD. Eschewing substantive policy initiatives on speculative activity, the Report merely called for more research and improved information flows. The document failed to endorse measures to delimit speculative activity, announcing simply that the G20 supports 'efforts made by the United States, the European Commission and others in addressing transparency and efficiency issues in futures markets' (FAO 2011: 23). The recent return to rapidly rising food prices notwithstanding, the Report called for mechanisms to assist in 'coping with volatility' rather than addressing the deep causes of the crisis (FAO et al. 2011b).

Justice Globalism's Food Policy Alternatives

As we noted in the introduction, our selected justice globalist organizations have articulated three main sets of policy alternatives pertaining to global food production and distribution: reregulation for food rights within an expanded 'market access' framework; delinking (and relinking) to achieve 'food security;' and transformation toward 'food sovereignty'. Outlining each of the three positions below, we show how the GJM has constructed alternative policy responses to the current global food crisis. To some extent, these approaches constitute competing alternatives. But they could also be considered a multidimensional progression toward desirable outcomes: each alternative seeks to change the current neoliberal status quo by improving global access to food for populations who presently struggle to secure those 'essentials of life' that are taken for granted by most people in the global North.

Reregulation: 'Food Equality' and 'Expanded Market Access'

At a basic level, this GJM perspective seeks to ensure that all people everywhere have access to adequate sources of nutritious food and are free from hunger. We refer to this policy approach as 'food equality' because it is grounded in the concept of equality of access to resources, opportunities, and outcomes that forms part of the ideological morphology of justice globalism as discussed in Chapter 2. To some extent, this approach incorporates market-driven mechanisms and thus may be characterized as an effort to 'reform' the market rather than fundamentally change the currently dominant regime of food production and distribution. Of the 45 WSF-affiliated organizations we examined for this study, only very few supported this perspective. As we discuss below, most groups promote either 'food sovereignty' or 'food sufficiency' as the most promising ways to tackle the global food crisis.

There are three key demands emerging from the food equality approach: expanding access to Northern markets for Southern producers; promoting consumer-driven fair trade to ensure equality, rights, and sustainability throughout the food production and distribution process; and strengthening 'right to food' clauses in national and international judicial practices.

Regarding the first demand we should note that GJM campaigns for food equality focus mainly on the market as a means of overcoming inequalities between Northern and Southern countries. The approach focuses primarily on the distribution and pricing of food supplies rather than interventions into agriculture per se. Market reregulation is central to this approach. Advocates promote specific policy mechanisms to achieve their goals: the expansion of market access for low-income countries to sell to high-income nations; consumer-led Fair Trade; and legal sanctions against the abuse of market power.

As noted above, the WTO's Agreement on Agriculture largely failed to achieve market access for Southern producers. Some GJM organizations seize on this failure, politicizing the disjuncture between WTO rhetoric and reality. Further, they contend that if market access were successfully implemented, it could alleviate global poverty. The Oxfam International 'Make Trade Fair' Campaign is a representative example of this approach (Oxfam International 2002). Other organizations have argued that overcoming the inequalities in global agricultural trade requires rules that are weighted in favor of low-income food producers. Northern countries should be required to remove barriers to agricultural imports, but at the same time Southern counterparts should be permitted to protect their domestic agricultural markets from Northern competitors. The Global Progressive Forum, for example, insists that developing countries should be 'given fair means to compete on world markets and ... the right to implement gradual measures with regard to the opening of their domestic markets' (GPF 2009b).

In part, some WSF-affiliated groups seem to have adopted this 'expanded market access' position because it helps expose the flaws in the WTO system and provides strategic leverage in policy discussions with governments and neoliberal economic elites. Certainly, by framing their advocacy from within the dominant rhetoric of market globalism, many Northern NGOs have gained significant access to Northern governments. In this respect, the relationship between the GJM-supported 'Make Poverty History' campaign and the Blair administration in the UK serves as an instructive example (Quarmby 2005).

Still, proposals to achieve food equality through market access remain highly controversial within justice globalist circles. The codification of a 'preferred option' for Southern producers is often defined as a breach of WTO 'equal treatment' provisions. Justice globalists suggest that attempts to gain access to Northern markets will always come at a price in terms of domestic protections, or trade-offs in other fields of WTO policy, which may negate any positive outcomes of increased access to Northern markets (Bello 2002). In addition, the assumed gains to be made from increased market access are themselves challenged as contingent upon global agricultural industry. This critique rejects the assumption that, once freed from government protection, Northern food markets will be more accessible. Indeed, access to Northern food markets is not just controlled by governments, but also concentrated amongst a small number of TNCs. The ability of small Southern producers to compete with these corporate powerhouses is by no means guaranteed, even if government controls of Northern agriculture markets were to be removed.

Furthermore, market access, if successful, leads to greater 'cash cropping' (producing large-scale amounts of a single product) in an effort to maximize returns. As critics have pointed out, however, cash cropping of luxury goods such as coffee, cocoa, cashew nuts, tobacco, and cotton for export into Northern markets is a recipe for dependence on highly volatile commodities, not for income security (Chossudovsky 2003; McMichael 2004: 10–11). Cash cropping

encourages monocultures and highly intensive farming, which, while producing short-term gains in income, represent long-term environmental – and
subsequently financial – losses and are ultimately ecologically self-destructive.
A further ramification is dependence on relatively low value commodity exports,
creating permanently negative terms of trade for countries that rely on exports of
basic commodities to pay for manufactures. Even if the government-sanctioned
barriers to market access are removed, there remain deeper structural factors that
will disadvantage Southern countries attracted to this option.

The current global food crisis has further undermined hopes for realizing food
equality through expanded market access as the crisis has highlighted fundamental failings of the entire market system. The goal of expanding market
access has become increasingly irrelevant for many justice globalists, particularly those advocating on behalf of Southern producers, such as the Africa Trade
Network (ATN). Campaigning against imports of Northern foods into Africa, the
ATN pressures African governments to protect their own industries, producers
and markets:

> We had a campaign on North-imported food products. Because these are products
> we can produce in our countries, but these products are massively imported into
> our countries because they are subsidized in the European Union or in the American
> countries. (Scerri 2011b)

For a growing number of GJM organizations, the answer to this problem no
longer can be found in appeals to Northern countries either to open up markets or to reduce subsidies on exports, but to strengthen domestic food producers to provide for domestic consumption. As the ATN suggests, 'Your subsidies,
your surpluses – keep them for you. Leave us to develop our own agriculture'
(Scerri 2011b).

A second key area of reform from the food equality perspective relates to consumer behavior and fair trade. The World Fair Trade Organization (WFTO),
formerly the International Federation of Alternative Trade, pioneered the conceptual and practical development of Fair Trade. While dominant neoliberal
conceptions of trade focus solely or primarily on the immediate direct costs and
benefits of a particular transaction, Fair Trade practices take into account indi-
rect costs as well, 'including the safeguarding of natural resources and meeting
future investment needs' (WFTO 2009: 5). Thus, the trading terms and conditions offered through Fair Trade promote economic, social and environmental
sustainability now and into the future (WFTO 2009: 5). Food equality advocates
emphasizing Fair Trade seek to raise awareness amongst rich consumers in the
global North about the origins of the food they consume, how it is produced,
and the effects of this process on humans and the environment. Other WSF-
affiliated organizations in our sample, such as the Global Progressive Forum,
encourage their members to contribute to this effort by promoting guides on
purchasing Fair Trade products.

Fair Trade advocates seek to reregulate markets as a vehicle for social change. In its various manifestations, Fair Trade constructs links between producers and consumers by revealing the impacts of commodity production. It invokes the power of consumers – consistent with market theories of consumer sovereignty – to reform existing neoliberal practices of production and distribution. Thus, Fair Trade often serves as a potent GJM campaign tool that opens a window from within the rhetoric of market globalism to target corporate players and practices and to construct alternative fair trading networks. Hence it is hardly surprising that the WFTO consider Fair Trade as a strong practical and pedagogical tool capable of demonstrating how to achieve 'poverty reduction through trade':

> Fair Trade organizations ... are engaged actively in supporting producers, awareness raising and in campaigning for changes in the rules and practice of conventional international trade ... Fair Trade is more than just trading: it proves that greater justice in world trade is possible. It highlights the need for change in the rules and practice of conventional trade and shows how a successful business can also put people first. (WFTO 2011)

The final approach to food equality seeks to strengthen the 'universal right to food' through legal means. The Food First International Action Network (FIAN), for example, works with victim groups in the EU and in developing countries whose right to food has been violated as a result of government actions, business practices, or international trade agreements (FIAN 2009). FIAN insists that access to food should not be dependent on charity or the free market. Rather, it constitutes a legally enforceable right. As such, food rights differs both from food security which may rely on technical measures of hunger, and food sovereignty which is seen as an aspiration rather than an obligation (Wilson 2009d). Pursuing its food equality approach within the context of a human rights discourse, FIAN has chosen a non-confrontational yet a highly political strategy:

> We know that it [human rights] has a political content, but it is a political issue that is accepted by the state parties when they sign the covenants. They say 'Ok this is political but we'll take this political struggle between different sides and adopt that as a common goal, which we can claim for'. And in this sense it goes from the just political or mere political dimension to the legal dimension, where you really can claim that and it is not just a struggle for a political position. (Wilson 2009d)

While FIAN does not promote models for global food production and distribution outside (regulated) market mechanisms, it emphasizes that the right to food, like all human rights, invokes a sense of human dignity that puts needs before profits or charity.

> We strive for the right to food, the human right to food, but particularly for people to get access to productive resources in order to feed themselves. This is important for us that they are not just given food, but that they have the ability to get the tools

and the resources to feed themselves, to do it in dignity … the rights-based approach is more with this human dignity where each one is able to claim their rights, they are rights holders. (Wilson 2009d)

In practical terms, FIAN focuses not only on introducing and monitoring food-related laws, but also on providing pragmatic assistance to states that struggle to meet their legal obligations. In the context of the global food crisis, FIAN's practical stance has increased its international profile and visibility:

There is now more attention, much more attention to this topic of hunger in the world. We've had much more requests to us as an organization, what is our analysis, what is our position towards the situation. There is a need for explanation and for more solid approaches on how to overcome it. (Wilson 2009d)

Advocating greater market access, Fair Trade, or rights protections, these three distinct currents within the food equality approach expose the worst abuses of market power that have contributed to the global food crisis while at the same time making the case for stronger regulation of global food markets. Yet, for many GJM organizations included in this study, these reformist initiatives and proposals remain inadequate. In their view, calls for more effective regulation rely too much on markets to deliver global food equality. These critics assert that market-friendly proposals fail to address the structural power imbalances that exist within the global system of food production and distribution. Instead of focusing on inconsistencies in WTO decision-making, they charge, justice globalists should target the agri-business sector that has been reaping rich prof-its from the global neoliberal food regime. Arguing for stronger rules may result in some minor gains, but does not address the question of who makes the rules and who benefits most from them.

More specifically, these critics in the WSF circles assert that greater market access, Fair Trade, and food rights policies are ultimately undermined by their failure to identify clearly the chief causes of food crises. They point to the fact that countries most adversely affected by market access rules governing global food trade are those with the least ability to influence and alter them (Menezes 2001: 40). Indeed, it could be argued that while GJM initiatives in favor of mar-ket reregulation may have gained some official recognition from public and private entities, global integration of food markets along neoliberal lines remains dominant. Relying on consumer practices, Fair Trade may fail to involve the governments and intergovernmental institutions that exert significant influ-ence on the global trading system. Equally, it is far from clear whether the existence of legally enforceable food rights makes any substantive difference in terms of food equality. Raising these concerns, most of our WSF-affiliated organizations stressed the limitations of a food equality approach in the context of the current global trade and finance system that governs the production and distribution of food.

Delinking and Relinking: 'Food Security' and 'Food Sufficiency'

A second justice globalism response to food crisis is delinking, an approach that represents the exact opposite of the market access approach. Advocates of this alternative policy path argue that delinking from global food markets enables a relinking among locally embedded networks of food producers and food consumers. From this perspective, food production should refocus on local contexts, albeit without losing sight of relevant global interdependencies. During the 1980s, delinking became more popularly known as 'food security' when some national and local governments asserted their right to protect domestic supplies of food staples from the vagaries of the world food market. Although these demands were backed by the FAO, a few years later the WTO Agreement on Agriculture recognized them only as a 'temporary deviation' from their free market access principles.

The notion of 'food security' implies the need for food production systems that are oriented to local development needs, rather than bent to the needs of Northern consumers. Menezes defines food security as 'the guarantee that everyone has permanent access to good quality food in sufficient quantities, based on healthy eating habits and without adversely affecting access to other essential needs nor the future food system, which should be implemented on sustainable bases' (Menezes 2001: 29). Mechanisms for relinking with local food needs and production systems are generally state-centered, although they may also be framed as local and regional responses reflecting varying degrees of popular participation. Such participation might take the form of local cooperative systems for relinking rural and urban sectors that promote more internally articulated development trajectories (Amin 2006).

Food security necessarily invokes the nation-state as arbiter at the international level, mainly in relation to the distribution and pricing of food (Ibase 2009). The first step is to delink from financial pressures and reverse the financialization of food. Several WSF organizations in our sample – including Focus on the Global South (2008), Jubilee South (2009), and the World Council of Churches (2009b) – argue for the immediate end to all speculative trade on food staples, such as wheat, corn, rice and maize, especially in light of the obvious links between speculation and rising food prices during the 2006 and 2008 food crises. This demand is echoed across all justice globalist groups campaigning for both food and financial reform. In short, government action on multiple levels is favored not only to protect food markets from global finance, but also from import surges resulting from the removal of trade barriers. Vulnerability to a glut of cheap imports is addressed by a shift to protectionism and market intervention, at least for the production and pricing of staples. From this perspective, intervention should include food aid and distribution programs that provide access to food for the poorest and most vulnerable within a country (PPEHRC 2003; Ibase 2009). The food available through these programs should be nutritious and culturally appropriate, not just what appears to be available from international markets (PPEHRC 2003). In addition, national governments should give priority to nationally produced food in contracts related to public spending, such as food purchased for 'schools, hospitals, prisons, food assistance programs' (Ibase 2009). Governments should also assist farmers in producing staples, replacing imports with food that can be produced nationally. An extended quote from the Citizens Association for the Defense of Collective Interests (CADCI), a member of the Africa Trade Network, provides a succinct description of the food security approach:

> We are not asking the European Union or America to stop subsidizing their farmers. It's a good thing to subsidize. But we are asking our own governments now to subsidize our own agriculture, so that we can face competition with the European Union and with the United States. So we are not asking them to stop their subsidies. We are encouraging subsidies. But we don't need the surpluses because we are capable in Africa of producing the food that we eat. We receive surpluses because they are subsidized. We are not subsidized. That's why we are faced with this unfair competition. (Scerri 2011b)

Many of these policy proposals attempt to improve access to food for poor and marginalized national consumers, reflecting once again the core ideological concepts of equality and social justice. Food security emphasizes bounded food markets, managed by governments to stabilize national and local chains of food production and distribution. Yet the ultimate goal of delinking and food security is to enable global food rights by relinking within stabilized local chains of production and consumption. Hence, it is important to keep in mind that these localization efforts occur within the larger global imaginary that animates global ideologies such as justice globalism or market globalism (Steger 2008).

Delinking advocates invest substantial faith in Southern governments and also in national systems of agricultural production, overseen by corporations and government-owned industry, with less consideration of subsistence farming, small-scale cash cropping, and cooperative or indigenous farming. As some critics within the GJM have noted, the food security approach fails to deal with many of the broader issues of injustice related to food crises. To be sure, food security and delinking initiatives may deliver room to maneuver by creating relatively autonomous fields of production and consumption that remain outside the strictures of the global food market and thus offer some immediate gains for local populations. However, it is hard to see how policies arising from the food security paradigm can be sufficiently grounded and pervasive to offer a long-term antidote to global food crises. In the absence of a broader transformation in food systems, delinking efforts might degenerate into a defensive and autarchic enterprise. As will be shown below, the majority of our WSF-affiliated organizations found that the food security approach and national delinking does not address the root causes of global food crises.

Transformation: Achieving 'Food Sovereignty'

By far the most prominent policy response to the food crisis offered by the GJM centers on the notion of 'food sovereignty'. In contrast to food equality, which aims to reform market practices around food, the goal of food sovereignty is to transform existing productive relations in agriculture. Directly addressing the anti-democratic nature of current global agricultural structures and the increasing concentration of agricultural control amongst global agri-businesses, food sovereignty promotes common ownership of the means of agricultural production by those who actually work in agriculture, thus endowing them with collective sovereignty over their food needs. This approach is anchored in the justice-globalist core concepts of paradigmatic change and participatory democracy and advocates a permanent shift from export-oriented agricultural industry or nationally oriented food systems to locally oriented control of land, production, and distribution systems. Advocates for food sovereignty emphasize that such a transformation ought to occur on the global level, not simply in the global South. Their chief target is the increasing corporatization of food worldwide and their overriding political objective is the removal of TNCs from agriculture and the return of control over food production to local farmers.

This food sovereignty approach addresses a seismic shift in the geographic scales of development. We noted in our discussion of the WTO Agreement on Agriculture that market globalists use the WTO and other institutions to neoliberalize models of national development. We also observed that food equality proponents aim to reregulate this market globalist regime in the name of universal food rights, while food security advocates seek to secure national-level food systems. Food sovereignty proponents, however, endorse a shift away from both neoliberal and national regimes to locally autonomous producers and consumers belonging to a worldwide network of like-minded social movements. Thus, the food sovereignty perspective expresses the global scope of justice globalism as it champions a *global* shift to local food autonomy in order to realize global norms relating to food production and consumption.

La Via Campesina (LVC), an international alliance of peasant-based social movement organizations, has been a global pioneer of food sovereignty. LVC first articulated the concept of food sovereignty at its second conference in 1996 outside the Rome World Food Summit, from which it had been excluded (Menezes 2001; Desmarais 2007; Bello 2008; Rosset 2008; Desmarais et al. (eds) 2011). For LVC, food sovereignty enables both food rights and food security:

> Food is a basic human right. This right can only be realized in a system where food sovereignty is guaranteed. Food sovereignty is the right of each nation to maintain and develop its own capacity to produce its basic foods respecting cultural and productive diversity. We have the right to produce our own food in our own territory. Food sovereignty is a precondition to genuine food security. (La Via Campesina 1996)

In the wake of LVC's successful agitation, policy proposals based on the food sovereignty approach quickly gathered momentum as a direct alternative to the neoliberal WTO agricultural regime. The 2001 World Peoples Conference on Food Sovereignty, held in Havana, demanded the WTO's Agreement on Agriculture be annulled, to 'Keep the WTO out of Food', contrasting with food equality and food security advocates, who have generally sought policy space within the existing WTO regime (Desmarais et al. 2011).

In 2003, the International Planning Committee for Food Sovereignty was established to ensure representation at FAO events and food sovereignty conferences have continued to shadow FAO meetings. The International Committee now refers to the Nyeleni Declaration – drafted at the 2007 Forum for Food Sovereignty in Mali – as the definitive model for food sovereignty. The Declaration offers the following definition:

> Food sovereignty is the right of peoples to healthy and culturally appropriate food produced through ecologically sound and sustainable methods, and their right to define their own food and agriculture systems. It puts those who produce, distribute, and consume food at the heart of food systems and policies rather than the demands of markets and corporations. It defends the interests and inclusion of the next generation. It offers a strategy to resist and dismantle the current corporate trade and food regime, and [defines] directions for food, farming, pastoral, and fisheries systems determined by local producers. (Forum for Food Sovereignty 2007)

Furthermore, the Declaration outlines six principles of food sovereignty with a focus on food as sustenance for people and not 'just another commodity'. The principles also assert the importance of valuing food providers, localizing food systems, putting control at the local level, building on existing cultural and indigenous forms of knowledge, and 'working with nature'. Recently, these six interlinked principles have been described as the key elements of 'the food sovereignty policy framework' (Forum for Food Sovereignty 2007), and we can see clearly how they are anchored in justice globalism's core concepts of participatory democracy, universal rights, sustainability, equality, and justice.

During the last decade, a large number of justice globalism organizations have adopted and promoted food sovereignty as an alternative food policy strategy, including a majority of the 45 organizations analyzed in this study. The MST, Brazil's Landless Workers Movement, has been a key food sovereignty player in the WSF and in the development of the concept of food sovereignty. LVC, CUT, and Ibase have also been at the forefront of this approach. In 2009, CUT released an influential statement arguing for government action to 'stop the rural exodus and affirm a new development model, self-sustained and based on ties of solidarity and complementarity' (CUT 2009). The statement also demanded a limit on land ownership and land reform, with recognition of the role of women and family-owned farms in producing most of the food that Brazilians eat. Since the 1980s, Ibase has promoted similar strategies and played a key role in the creation of the Ministry for Agrarian Reform in Brazil in 1985. Ibase now focuses on the policy frame and has outlined 13 steps to 'guarantee the human right to adequate and healthy food'. For Ibase, the state has a critical role to play in the creation of local networks of food production and distribution. They argue that national governments must create the policy infrastructures to support family farming, including land reform, rural schooling, rural credit and tax incentives, support for farmers' cooperatives and 'public channels of supply' from farm to market, with a 'networking of food production' (Ibase 2009; Steger 2010b).

Still, organizations like CUT and Ibase occupy a policy position that sometimes sits uncomfortably between the delinking/relinking and transformation approaches. In essence, food sovereignty is an attempt to 'deglobalize' food production and distribution, that is, to shift the focus away from the needs of business and the economy towards the needs of local communities and the environment (Bello and Baviera 2009; Focus on the Global South 2009). One of the main tenets of food sovereignty is that the production of food for export should be a secondary consideration to the production of food to feed the local community (MST 2009; La Via Campesina 2009a, 2009b). According to this vision, 'deglobalization' requires that the needs of local communities and ecosystems should override the profit motive of global markets and corporations. Again, this does not necessarily entail shifting away from global relationships, or from a global imaginary, particularly given the strong network solidarity that exists among food sovereignty advocates around the world. As we have emphasized, justice globalists do not oppose globalization *per se,* but rather its dominant market-driven and corporate form.

Proponents of food sovereignty also highlight the lack of democracy within current structures of global governance for agriculture and food production. Farmers and local producers are excluded from discussions and decision-making processes, decisions that often result in the forcible removal of small-scale and peasant farmers from their land. Such 'land-grabbing' measures benefit corporate agri-businesses engaged in the mass production of monoculture cash crops. Hence, a key political step required for the transformation toward food sovereignty is profound land reform and land redistribution, which must include small-scale farmers in any discussions around the use of land for the production and distribution of food (CTA 2009b; CUT 2009; Ibase 2009; La Via Campesina 2009b; Wilson 2009d). MST, LVC, and other food sovereignty advocates argue that small-scale farming, unlike industrial agriculture, ensures that sufficient food of good quality is produced and equitably distributed to meet the needs of local populations rather than the demands of the global market. In contrast with intensively cultivated single plant varieties that require chemical fertilizers, pesticides, and herbicides, mixed farming practices are more reliable and ecologically sustainable (Ibase 2009). Locally produced foods also have a lower carbon footprint, since the distances they are transported are much shorter (Focus on the Global South 2008).

Food sovereignty advocates point to the integration between food systems and community ways of life, especially in many agrarian societies in the global South. The connection between local culture and food production further reinforces the importance of local and indigenous ownership. Organizations like FIAN, Focus on the Global South, Ibase, CTA, MST, and CUT have spoken out against forcing local farmers to adapt to the corporatized, urbanized agri-business model that is part of globalized food production. Rather, they insist, the agrarian lifestyle of local people should be honored, protected, and upheld as the foundation for sustainable food production. This argument reflects their core ideological concepts of sustainability and restorative justice. On a more pragmatic level, food sovereignty proponents suggest that promoting models of local, indigenous and peasant farming would increase employment in comparison with dominant agri-business models.

Finally, food sovereignty approaches assert the transformative agency of the peasantry in a new development model. The 2007 Nyeleni Declaration, for example, celebrates food sovereignty not simply as an alternative, but also as 'a strategy to resist and dismantle the current corporate trade and food regime', that offers new hope for peasant-based global justice movements (Forum for Food Sovereignty 2007). The food sovereignty paradigm refuses to see farmers as the historically necessary victims of industrialism. Rather, it rehabilitates the peasantry as a leading stratum of society capable of enacting transformative change. Reflecting the growth in mass-based movements of dispossessed peasants, such as La Via Campesina – literally 'The Peasants' Way' – advocates for food sovereignty have been able to make some significant political advances (Davis 2005; Roisin et al. 2011). Building on shared experiences of dispossession and with a clear emphasis on the importance of solidarity, land reform movements across many countries have become interlinked in worldwide networks. Longstanding demands for land redistribution – an unresolved problem in many postcolonial countries – have as a result been reinvigorated by social movements engaged in the direct occupation of vacant land.

The MST, for instance, has played a particularly significant role in campaigning for land redistribution within the broader framework of food sovereignty. Established in 1984 to campaign for land reform and for a 'just society', the MST led a movement of land occupation that has successfully redistributed 7.5 million hectares to close to 400,000 households (MST n.d. a). Its land occupations are legitimized under the 1988 Brazilian Constitution, which at Article 184 empowers the government 'to expropriate on account of social interest, for purposes of agrarian reform, the rural property which is not performing its social function' (Government of Brazil 2010). In a country which is still said to have the world's largest concentration of land ownership, the MST calls for a limit on how much land can be owned personally or by a corporation, and campaigns 'to organize the national agricultural production with the main objective of the production of healthy food, free from pesticides and genetically modified organisms for the entire population, thus applying the principle of food sovereignty' (MST n.d. b). Other key justice globalism organizations such as Ibase (2009), CUT, and La Via Campesina have long supported these calls for limitations on land ownership.

Given its focus on smallholders, however, food sovereignty has not gained significant traction beyond Southern countries. In Northern contexts, most farming is integrated into agricultural industry. Highly intensive and industrialized, farming long ago ceased to employ a significant proportion of the workforce. As a result, food sovereignty initiatives in the global North focus on the perspective of the consumer. Food consumers in developed countries also bear the risks associated with corporatization of nutrition, exemplified in food scares and dietary disorders linked to the industrialization of food production. The remarkably pervasive movement against genetically engineered foods, for example, has gained traction mainly from a consumer perspective. Hence, the desire for alternative food systems – expressed in the GJM's food sovereignty approach – is not confined to the global South (Responses to Crisis Workshop, Session Three, Global Food Crisis, 1 July 2011). Yet, Northern mobilizations for food sovereignty like the LVC-affiliated French Peasant Union, *Confédération Paysanne* (best known internationally for the 1999 dismantling of a McDonald's franchise in Aveyron, France, under the leadership of the charismatic French farmer José Bové) remain relatively rare, though symbolically effective.

To summarize, food sovereignty perspectives generate alternative policies based on core concepts of justice globalism, specifically social justice, participatory democracy, sustainability, global solidarity, and transformative change. Concerned not merely with unequal access to food but also with the historical dispossession of farmers in favor of agribusiness, food sovereignty proponents seek to restore and redistribute land to local peasants, and indigenous peoples, and women to enable greater access to sufficient nutritious food for the local community (Wilson 2009d). Second, they challenge the authoritarianism of industrial agribusiness, demanding that a more decentralized food policy be developed democratically with the participation of the entire local community. La Via Campesina, Ibase, Focus on the Global South, FIAN, and the CADCI all exemplify this emphasis on participatory democratic practices. Third, food sovereignty advocates promote social and ecological sustainability by prioritizing traditional forms of food production independent of energy-intensive chemical fertilizers, linked-in with local food markets. Fourth, food sovereignty strengthens solidarity amongst indigenous and peasant populations in campaigning together for a new model of food production and distribution to enable greater control at the local level. Finally, in contrast to food equality and food security approaches, the food sovereignty paradigm seeks to supersede the dominant WTO-led global regime around food production and distribution.

It is worth emphasizing that advocates of food sovereignty do not reject food equality and food security approaches out of hand. As we noted above, some of our WSF-affiliated organizations like FIAN or Ibase support elements of both strategies in their work to legally institute the right to food and support campaigns for land reform. Focusing on food sovereignty as their ultimate goal, members of the Africa Trade Network expressed a similar idea by supporting policies that weave together a range of alternative approaches (Scerri 2011b). Still, as LVC has argued, it is difficult to achieve either food rights or food security without food sovereignty. Indeed, the vast majority of the GJM organizations analyzed in this study opted for food sovereignty as the policy alternative most capable of tackling the causes and impacts of the global food crisis.

Conclusion

This chapter has shown that justice globalists provide a rich set of policy alternatives to address the serious challenges posed by the global food crisis. Consistent with their core ideological concepts and central claims, the 45 WSF-affiliated organizations examined in this study offer creative approaches to worldwide food production and distribution that adhere to the same three-tiered policy framework that characterizes the GJM responses to the GFC we discussed in the previous chapter. These alternative food policy proposals range from reregulation within an expanded market access framework and delinking (and relinking) in order to achieve food security, to the transformation of the dominant food production system toward locally oriented networks of food sovereignty.

Each of these three policy packages contrast sharply with the neoliberal development approach that continues to animate the dominant WTO-led market regime. Ultimately, the policy paths forged by GJM organizations reflect what we consider to be key ideological differences between market globalism and justice globalism, centrally in relation to how global development should be defined and pursued, over what the main drivers of globalization should be, and over what political objectives and ethical norms should shape the public discourses in tackling the major global crises of our time.

7

CLIMATE CRISIS AND JUSTICE GLOBALISM

Introduction

In our final chapter, we examine justice globalist alternatives generated in response to what is arguably the most serious challenge of our time: the global climate change crisis (GCCC). While the social devastation caused by the GFC and global food crisis could be ameliorated rather quickly, the impacts of climate change are largely irreversible and will affect every aspect of life on the planet. An inter-governmental conference convened in Toronto a quarter-century ago already described the threat of climate change as 'second only to a thermonuclear war' (Toronto Statement 1988: 1). More recently the high-profile Stern Review pre-dicted climate change would cause disruption 'on a scale similar to [that] associ-ated with the great wars' (Stern 2006: 2).

If the impact of climate change can be likened to a new world war, then the global South is directly in the firing line. Both Oxfam International and the Intergovernmental Panel on Climate Change (IPCC) predict that the most immediate and catastrophic impacts of climate change will disproportionately affect low-income peoples in countries where urbanization and industrializa-tion are already putting pressure on scarce resources and adaptation capacity is relatively weak (IPCC 2007a; Oxfam International 2009). Major water shortages could potentially halve agricultural production in some regions of Africa by 2020, and reduce yields in Central and South Asia by one third by 2050. This serious situation will add further to the existing pressures associated with the food crisis that we encountered in Chapter 6. Alongside this strain on agricul-ture, the IPCC also predicts mass inundation of the densely populated mega-deltas of South and South-East Asia due to rising sea levels, placing further stress on weak urban infrastructure around housing, health, sanitation, and energy (IPCC 2007a).

The climate crisis is clearly a social crisis as much as an ecological crisis. It not only affects our planet's natural dynamics such as weather patterns, loss of species, and transboundary pollution, it also produces a crisis of social justice. The most immediate and damaging effects of climate change will be felt by the people who are least responsible for greenhouse gas emissions, have the least capacity to adapt, and are the most excluded from the international climate negotiations. These asymmetries directly reflect global development divides, and make the question of how to address climate change unalterably a question of justice. As expressed in the title of a 2008 report from the United Nations Development Program, *Fighting Climate Change* is centrally about 'Human Solidarity in a Divided World' (UNDP 2008).

In this chapter, we explore the main features of the GCCC as well as relevant justice globalist policy responses. We begin by outlining the two perspectives that dominate debates on the climate crisis and how it should be addressed – namely elite Third-World developmentalism and market globalism. We note how these positions have shaped the global climate regime and undermined effective action. Although approaching the crisis from different perspectives, both elite Third-World developmentalism in the global South and Northern market globalism coincide on how to protect vested interests and maximize economic growth and industrialism. As with the global crises discussed in previous chapters, current intergovernmental action on climate change is designed to be market friendly in accordance with market globalist precepts. Indeed, as we note below, government and intergovernmental efforts to address climate change have primarily focused on market-based solutions, such as carbon taxes and emissions trading schemes. Yet, as justice globalists highlight, market-based mechanisms that rely on competition, markets and the chimera of endless resources simply cannot provide long-term solutions to a crisis embedded in our finite and fragile global climate system.

In the second half of this chapter we discuss justice globalist perspectives on the climate crisis. In contrast to Southern pro-development elites and Northern market globalists, who focus primarily on the economic impacts of any efforts to address climate change, justice globalists are more concerned with its social and ecological consequences. While supporting the developmentalist view that Northern emitters are primarily responsible and should therefore take the lead in reducing emissions, justice globalists argue that Southern emitters must also take action. It is not just the issue of emissions, however, that concerns justice globalists. They also criticize the opaque nature of global climate negotiations, evident in the exclusion of the people who most directly feel the impacts of climate change. Beyond the immediate issues of interstate and historical North–South ecological debts, justice globalists also highlight critical questions concerning inter-generational, inter-cultural and inter-species justice.

Emerging from their comprehensive analyses of the key problems and challenges posed by climate change, justice globalists present a series of alternatives to the prevailing official responses. We present these alternatives in the final section of the chapter. As in the two previous chapters, the alternatives fall into three major categories, in this case climate action, climate autonomy, and climate justice. Each of the perspectives draws on core values identified in Chapter 2 that combine in the ideological fingerprint of justice globalism: sustainability, universal rights, participatory democracy, equality, and transformative change. While several organizations selected for this study are engaged with more than one of these approaches, the climate justice position was by far the most popular approach. Our analysis of the GCCC confirms once again that justice globalism should be considered a maturing political ideology endowed with core concepts and with claims that translate into practical policy alternatives addressing the most significant challenges of the global age.

The Global Climate Regime: Market Globalist and Global South Developmentalist Perspectives

The global climate regime is a remarkably complex social construction. Institutionally, it incorporates climate action NGOs, the IPCC, the Conferences of the Parties to the UN Framework Convention on Climate Change (the UNFCCC COPs), and national and local policy frameworks. Each of these elements are brought together under the 1992 UNFCCC and the resulting obligations that arise out of the 1997 Kyoto Protocol. Aside from its extensive and highly bureaucratic network of global actors, the most significant feature of the global climate regime is its symbolic status as a reflection of the failure of the global market-based development projects. Its uneven attempts to reduce greenhouse gas (GHG) emissions clearly demonstrate the ecological bankruptcy of the prevailing market-embedded development model. Indeed, by recognizing the uneven responsibility across global North and South for emissions reduction, the global climate regime acknowledges and institutionalizes global development divides – those countries with the highest levels of income per head are also those most responsible for climate change. The climate regime thus makes visible structures of economic and ecological inequality on a world scale.

In addressing and expressing these global climate asymmetries, the climate regime appears to be self-contradictory. It weaves together some of the worst aspects of elite developmentalism in the global South with some of the most mythic constructions of market globalism. These two separate perspectives previously dominated climate change negotiations, which ultimately resulted in a policy impasse. The postcolonial 'Group of 77' (G77) countries, embodying the elite Southern developmentalist approach, played a key role in shaping the UNFCCC and the resulting Kyoto Protocol (Williams 1997). The key distinction embedded in the UNFCCC, between the 37 'Annex 1' developed countries (41 countries in 2011) and the rest of the globe, is founded on the principle of 'common but differentiated' responsibilities for GHG emissions. Under this principle, the present-day obligation for emissions reductions rests with those countries most responsible for historical rather than present-day emissions (the Annex 1 countries). For elite developmentalists in the G77, the implication of this principle is that developed countries must radically and immediately reduce their GHG emissions, while developing countries may maintain and increase theirs, at least until their level of development is commensurate with that of the global North. This interpretation remains strongly contested by the political and corporate elites in the global North.

First articulated at the 1992 UN Conference on Environment and Development (UNCED) that resulted in the UNFCCC, this elite developmentalist position shaped global climate action from the very beginning. Global South governments refused to compromise control over their own economic development to solve a problem produced mainly by the industrial North. Indeed, in 1990 the OECD emitted three-quarters of global GHG emissions, and was overwhelmingly responsible for the historical build-up of emissions (Jordan 1994). At UNCED the 128 less developed countries grouped under the G77 presented their demands as follows:

> We have not come here to negotiate away our permanent sovereignty over our natural resources ... . Those who have come to these negotiations to make arrangements for a free ride on developing countries should therefore re-examine their positions ... [we call for] a clear differentiation between the actions required to be taken by the developed countries and those to be taken by developing countries, in accordance with their differentiated responsibilities. (cited in Kufour 1992: 8)

The refusal by Southern elites to accept responsibility for reducing GHG seriously undermined efforts at emissions reduction. In the first instance, the UNFCCC created a window for carbon intensive development in the South. As a result, by 2004, non-Annex 1 countries accounted for more than half of global emissions (IPCC 2007a).

At the same time, the elite Southern developmentalist position inadvertently aligned with the interests of market globalists to keep commitments to cut emissions to a bare minimum. Northern elites used the anticipated competitive threat from an emissions-intensive development drive in the South as a key argument against 'unilateral' Northern emissions reductions. Consequently, international emissions targets between 1988 and 1997 were heavily reduced. The 1988 inter-governmental conference in Toronto saw the representatives of leading industrialized countries commit to a voluntary reduction of 20% below 1988 levels by 2005 (Toronto Statement 1988: 1). Yet, despite mounting scientific evidence for climate change since 1988, the targets outlined in the Toronto statement remained the high-water mark in the negotiation process. In fact, the Toronto goal was abandoned in 1992. Instead, under the UNFCCC, industrialized countries were simply committed to reducing emissions to 1990 levels by 2000 (UNFCCC 1992: A.4.2a, b). Worse still, the UNFCCC stopped short of establishing obligations that would ensure this commitment was achieved.

Negotiations proceeded for another five years, culminating in the 1997 Kyoto Protocol, which set a new emissions reduction target of 5% below 1990 levels for all Annex 1 countries to be achieved by 2012. It also allowed considerable variation in the commitment levels of individual countries. For example, the EU committed to an 8% reduction while Australia actually projected an 8% increase in emissions (Kyoto Protocol 1997: A.3.1).

In addition to its failure to lock in substantive targets for emissions cuts, the UNFCCC insisted that international climate policies be 'market-friendly'. Indeed, the Fifth Principle of the 1992 Convention stated that 'measures taken to combat climate change, including unilateral ones, should not constitute a means of arbitrary or unjustifiable discrimination or a disguised restriction on international trade' (UNFCCC 1992: A.3.5). Conversely, the highly successful 1987 Montreal Protocol on Substances that Deplete the Ozone Layer had explicitly provided for sanctions on trade in ozone-depleting chlorofluorocar-bons (CFCs) to be imposed against non-signatories of the Protocol. As noted in Chapter 6, however, the GATT Uruguay Round negotiations proceeding in the intervening period had by 1992 drafted its 'final act', which enshrined the principle of 'non-discrimination' for the emergent global trade regime. The same principle was simply carried across into climate policy (Eckersley 2009). From the very beginning, therefore, market globalism constituted the ideological core of the global climate regime.

The 1997 Kyoto Protocol went much further than the 1992 Convention, not just limiting climate action to mechanisms that were market friendly, but actually introducing an entirely new market in carbon emissions. This new market was established through a series of substantial offsetting loopholes in the Protocol that further undermined the already weakened emissions reduction targets. Under Kyoto, 'national measures' for emissions reduction could be 'supplemented' by market measures, allowing countries to meet their targets partly through the purchase of international carbon credits. These carbon credits were created on the basis of equivalences across sites of excess emissions, sites for emissions reduction, and increases in sink capacity. Carbon credits could be bought from other Annex 1 countries that had exceeded their target reductions, or generated from 'joint implementation' projects in other Annex 1 countries. Credits could also be generated through 'clean development' projects in non-Annex 1 developing countries. With the equivalences verified by the UNFCCC, the scope to use 'market measures' under the Protocol encouraged the creation of national emissions trading schemes, leading to the neoliberalization of climate policy (Okereke 2008). Predictably, the ideological assumption was that markets would deliver the most efficient, lowest-cost, emissions reductions. The role of government was simply to establish the cap on emissions, issue the permits, and support market dynamics (Lohmann 2006). The Kyoto Protocol thus enshrined market globalism as the primary solution to the climate crisis – rather than recognizing its potential to contribute to the further degradation of the environment.

Today's dominant climate regime bequeathed to the world by the UNFCCC and the Kyoto Protocol rests on the twin influences of global South developmentalism (articulated by Southern elites) and market globalism. The policy dynamics fueled by these two perspectives have been mutually reinforcing: the more Southern countries have exploited their emissions window, the more Northern countries have sought to displace emission reductions onto 'the market'. As a result, emissions have been escalating across both the North and South (CSIRO 2010). Although climate change is already creating humanitarian crises (Oxfam International 2009), negotiations for a legally binding international agreement post-2012 have been delayed to 2020 (UNFCCC 2011b). The hiatus in global climate policy suggests the urgent need for a different approach, and offers opportunities for advancing alternatives proposed by the GJM.

Analyzing Global Climate Change:
The Justice Globalist Perspective

Although the current policy impasse has severely hampered efforts to produce both concerted and effective global action on climate change, it also draws acute attention to the need for alternatives. In the context of stalled climate policy, new political spaces have opened up for the alternative critiques and approaches promoted by justice globalists. As with the finance and food crisis, the failure of the existing market globalist climate regime lends new credibility to these alternative approaches that seek to address the causes of the crisis rather than find ways of managing it. In this section, we outline the main features of the dominant justice globalist analysis of the climate crisis. This analysis forms the foundation for the GJM's policy alternatives, which we present in the final section of the chapter.

Unsurprisingly, the justice globalist assessment of the GCCC starts as a critique of market globalist ideology by arguing that two of the central claims of market globalism – that market globalization is irreversible and everyone benefits from the global integration of markets (Steger 2009) – are actually the primary causes of the GCCC. The same inverse relationship noted between finance and food also applies to finance and climate: the levels of global emissions fall when the financial system is in crisis. The European Union is a case in point. It was one of the few state blocs that met its emissions reduction obligations under the Kyoto protocol, yet this was mainly because of the economic collapse in post-Communist 'Economies in Transition' (EIT) rather than any real reduction in emissions. Indeed, the reported reduction in emissions by Annex 1 countries, from 19,000 to 17,800 million metric tons CO_2 equivalent ($mtCO_2e$) for the 1990–2008 period is entirely due to the economic collapse in EIT countries (over this period EIT emissions dropped from 5900 to 3800 mtCO$_2$e while at the same time non-EIT Annex 1 countries' emissions rose from 13,000 to 14,100 mtCO$_2$e) (UNFCCC 2011a).

The GFC reinforced this inverse relationship between the economic growth and GHG emissions. While the emissions of non-EIT Annex 1 countries rose 14.9% during the boom years of 1990 to 2007, the collapse of financial markets starting in 2008 nearly halved this overall increase to 8.4%. But even this reduced rate is still significantly above the Kyoto target. If we accept the mainstream economic view that the EIT recession and the GFC were large-scale events unlikely to be repeated on a regular basis,[1] then the non-EIT 1990–2007 growth in emissions of 14.9% reflects an emerging trend across industrialized countries, as such carbon emissions in industrialized countries are rising, not falling (UNFCCC 2011a: 11, Figure 2).

Ideologically, this widely acknowledged inverse relationship between climate crisis and market-driven development undermines the market-globalist claim that neoliberal globalization brings universal benefits. On the contrary, as argued by justice globalists, market-based globalization is producing the global climate crisis. Many of the GJM organizations analyzed for this study emphasize that the market globalist principles embedded in the global climate regime are fundamental to understanding the causes of the climate crisis. Indeed, the evident link between emissions levels and the health of the financial sector suggests that a dramatic reordering of the relationship between the market and the climate is urgently needed (WCC 2009b, 2009c).

In addition, justice globalists point to the spatial injustices of climate change to debunk what they consider to be the market globalist myth of the universal benefits of global financial integration. Several organizations stress that Northern emissions have wide-scale detrimental impacts on the South and, on this point at least, justice globalists converge with the critique from Southern developmentalist elites. However, justice globalists also point to growing Southern GHG emissions that benefit Southern industrializing elites at the expense of the wider populace. Northern ecological debts to Southern peoples may remain unpaid, but many in the GJM also recognize that new debts are now being generated by Southern elites in their pursuit of market-led growth and 'development'.

Indeed, it is now widely accepted that the survival of the global North, and of future generations globally, is dependent on the willingness of Southern industrializing countries, as well as Northern countries, to reduce their emissions levels. As we noted above, in 1990 non-Annex 1 countries accounted for approximately a quarter of global emissions; by 2004 non-Annex 1 countries, led by industrializing states such as China, India and to a lesser extent Brazil, accounted for more than half of current world emissions (IPCC 2007b: 1.3.1, Fig. 1.4a). This shift in current responsibility for GHG emissions is producing a shift in the geopolitics of climate governance and, as discussed below, is foregrounding the questions of global justice in climate change that are being addressed by the GJM.

The North–South reordering in climate governance opens up new challenges for climate policy, but also presents new possibilities for Southern leverage. In 2000, when the IPCC sought to predict Southern and Northern GHG emissions, it came to the conclusion that even in the most optimistic scenario (see the dark solid line in Figure 7.1 below), unchecked Southern emissions would compensate for any reductions that Northern states could implement (Obasi and Topfer 2000; EcoEquity 2008: 14). Since 2000, however, with Southern emissions rising faster than the IPCC predicted, the prospect of Southern emissions simply replacing Northern emissions by mid-century has become very real. With aggregate Southern and Northern emissions now nearly equal, a qualitatively different North–South power dynamic exists. Both hemispheres are now equally dependent on one another as the survival of each rests to a large extent on the willingness of the other to adopt low-carbon development and production pathways. With the expiry of the Kyoto Protocol in 2012, any new deal at the international level has to secure emissions reductions in the South as well as the North. Since the global South has to be included in any future agreement, it finds itself in an excellent position to negotiate for substantial concessions (Baer and Mastrandrea 2006; Depledge 2006; Okereke et al. 2009).

While justice globalists recognize the growing power of the South in climate negotiations, they nonetheless criticize the current dominance of the political and corporate elites of Southern countries. They insist that the interests of people most directly and negatively affected by climate change – peasants, urban poor,

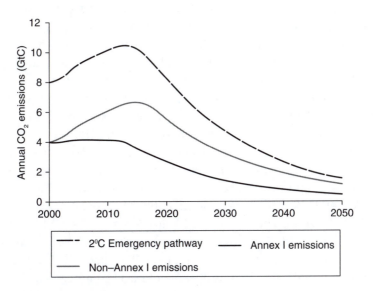

Figure 7.1   The South's Dilemma
The dashed line shows the 2°C Emergency Pathway, in which global CO_2 emissions peak in 2013 and fall to 80% below 1990 levels in 2050. The dark solid line shows Annex I emissions declining to 90% below 1990 levels in 2050. The light solid line shows, by subtraction, the emissions space that would remain for the developing countries. (Source: EcoEquity 2008: 14)

and other low-income and marginalized groups – should be represented as well. Indeed, justice globalists point to the fact that the industrialization of key Southern countries, notably India and China, has sharpened the global power divide between elites both in the North and the South, who are the principal beneficiaries of carbon-intensive development, and those at the grassroots level who bear the costs of neoliberal growth, are most vulnerable to the impacts of climate change and simultaneously have the least capacity to adapt to it.

Confrontations over climate policy between the UNFCCC and its state elites on the one hand, and the GJM on the other, have intensified. At the 2009 Copenhagen UNFCCC Summit, for example, civil society groups found themselves abruptly excluded from the final days of negotiation – in particular, groups representing the interests of indigenous peoples, peasants, feminists, and ecologists associated with the GJM (Riedy and McGregor 2011). This heavy-handed action by the UNFCCC provided further support for the justice globalist contention that those people most directly affected by climate change are marginalized and excluded from the mainstream negotiating process.

Indeed, at Copenhagen, the conflict between the North and South reached a new climax when the G77 countries defended the existing UNFCCC model, arguing that Annex 1 countries had failed to significantly reduce their emissions. Annex 1 countries meanwhile argued for a new 'comprehensive agreement' to replace Kyoto, or to exist side-by-side with it. Faced with the threat of a G77 walkout, several Annex 1 countries, supported by 'emerging economies' including China and India, initiated their own agreement, dubbed the 'Copenhagen Accord'. UNEP analysis estimates that the commitments agreed to under the Copenhagen Accord would do nothing to prevent a 'likely 2.5–5.0°C rise by 2100' (UNEP 2010: 47). The scenario would mean the disappearance of land, cultures, and species as a result of rising sea levels and extreme weather patterns, and would create new 'tipping points' into more global warming.

After two years of inadequate voluntary commitments under the Copenhagen Accord, the UNFCCC's 2011 Climate Change Conference in Durban again shifted the negotiating framework, generating new strategic challenges and opportunities for justice globalists. The Durban Conference introduced a twin-track process to re-formalize emissions reductions. The first track entailed a second Kyoto commitment period for 2013–17, reaffirming the distinction between Annex 1 countries that are legally obliged to reduce emissions, and the rest (UNFCCC 2011a). The second track departed from the UNFCCC model in establishing negotiations for a new agreement 'with legal force' that would be 'applicable to all Parties' (UNFCCC 2011b: para 2). Dubbed the 'Durban Platform for Enhanced Action', this second track would lead to a negotiated agreement by 2015, and ultimately come into force in 2020.

The new negotiating arrangement potentially takes climate policy beyond a Southern developmentalism model, since for the first time countries most affected by current climate change (in particular the Association of Small Island States) will be directly involved in negotiating a global deal to reduce GHG emissions. The revised framework offers at least the possibility of a more genuine process of North–South reciprocity to mitigate GHG emissions (Depledge 2006; Roberts and Parks 2006). This shifting geopolitics of climate change is, therefore, forcing a refiguring of North–South relations, changing the meaning of the 'global South'. Although this process suggests that new political possibilities may be emerging, the market globalist bias of the regime remains. In the post-Kyoto context, a myriad of mechanisms are available for states to displace emissions reductions into emergent carbon offset markets that, in reality, do not reduce emissions at all.

Justice globalists have responded to the shifting framework by moving toward a 'climate justice' model that breaks with both Southern developmentalism and market globalism, and instead addresses climate change from the perspective of the grassroots – often referred to as 'globalization-from-below'. This grassroots approach shifts the justice globalist analysis – and consequently their policy responses – away from the focus on economic development and markets toward the social and ecological dimensions of the GCCC, in particular its impacts on the health, education, living conditions, culture, and wellbeing of the most vulnerable. While the North–South divide is still important in the justice globalist analysis, many GJM organizations are much more focused on the impacts of climate change on the poorest and most marginalized globally, not simply on the consequences for economic development in the global South. This grassroots perspective also enables justice globalists to move their critique beyond the question of simply reducing emissions to address the multiple dimensions of climate injustice.

The unique notion of 'intergenerational justice' is especially important for the justice globalist analysis of the GCCC. Developmentalists in the global South focus on historically accumulated emissions and therefore argue that Northern countries are most responsible for environmental degradation. Northern market globalists, conversely, concentrate on present-day emissions and thus insist that the global South must be prepared to shoulder its share of responsibility. Justice globalists argue that Northern countries should lead the way, but that the global South must also take substantial measures to reduce their own emissions. While the Northern market globalist approach does not address the historic injustices of the unequal development process, the elite Southern developmentalist approach pits the development rights of the present generation against the development rights of future generations. Hence, justice globalists conclude that only an approach that considers all of these dimensions best meets the formidable challenges posed by the climate crisis.

Justice globalists also do not simply focus on the question of emissions produced by each country but on the particular sources of those emissions, highlighting the implications of international trade in this equation. Interstate

injustices, they argue, are compounded by the UN's country-based policy framework that ignores cross-state transfers of emissions-intensive commodities,
whether of fossil fuels or carbon-intensive manufactured goods. Here Northern
consumers reap rewards from rapidly rising emissions in late industrializing
countries, enabling them to maintain living standards while offsetting the emissions from that lifestyle. Thus, the issue of interstate justice is not merely a question of historical responsibility for emissions production but must also take into
consideration contemporary trading relationships.

For many justice globalists, climate change poses a fundamental threat to the
very survival of some Southern countries. The potential of ensuing cultural
genocide – especially where high emitting countries are willfully culpable – poses
profound questions of cultural justice: should one culture or group of cultures
have the power and the right to determine whether another culture survives
or not? In addition, there is the injustice of species extinction. Rates of climate
change deemed acceptable under the UNFCCC are already increasing rates of
extinction. Thus the question arises: should one species be able to decide which
other species will survive and which won't? To what extent are these injustices
morally acceptable or should they just be seen in instrumental terms as the 'price
to pay' for 'market-friendly' climate policies?

One way of interpreting the current challenge of global climate change is to
view it as an instance of 'reflexive development', where shared problems, North
and South, have to be addressed through mutual recognition, dialogue, and common action (Pieterse 1998, 2004). As revealed in the failure to achieve Annex 1
emissions reductions, the GCCC challenges developmentalist models that measure success against Northern standards (Biel 2000; McMichael 2003). Here, rather
than looking to the North as a guide for development, or indeed to the South
for postcolonial developmentalist scenarios, a 'reflexive development' approach
focuses attention on the ways that mutual problems are confronted and addressed
(Pieterse 2004). The GJM and its attempts to conceptualize development as a collaborative, dialogic endeavor grounded in global solidarity and social justice
exemplify this alternative model.

Justice Globalist Policy Alternatives

We again identified three sets of policy alternatives in the GJM with regard to
climate change. We refer to these as 'climate action', 'climate autonomy', and
'climate justice'. However, these three strands should not be seen as mutually
exclusive visions, but as distinct currents that sometimes promote overlapping
alternative policies. And yet, these approaches clearly diverge over the issue of
market-based strategies for reducing carbon emissions. There was a clear preference for 'climate justice' amongst the organizations we examined, mirroring the

preference for food sovereignty as observed in Chapter 6. 'Climate action' inter-acts most intensely with global institutional, market-based frameworks whereas 'climate autonomy' shows clear affinities with the Southern developmentalist perspective. 'Climate justice' is by far the most radical of the three GJM positions on climate change and thus favors policies intended to bring about wide-reaching changes in currently dominant social and ecological relationships.

Climate Action

Climate action approaches have their origins in the late 1980s and early 1990s when various environmentalist groups sought to persuade governments that GHG emissions were seriously threatening the health of our planet and thus that urgent action was required to remedy the situation. Demanding primarily gov-ernment action to force a reduction of emissions worldwide, these 'Green' advo-cates were relatively agnostic on the question of how this should be achieved. The Climate Action Network (CAN) embodies this position. The Network was created by a coalition of environmental organizations with the central objective of ensuring the 1992 UN Conference on Environment and Development (UNCED) would implement strong emissions reductions. One of its key priorities was to counter the international fossil fuel lobby, which, in 1988 had established its own (now defunct) Global Climate Coalition to campaign against regulatory climate policy.

Throughout the 1990s, this battle over climate action shifted substantially from a Green minority position to a growing international consensus in favor of *some* sort of regulatory climate action. As a result, GJM organizations like CAN grew in stature and turned into key players in the UNFCCC process by marshal-ing international opinion and interpreting policy developments for country delegates. Over time, CAN positions became increasingly aligned with the UN negotiations, reflecting its approach of close engagement with a regulatory pro-cess involving mainstream players and their associated worldviews. Indeed, its key priority remained securing aggregate emissions reductions rather than gen-erating critical questions of how such goals could be achieved within the domi-nant policy framework. In many respects, climate action directly replicated and promoted the dominant assumption that regulatory measures could enable a decoupling of economic growth from environmental impacts. Policy proposals were assessed against the instrumental yardstick of 'emissions' rather than nor-mative criteria of justice or solidarity. As a result, CAN never emerged as a strong critic of the neoliberalization of climate policy as it proceeded through the Kyoto process (Pearse 2010). Climate action advocates acknowledged the need to accommodate the historical injustices of climate change and accept differentiated responsibilities, provided these did not become a barrier to negotiated emis-sions reductions. Partly reflecting the success of CAN, climate action in the 2000s broadened into a large tent capable of housing government and business players as well as other NGOs under the leadership of CAN.

In the 2010s, the climate action approach has certainly retained a strong influence on the GJM in general. Several organizations in our sample advocated relatively strong variants of ecological modernization to address the climate crisis. Specifically, climate action measures now highlight 'cooperation' at the global institutional level to develop agreements around emissions reduction targets. In addition, climate change proponents support technology transfers between North and South, seek the establishment of adaptation and mitigation funds to support developing countries, and favor the implementation of emissions trading schemes. To that end, they call for carbon taxes, cap-and-trade systems, and the exploration of technological alternatives such as 'clean' coal and carbon sinks. Trade unions affiliated with the World Social Forum saw the implementation of such measures as a key way to preserve economic growth and, therefore, to secure jobs for their members. Frequently, they made this argument by pointing to the 'economic imperative' forcing countries to position themselves favorably in the new 'green' economy. For example, the Australian Council of Trade Unions' (ACTU) *Jobs and Rights Charter for Working Australians* (2009) called for 'investment in new, clean energy' and emissions trading under the Carbon Pollution Reduction Scheme (CPRS). More recently, the ACTU published an influential pamphlet supporting the introduction of a price on carbon as 'crucial to combating man-made climate change' (ACTU 2011: 7).

Moreover, trade unions often address the impacts of climate policy on carbon-intensive sectors. They argue that climate policy should prioritize a 'just transition' that protects the rights of workers in existing carbon intensive industries, incorporate a 'social dialogue' involving workers and unions in decision-making, and promote North–South justice through transitional funds and technologies (Wilson 2009a). Likewise, the AFL-CIO representative we interviewed raised the political question of how to pursue climate policy in the context of recession. Ultimately, he called for increased government spending to resolve both the jobs crisis and the climate crisis, 'to create good work there while we lower our carbon footprint' (Wilson 2009g). Other organizations, such as the Global Progressive Forum (2011), the ETUC (2010), and, to a lesser extent, the Council of Canadians (2010), support the introduction of consumption taxes, emissions trading schemes, cap-and-trade programs, and other similar market-based mechanisms designed to reduce carbon emissions worldwide.

Beyond their support for market-based solutions, climate action advocates also endorse technology transfers and regulatory schemes at the global level. This includes some support for biofuels as an alternative energy source and the development of 'green' technology (AFL-CIO 2007; ACTU 2009; GPF 2009a). As we shall see, these policy proposals are highly contested by climate justice advocates. As we pointed out in Chapter 6, several GJM organizations argue that the recent move to biofuels has contributed to the rising price of food staples such as corn and maize, and is therefore in part responsible for the recent global food crisis (Chand 2008; Wilson 2009d).

Other climate action policy recommendations include the establishment of global funds to finance climate change adaptation and mitigation, particularly in developing countries. In 2011, the ITUC proposed using the revenues of a global financial transactions tax ('Tobin Tax') to fund climate change adaptation and mitigation measures, especially in the global South (ITUC 2011). Finally, climate action advocates also support the notion of common but differentiated responsibility, arguing that developed countries should transfer technologies to developing countries for adaptation and mitigation 'without the penalties and restrictions currently being encountered as a result of Intellectual Property Rights' (TWN 2007; CCSCS 2009).

Climate Autonomy

In contrast with climate action adherents, who focus on achieving a global agreement on climate policy, climate autonomy groups incorporate a range of more local perspectives that stress the necessity for more engaged and embedded strategies to address climate change. From this perspective, global climate policy that seeks to manage global resources for climate stability is authoritarian, and far removed from the concrete local contexts in which more sustainable livelihoods are maintained. Climate autonomists suggest that the global policy framework can actively undermine and displace embedded sustainable practices. Thus local populations, especially in the global South, might experience them as neocolonial impositions rather than as a globally rational response to a global problem. For many climate autonomists, the climate action approach amounts to a veiled power grab by new 'global resource managers' whose supposedly noble goals and activities actually disempower the very people that ought to be at the core of designing meaningful climate action at the local level (Goldman (ed.) 1998).

Similar to the financial delinking approach discussed in Chapter 5, climate autonomy should not be seen as embracing total autarchy. Rather, it seeks to achieve global ends through local means, and to enhance, rather than undermine, local autonomies. One key aspect of this approach is its strong emphasis on the intrinsic value and incommensurability of local practices – actions to address climate change should be pursued through established forms of knowledge within local contexts. Hence, climate autonomists reassert the constitutive power of locally meaningful sustainability against the 'false' claims of 'would-be' global policy makers. At one level, then, climate autonomy contests the discursive privileging of global and national elites by asserting the sovereignty of the local. More substantively, however, this perspective considers 'sustainability' as a locally embedded value, which means that global sustainability can only be achieved through the collective efforts of myriad local communities. Hence, the key foundations for emissions reduction are to be found by building on existing local practices, not in global policy 'fantasies' that are more likely to legitimize expanded emissions and displace locally sustainable practices.

For example, the response of indigenous peoples' organizations to the UNFCCC policy Reducing Emissions from Deforestation and Degradation (REDD) reflects the core positions of climate autonomists. Leading industrialized countries have supported UN efforts to protect existing forests as carbon sinks with special enthusiasm, seeing REDD as a means of offsetting their industrial emissions. In 2009, the G8 specifically cited REDD as its preferred carbon policy mechanism (G8 2009: para 78b). In contrast, a wide range of indigenous peoples' organizations have claimed the REDD proposals will recolonize lands for offset trading and will undermine sustainable practices currently undertaken by indigenous custodians (Goodman and Roberts 2011). Not surprisingly, REDD has become a key flashpoint in climate negotiations. The controversy around REDD and similar initiatives has opened up considerable policy space for the climate autonomy position. While global policy is geared to protecting the interests of large emitters, struggles for local autonomy have gained considerable symbolic power as legitimate defenders of meaningful forms of sustainability.

The need to localize solutions is often couched in the language of sovereignty and rights. For example, there are strong links between arguments for autonomy in responses to climate change and calls for land reform in response to the food crisis. Organizations such as Corpwatch (Bruno 2002: 14), Focus on the Global South (2008), Jubilee South (2008), Grassroots Global Justice (2009), and La Via Campesina (2007) all emphasize local indigenous and peasant populations having control over land, water, seeds, fisheries, and local renewable energy sources, amongst others, as a key mechanism for combating climate change. These organizations also promote the purchase of locally produced food and goods in an effort to reduce carbon emissions through transportation of products over long distances.

Although the above WSF-connected organizations also emphasize autonomy at the level of the nation-state, they do not consider national policies as an alternative to globally agreed climate policies. They view the primary role of national governments on this issue is to hold corporations accountable for environmental damage (Bruno 2002; People's Health Movement 2004). Most agree that all countries should reduce emissions. Recognizing the need for developing countries to adopt low-emission pathways, they nonetheless suggest such policies should be implemented in accordance with the principle of common but differentiated responsibility. Thus, echoing similar concerns expressed by Southern developmentalist elites, climate autonomists stress the historical responsibility of developed nations in the deterioration of our planet's natural environment (Third World Network 2007; Focus on the Global South 2008).

Climate Justice

The climate justice position emerged out of the earlier climate action and climate autonomy approaches, although in a significantly revised and more radical form. Although climate justice advocates recognize the importance of drawing together a transnational coalition across global civil society to put pressure on states on environmental regulation, they also realize that state action – even at the global level – is insufficient. In their view, states will always fall short of comprehensive climate change reform; hence they promote mass collective action through social movements to transform the dominant policy framework. As part of this broadly transformative orientation, activists arguing for the climate justice position are also most likely to push for food sovereignty in relation to the food crisis and democratic transformation in relation to the financial crisis.

Climate justice was first enunciated as a global set of principles at the United Nations World Summit on Sustainable Development in Johannesburg, South Africa, August 2002 (International Climate Justice Network 2002). A manifesto containing 27 'Principles of Climate Justice' was written by a group of 14 Northern and Southern NGOs, including CorpWatch, Friends of the Earth International, Greenpeace International, the Indigenous Environmental Network, and the Third World Network. On the one hand, the Principles emphasized ecological debt, stating Northern states and corporations 'owe the rest of the world as a result of their appropriation of the planet's capacity to absorb greenhouse gases'. On the other, however, the climate justice manifesto also prioritized stronger involvement from affected peoples in the South to allow local control and conservation with 'clean, renewable, locally controlled and low-impact energy'. The Principles further rejected commodification and existing corporate control, although market solutions were deemed acceptable provided they conformed to 'principles of democratic accountability, ecological sustainability and social justice' (Article 13 of the Bali Principles of Climate Justice, International Climate Justice Network 2002).

Two years later, a climate justice critique of 'false solutions', in particular regarding carbon emissions and trading, was developed in conjunction with the 2004 Durban Climate Justice Summit. Spearheaded by the Durban GJM group 'Carbon Trade Watch', the Summit gathered 20 organizations from Europe, the USA, Latin America, India, and Africa. The resulting 'Durban Declaration on Carbon Trading' outlined various ways in which emissions trading both undermines existing sustainable practices and contributes to climate change. Moreover, it pointed to the irony that with 'this process of creating a new commodity – carbon – the Earth's ability and capacity to support a climate conducive to life and human societies is now passing into the same corporate hands that are destroying the climate' (Carbon Trade Watch 2004). The Declaration quickly spread across the GJM, ultimately garnering support from a further 163 organizations.

Drawing major climate justice groups together, a 'Climate Justice Now!' coalition was established at the 2007 UNFCCC Summit in Bali. This alliance included a range of Southern and Northern-based NGOs and social movements, which had been playing a central role in the GJM, such as Focus on the Global South, the International Forum on Globalization, La Via Campesina, the World Development Movement, the Transnational Institute and Third World Network, as well as a good number of signatories of previous climate justice statements. Criticizing 'false solutions … such as trade liberalization, privatization, forest carbon markets, agro-fuels, and carbon offsetting', Climate Justice Now! emphasized the need to abandon fossil fuels, reduce elite consumption, entrench resource rights, pursue food sovereignty, and repay climate debts through North–South wealth transfers (Climate Justice Coalition 2007). At the 2008 UNFCCC Summit in Poznan a year later, the coalition arrived at an even more critical position, claiming that 'we will not be able to stop climate change if we don't change the neoliberal and corporate-based economy which stops us from achieving sustainable societies'. They urged the UNFCCC to break decisively with 'market ideology' and help develop sustainable and equitable practices in the global South, as 'effective and enduring solutions will come from those who have protected the environment' such as peasants, women, and indigenous peoples (Climate Justice Now! 2008).

Representatives from Focus on the Global South have produced a clear summary of the climate justice approach by emphasizing four major points (Wilson 2009e). First, it is necessary 'to confront what each other's responsibilities are', including historical responsibilities and humanitarian duties with regard to environmental impacts. This question of historic responsibility is often reframed as 'ecological debt'. Part of the Jubilee Movement, the WCC played a key role in conceptualizing ecological debt after spending several decades campaigning against the financial indebtedness of low-income countries. A WCC representative we interviewed was particularly pleased to see this concept being deployed by many NGOs and governments in the context of the UN negotiations. In her view, this amounted to a major shift in consciousness:

> As you think, so you are. So if you think you are a debtor you act in one way, if you are a creditor you act in another way. So the question is, who owes whom for their ecological debt? Who's been having free rein on the ecological dumping ground to the atmosphere? Well it hasn't been the poor. It's the creditor there, and how do you call in that debt? … If you start to switch the perception, then you switch the solutions too. And that is what we've tried to do all along is to say, what is the way we can frame this that brings the truth into focus? (Wilson 2009h)

Second, for Focus on the Global South, climate justice aims at a *real* reduction in emissions rather than just cosmetic fixes rooted in the commodification of carbon emissions and the expansion of carbon sinks. As Joy Chavez from Focus on the Global South states, people must recognize that 'we will be kidding ourselves to say that we will always come up with technology and the earth and human capacity can keep on growing' (Wilson 2009e). Implied in this second point

is the central characteristic of the climate justice perspective, namely its opposition to primarily market-based solutions. The WCC, for example, has been
highly critical of efforts to commodify the ecological commons, for they constitute a 'public good', which needs 'to be treated as a sacred gift for use not abuse'
(Wilson 2009h).

Echoing the criticisms of the market raised in Chapter 5, climate justice advocates
are opposed to emissions trading schemes because they cannot address the real,
everyday lived problems that communities face as a result of climate change and
environmental degradation. As members of Focus on the Global South observed:

> [T]he kind of solutions being dangled or battled at the international level will not
> really solve for example the rising sea level … a city like metro Manila, 80% of it will
> be submerged in water by carbon trading or by clean development mechanisms.
> (Wilson 2009e)

In similar fashion, the Transnational Institute addresses this crucial disconnec-
tion between socially constructed markets and living environments:

> Carbon trading and emissions trading inside of a market system will never be able
> to address the real problems on the ground … it acts to privatize and commodify a
> global commons and put a price tag on something that is or should be a global
> commons … how can something like the atmosphere survive in a market that relies
> on growth … . We are talking about limited resources. (Wilson 2009i)

In short, mainstream market-based climate policy profoundly demonstrates the
rift between material accumulation and eco-systemic survival. For many of our
selected GJM organizations, the 'fraud' of carbon trading prioritizes cold cash
over and above warm bodies, especially in the global South: 'Companies in the
North buy those [emissions] credits, to do what? To continue polluting; to actually go above a cap. It's a fraud, it's an easy way out' (Wilson 2009i).

For climate justice activists, overcoming the GCCC cannot be limited to
abstract economic or scientific concerns. Rather, as a system-wide crisis affecting
all life on this planet, it requires a transformation of prevalent social systems.
A representative from OneWorld put it well:

> Climate change to me isn't an environmental issue, it's a people issue and it's a sys-
> temic issue, talk about systems, inter-dependent systems, there is nothing that
> proves that more than climate change. As a systemic issue it forces societies to reas-
> sess the dominance of materialism and money as a means to status, and to move to
> a less status-mad kind of culture. (Wilson 2009f)

Similarly portraying climate change as a systemic crisis, the WCC has warned
against the 'reductionist' approach of focusing on air pollution: 'This is why we
talk about system change more than climate change'. The climate crisis is bound
into the broader systemic crisis around finance, poverty, marginalization, and
disempowerment, and both are framed in terms of justice: 'eco-justice actually

complements ecology, and also is balanced in a way that can offer justice to the Earth and to the people. Because if you reap lavishly from the Earth you are also doing an injustice to it' (Wilson 2009h). The WCC derives this position from several decades of climate campaigning that emphasized the connections between justice, peace, and the integrity of creation. For this GJM organization, the question of moral integrity underpins the idea of sustainable development and thus serves as an ethical guide to environmental action: 'If we truly loved ourselves and our neighbors, it's really simple, we wouldn't exploit, we wouldn't over-appropriate the ecological space, we wouldn't do what we do and leave nothing for the future' (Wilson 2009h).

Building on similar ethical concerns, the GGJ has focused on the concept of 'global well-being', derived from indigenous Latin American affinity for *'e buon de vire'*. Linking this concept to radical slogans such as 'system change not climate change', GGJ deployed 'global well-being' with much success at the 2009 Copenhagen Climate Summit. Many GJM organizations also connect it to the older notion of 'a paradigm shift', enabling 'much more synergy and movement and ability to move forward' (Steger 2010a). The frequent usage of such key phrases reflects the ideological influence of justice globalism's core value of transformative change.

The third major feature of the climate justice perspective challenges an assumption pervading mainstream environmental policy, namely, that it might be acceptable for certain countries (like the Pacific island nation of Kiribati), peoples, and species, to be simply 'written off', while others might be 'saved'. This argument also extends to support for significant reparations provided to ecologically damaged regions by historically culpable parties. Reflecting this, a number of climate justice organizations argue that the global North should pay reparations to the global South for the historical damage caused as a result of industrialization. In addition, they insist that developing countries should not have the same pressures placed on them to reduce their emissions until they have reached an acceptable level of development (see EcoEquity 2008).

On this issue, the climate justice position is in danger of collapsing back into Southern elite developmentalism or climate autonomy. But we should note that climate justice advocates are not suggesting that developing countries are excused from making alterations or adjustments to their emissions outputs. Indeed, they remain highly critical of the G77 position that developing nations need not act until the global North has first made its own adjustments (Bello n.d.). For climate justice proponents, the GCCC requires global action simultaneously involving all parties, albeit mediated through the principle of common but differentiated responsibility. This stance highlights the GJM's strong commitment to social justice. Even for organizations employing a more judicial understanding of justice, such as the Federation Internacional Direitos Humanos (FIDH), enforcement should be geared to developing a legal concept of environmental justice, which recognizes historical environmental injustices and holds those responsible for environmental crimes accountable (Goodman 2010b).

The fourth and final key point of climate justice involves its commitment to participatory democracy by means of greater transparency and the active inclusion of the peoples most affected by climate change. Hence the importance of a democratic decision-making process that assures that 'those who are the victims, who are going to be heavily impacted by a change in the climate, have a say' (Wilson 2009e). Indeed, climate justice advocates have long criticized global climate governance mechanisms for excluding people who have been most affected by the impacts of environmental degradation. While the UNFCCC constitutes one of the most democratic UN institutions – each country has one vote and agreements are based on unanimity – NGOs and other civil society groups often are excluded from the discussions as demonstrated at the 2009 Copenhagen Conference (Riedy and McGregor 2011). Corporations and governments, on the other hand, hire consultants and send huge delegations of lobbyists to UNFCCC meetings who are permitted to remain in the thick of discussions. Several representatives have stressed the need for locally grounded forms of indigenous knowledge to be directly included as well. A WCC representative openly doubted whether mainstream UNFCCC policy-makers had a genuine interest in facilitating the 'inter-connection of people, the natural resources of the planet, and sustainable communities', adding that 'Indigenous communities have a lot to teach us about sustaining communities over millennia' (Wilson 2009h). Most importantly, climate justice advocates insist that overcoming the GCCC will require meeting dramatically reduced carbon emission targets resulting in significant adjustments in lifestyles, particularly in the Global North (Vittachi 2007; Grassroots Global Justice 2009; Wilson 2009e). Overall, this position translates into concrete policy terms justice globalism's underlying core concepts of transformative change, sustainability, global solidarity, and social justice.

Conclusion

Providing a general overview of the global climate regime as well as justice globalist perspectives on global climate change, this chapter suggested that GJM policy responses to the GCCC fall into three broad approaches: climate action, climate autonomy, and climate justice. These approaches are broadly commensurate with the three major policy perspectives identified in Chapters 5 and 6 with regard to the GFC and global food crisis. We observed that the 'climate justice' approach departs significantly from both climate action and climate autonomy strategies.

Generally speaking, the climate justice perspective argues that 'market-friendly' and technology-based solutions are aimed at maintaining growth

(Continued)

(Continued)

rates rather than reducing emissions (Gilbertson and Reyes 2009). Putting forth radical policy alternatives to dominant market globalism and Southern developmentalism, climate justice advocates in the GJM call for a fundamental transformation of social and ecological relationships, lifestyles, global governance mechanisms, and property relations. These alternative policy proposals have gained political traction in the wider movement, and have been taken up by some governments, notably the Bolivian Government of Evo Morales, which in April 2010 convened the People's World Conference on Climate Change and Mother Earth's Rights, to provide a counterpoint to the failing UNFCCC process.

Finally, it is important to note that the alternatives offered by justice globalists to the three global problems discussed in this book all converge in the core ideological claim that market globalism generates global crises. Positing an inverse relationship between marketization and sustainability, our select WSF-connected organizations contend that global markets must at least be severely constrained, if not radically transformed. Thus, the ongoing policy debate surrounding these three global crises reflects the great ideological struggle between market globalism and justice globalism. The ultimate outcome of this contest will dramatically affect the future course of human history and the planet.

Note

1 As discussed in Chapter 5, however, it is possible that global financial crises will occur with increased regularity and severity if little is done to dramatically transform the global financial system. Financial collapse benefits emission reduction by massively destabilizing the global economy. This situation provides some evidence to support the view that neoliberalism is incompatible with efforts to address climate change and promote sustainability.

8

CONCLUSION

Based on the wealth of data generated by our analysis of 45 selected GJM organizations affiliated with the WSF, we call into question market-globalist critiques of the GJM as a simplistic and incoherent catch-all movement characterized by an unproductive 'anti' attitude toward 'globalization' (Friedman 2000, 2005; Stiglitz 2003; Wolf 2004; Bhagwati 2004; Greenwald and Kahn 2009; Wilson 2009e). Employing Michael Freeden's criteria for ideological maturity in our morphological discourse analysis of the central texts and interview materials, this study has demonstrated the ideological coherence of 'justice globalism'. A mature ideology with global reach, justice globalism constitutes the normative-conceptual glue binding together the global justice 'network of networks' while at the same time to helping to generate policy alternatives to the neoliberal framework of market globalism.

Thus, this original study offers clear answers to the two main research objectives of this book: the in-depth examination of the ideological structure of the GJM, and the detailed assessment of the connection between ideology and policy in the context of global crises. Unlike its reliance on ideological coherence, however, the GJM shapes and articulates its policy alternatives by following three distinct approaches or strategies: reform, autonomy, and transformation. Still, it is important to remember that these approaches are united in their global orientation in terms of their common translation of the rising global imaginary into concrete policy alternatives that respond to the major global crises of the early 21st century.

The outcomes of our comprehensive examination of the GJM's ideology and policy proposals also raise additional questions about the future trajectory of the movement. Our study indicates that the GJM generates multiple policy alternatives to those offered by market globalism, and that these especially gain a degree of traction in the context of the global crises that they seek to address. Influence over the global political agenda, by pressuring political elites to accept and implement recommendations, has been realized to a limited extent in relation to the reform and autonomy-centered alternatives. The movement has also had some success in constituting and enacting alternatives through mobilization, in some cases helping displace and supplant existing elites, including state elites. Despite these limited gains, market globalism remains the dominant global policy framework, and global justice values remain subordinate. This concluding chapter is a good place to reflect on these implementation difficulties, and also draw on the findings of this study to offer suggestions for how the GJM might move forward.

Coherence and Distinctiveness

Our study reveals a surprising degree of shared ideational alignment around core ideological concepts that reflect deep-seated norms and values. Sharing some affinity with liberal and social-democratic aspirations, justice-globalism rearranges and recombines these values, endows them with new meanings, and invigorates new values such as 'sustainability'. The outcome is a fundamentally new ideological morphology reconfigured around a rising global consciousness rather than a more defensive national imaginary. As we discussed in the early chapters of this study, justice globalism's normative commitments to democracy, equality, justice, rights, solidarity, sustainability, and social change are reflected in seven core concepts, which, in turn, are mobilized in five central claims against the dominant assertions of market globalism. This dynamic is outlined in Table 8.1.

Table 8.1 Values and Core Concepts: Market Globalism and Justice Globalism

Values	Market Globalist Core Concepts	Justice Globalist Core Concepts
Democracy	Liberal representative democracy	Participatory democracy
Equality	Formal equality	Equality of outcome and access
Justice	Procedural justice	Social justice, restorative and (re)distributive
Rights	Civil and political rights	Universal rights, including economic, social, and cultural
Social solidarity	Civility under the state	Global solidarity in social movements
Sustainability	Sustainable economic development	Sustainable ecologies and societies
Social change	Market-led social change	Transformative change 'from below'

While market globalism clings to the neoliberal mode of minimalist representative democracy, justice globalists assert the necessity for much deeper forms of participatory democracy. Market globalism limits equality claims to formal equality before the law, while justice globalists assert the necessity for equality of access to resources and equality of outcome. The same logic applies to the idea of 'justice'. Market globalists embrace procedural and retributive justice while justice globalists assert substantive social justice. Justice globalists focus particularly on the need for restoration and redistribution in light of past injustices. Market globalists promote political and civil rights as defined by the liberal state (for instance the right to property), while justice globalists promote universal rights across all fields especially in relation to economic, social, and cultural rights. In terms of social solidarity, market globalists promote functional civility amongst the citizenry while justice globalists promote an ethic of people-to-people global solidarity directed towards societal transformation. More recently, market globalists have begun promoting the idea of 'sustainable economic development' (partially as a result of justice globalist influence). Justice globalists, on the other hand, ground their core concepts in the intrinsic value of ecological and societal sustainability. Finally, while market globalists promote a model of social change fueled by largely unregulated markets, justice globalists promote ethical models of market regulation, community embedding and transformative change brought about by global social movements 'from below'.

As demonstrated in Chapter 2, these core concepts are widely accepted among organizations associated with the GJM. The assertion of an agenda for substantive outcomes rather than simply formal commitments is a central aspect linking the core concepts together. Democracy, equality, justice, rights, solidarity, sustainability, and social change are promoted only to the extent that they are capable of delivering outcomes that particularly address the needs of the most marginalized in contemporary global society. Significantly, these outcomes are seen as open-ended, allowing for the normative evolution of the core concepts. There is an active rejection of market globalist-imposed preconditions to or limitations on the realization of these values. In particular, justice globalists forcefully reject the notion that ethical commitments must not impinge on the self-regulating operations of the market. Rather they define and promote an expansive re-embedding of markets in society, thus privileging the social sphere over the economic domain.

As we noted above, the core global justice concepts generate a series of central ideological claims that guide collective action in the wider GJM. These claims decontest core concepts and thus operationalize normative commitments by targeting market globalism and the neoliberal models it promotes. Hence, the first two claims that we identify in Chapter 3 define neoliberalism as producing global crisis, and market-driven globalization as increasing global disparities. The remaining three claims prioritize democratic participation and 'people power', ultimately asserting that 'another world' is possible. Like the core concepts of justice globalism, these five central claims have wide currency among the organizations investigated for this study for they define and articulate a worldview that serves as the normative foundation for the development of shared policy alternatives.

In Chapter 4, we discussed the ways in which global justice organizations translate ideology into policy alternatives. Seeking to exemplify their own values, many WSF-affiliated groups engage in a democratic process of developing strategy 'from below', embedded in dialogue and reflexivity. The diverse approaches to strategy demonstrate a shared openness to emerging agendas. Organizations focus on agenda setting beyond more reactive approaches, in the process constructing a range of framing mechanisms to ensure their messages gain wide resonance. These mechanisms are developed in tandem with other global justice organizations, through structures designed to generate movement dialogue. Central to this dialogue is the core concept of 'solidarity', applied through various modes of organizational reflexivity across both geographical and issue divides, and between organizational elites and grassroots groupings. These agenda-setting strategies are never perfected, but help to produce what we call 'generative issues' – key socio-political problems and events around which justice globalists mobilize wider publics. As such, these generative issues build relevance for the movement, translating core concepts and claims into movement agendas.

Political Responsiveness

Our second main task was to investigate the extent to which the ideology of justice globalism translates into substantive responses to political contexts. Building on the general insights of Chapter 4, the ensuing three chapters focused on specific policy responses to the global finance crisis, the global food crisis, and the global climate crisis. Table 8.2 outlines the range of positions and common themes we identified. Indeed, our analysis demonstrates that justice globalism responds well to pressing political issues, suggesting it has matured as an ideology. Significantly though, justice globalism does not produce policy uniformity in terms of political responsiveness. While we found surprising convergence in key values, core concepts, and central claims, there remain in the GJM significant differences in terms of approaches, agendas, and ultimate policy objectives. Yet, the contestation and debate over policy alternatives does not undermine justice globalism's overall ideological coherence. Market globalists, too, frequently disagree on policy issues, all of which are nonetheless consistent with their underlying ideological political commitments. Rather, the presence of multiple policy alternatives in the GJM points to justice globalism's ideological maturity and conceptual depth, reflected in the richness of normative resources for the development of movement strategies.

Table 8.2 Global Justice and Global Crises, Summary of Responses

Crisis	Reform	Autonomy	Transformation
Finance	Regulation for the public good	Delinking-to-relink	Democratizing finance
Food	Food equality and market access	Food security and sufficiency	Food sovereignty
Climate	Climate action	Climate autonomy	Climate justice

Our tripartite schema echoes other typologies of movement politics under conditions of intensifying globalization. Manuel Castells' model presented in his 'Power of Networks' series, for example, suggests that under the domination of global network politics, social movements take on legitimating, resistance and project identities (Castells 1997). Castells defines these as alternatives that produce radically different political outcomes. In the abstract, they reflect the series of different options that may present themselves to movements in confronting the dominant dynamic of 'globalization-from-above', namely, i) to seek some incremental accommodation that is legitimated by the hegemonic network, ii) to resist the network through an alternative 'communal heaven', or iii) to pursue a project that transforms the network. Reitan and Gibson (2012) also develop a tripartite typology in their recent analysis of global social movements and climate politics, finding that pre-existing ideological formations of liberal-reformism, anarchism and socialism are reproduced in these international settings. Our analysis of global justice organizations also found a broad range of postures that seek to enact the shared normative commitments. We do not suggest, however, that conventional political ideologies are replicated at the global level. Rather, we argue that the process of translating the global imaginary is producing new overarching ideological formations, including justice globalism, that generate substantive and distinct alternatives.

Our analysis of the GJM responses to global crisis makes clear there is no unified position in the GJM regarding which approaches and policy alternatives are the 'best'. Rather, a series of perspectives come into play, producing different diagnoses and alternatives. Indeed, in the context of real-world crises, the ideological consensus on core concepts and central claims shifts into an open-ended series of debates about concrete policy alternatives. These differences reflect, in part, the different geographical impacts of the global crises we discussed in this study. While all three crises have their origins in Northern contexts, they have radically uneven effects across the globe. The GFC was mainly felt in the North and in exposed Southern countries. Countries that had maintained strong controls on capital flows, such as the People's Republic of China, escaped relatively unscathed. The global food crisis, in contrast, was largely a Southern problem felt most keenly by countries most exposed to the pressures of the global food trade. The GCCC, in theory, is a worldwide crisis, but, in practice, it currently impacts most severely on those living in exposed and marginal areas of the global South. Not surprisingly, these divergent impacts and experiences generate differences of interpretation and in the development of policy alternatives.

At the same time, however, we also noticed a degree of convergence, including a discernible shift from food rights to food sovereignty and from climate action to climate justice. We suggest that this convergence stems from an underlying shared critical stance among justice globalists. This critical perspective focuses on systemic contexts and explanations rather than superficial face-value diagnoses. As we noted in Chapters 5–7, the majority of our WSF-affiliated organizations attend to the causes of global crises, rather than their symptoms. In terms of the GFC, financial 'irregularities' are not the issue, but the power and influence of corporate and financial actors. For the global food crisis, it is not problems with food supply that generate crisis but marketization, agri-industry and financialization. Likewise for the GCCC, emissions reduction and temperature rises are seen as only a small part of the story; the main concerns lie with the systemic drivers of the growth economy and climate injustice. Most justice globalists reject market-based solutions that exercise power through markets and commodities, whether in the form of derivatives, food futures, or carbon credits. Instead, GJM activists promote government regulation, delinking from global markets, or the transformation of the dominant market-globalist ideological and policy framework. Moving beyond sectoral alternatives to an overarching critique that rejects commodification and financialization as such, global justice organizations bring their integrated holistic analysis to bear in their formulation of socially embedded policy alternatives.

All of these alternative proposals – albeit in distinct ways – are geared to subjecting economic forces to popular control. Thus, they implicitly accept Karl Polanyi's (1944) solution of subordinating economy to society rather than the other way round. Consistent with their core ideological concepts and central claims, WSF-affiliated organizations aim to deepen democratic participation in global agendas that are primarily implemented and enacted at the local level. One of their main priorities is to strengthen the ability of local peoples to shape their own economies and environments and thereby exercise democratic agency, whether on issues of finance, food, or climate.

The findings presented in this study suggest that the GJM serves as a striking example of the complex interweaving dynamics of globalization. As the old nested geographical scales of the local, national, regional and global collapse into each other, the newly emerging spatial arrangements favor differences between diverse locations and communities. Rather than market globalism's prescription of 'one-size-fits-all', justice globalism encourages a diversity-within-unity attitude designed to forge transnational people-to-people linkages.

Quo Vadis, GJM?

History teaches us that new ideologies and movement mobilization do not necessarily ensure that policy alternatives will be implemented. The evolution of the GJM attests to this wisdom. Perhaps the most instructive example is the GFC, which marked a critical moment of opportunity for the GJM. Generating a profound legitimacy crisis for market globalism, the GFC represented a damning indictment of the utopian ideal of the self-regulating market. The extent of market failure became obvious even to ordinary citizens when their governments authorized corporate bailouts and stimulus packages equivalent to a fifth of global income. Although justice-globalist claims regarding the inherent weaknesses of neoliberalism were borne out, the GJM was only a marginal player in the ensuing public debate. At this critical juncture, justice globalists advanced numerous proposals yet signally failed to advance political alternatives that captured the imagination of billions of disillusioned working people.

The GJM's inability to affect change in its principal arena of criticism at a moment of severe instability and uncertainty raises significant questions about its overall ideological appeal and political effectiveness. As several of our interviewees noted, this failure to shift the dominant paradigm in a more progressive direction invites serious reconsiderations regarding the GJM's strategizing, campaigning, and mobilizing. Indeed, the early 21st century marks a critical moment for the GJM. The movement has developed beyond its initial stage of raw protest to a point where it can offer substantive alternatives to the ideology of market globalism and its associated neoliberal policy agenda. The question the movement faces is how to capture and sustain the political imagination of the masses. To do this, it must complement its well-established models of refusal and dialogue with more effective ways of disseminating its ideological concepts and claims and thus challenge the still dominant slogan that 'there is no alternative' to market globalism. One way of doing that would be for the GJM to consciously transform itself from a social into a political movement.

If we look back in history, we find many similar moments where progressive movements have made the transition from social movement to political movement. One example is the international socialist movement, which self-consciously established the first 'International Workmen's Association' in 1864 in order to constitute a political formation capable of challenging capitalism. Another moment might be the 1955 Bandung conference of colonized and post-colonial leaders, which sought to give birth to a political force – a Southern Non-Aligned Movement – capable of transforming a world created by Northern imperialism and colonialism. The 2001 World Social Forum, heralded by Michael Hardt (2002) as the 'New Bandung', was surely a moment of similar significance for the GJM, in establishing a social movement configuration beyond both neoliberalism and statism. As we look back on the achievements of that formation, we may apprehend and appreciate the centrality of political aspiration – despite the self-definition of the WSF as primarily a dialogic forum, rather than as a new political force in its own right entering the world stage.

The findings presented in this study suggest that the GJM needs to become more 'political', harnessing its values and strategies in order to arrive at a coordinated political agenda. One possible way forward may be the establishment of a World Political Forum. As we highlighted above, the WSF and its dialogic method of engagement have played a central role in strengthening the GJM and in generating its alternative agendas. Yet the dialogic model is also inherently limiting. Although the organizations we selected for this project are all members of the International Council of the WSF, they nonetheless retain a degree of (healthy) scepticism about the WSF model. Some believed the model has become too focused on opposition rather than on alternatives (Wilson 2009f). Others pointed to a gulf separating WSF theoretical critiques and their campaign language on the grassroots level (Wilson 2009c). For many, the WSF constituted not only an important sounding board, but also a place where new trends and strategic possibilities could be discussed – yet mostly in the abstract (Steger 2010b; Wilson 2009b). Thus many GJM organizations have developed their strategic agendas independent of the WSF or, at best, within WSF-related networks that meet at the margins of the Forum itself.

As an increasing number of scholars and activists within and outside the GJM have noted (including many of our interviewees), the WSF's dialogic politics has perhaps run its course. What may be urgently required today is not just open dialogue, but effective political strategy and policy leverage. At one level, this would require shifting the GJM from a social movement engaging primarily in the meta-politics of values and ideology into a political movement seeking to capture political power. Given the continued dominance of market globalism and of neoliberal governance, this is not an easy task. Yet there are signs that this is precisely the direction in which the WSF is moving. At the UN's 2012 Rio+20 Conference on Environment and Development, the WSF presented a counter-agenda embodied in the consensus report, 'Another Future is Possible'. Not only did the report offer concrete alternatives to the UN's 'green economy' agenda, it also offers the first approximation of a manifesto for justice globalism (Thematic Social Forum 2012).

This study contributes to this necessary process of politicization. Our analysis has provided ample evidence – for the first time on such a comprehensive level – of the ideological capacity of justice globalism to serve as a powerful conceptual map for moving our crisis-ridden world beyond the spirals of injustice that have relegated the majority world, and now impose intensifying ecological degradation on the planet as a whole.

REFERENCES

Africa Trade Network (2009) 'Africa and the global crisis: time to throw away neoliberalism', Africa Trade Network statement released 24 August 2009. Available at http://twnafrica. org/index.php?option=com_content&view=article&id=197:12-atn-statement-qafrica-and-the-global-crisis-time-to-throw-away-neo-liberalismq&catid=47:atn&Itemid=72 (accessed 27 August 2009).

Albrow, M. (1996) *The Global Age: State and Society beyond Modernity*. Cambridge: Polity Press.

Aldrick, P. (2011) 'EU Parliament approves Tobin Tax on transactions', *The Telegraph*, 8 March 2011. Available at www.telegraph.co.uk/finance/economics/8368563/EU-Parliament-approves-Tobin-tax-on-transactions.html (accessed 2 June 2011).

Allianza Social Continental (n.d.) 'Health and free trade'. Available at www.asc-hsa.org/node/567. Translated by Kevin Wood (accessed September 2009).

Allianza Social Continental (2008) 'Before the financial crisis, ASC demanded change to the model', 25 November 2008. Available at http://www.asc-hsa.org/node/663. Translated using PROMPT Online translation (accessed 15 June 2009).

Althusser, L. (1969) *For Marx*. London: Allen Lane.

American Federation of Labor – Congress of Industrial Organisations (AFL-CIO) (2007) 'Labor leaders back "Cap and Trade" plan to cut carbon emissions'. Available at http://blog.aflcio.org/2007/07/11/labor-leaders-back-cap-and-trade-plan-to-cut-emissions/ (accessed June 2011).

Amin, S. (2006) 'The Millennium Development Goals: a critique from the South', *Monthly Review*, 57(10). Available at http://monthlyreview.org/2006/03/01/the-millennium-development-goals-a-critique-from-the-south (accessed 11 November 2011).

Anderson, B. (1991) *Imagined Communities: Reflections on the Origin and Spread of Nationalism*, rev. edn, London: Verso.

Appadurai, A. (1996) *Modernity at Large: Cultural Dimensions of Globalization*. Minneapolis, MN: University of Minnesota Press.

Archibugi, D. (2008) *The Global Commonwealth of Citizens: Toward Cosmopolitan Democracy*. Princeton, NJ: Princeton University Press.

Articulacion Feminista Marcosur (2009) 'About the current campaign – Against Fundamentalisms'. Available at www.mujeresdelsur-afm.org.uy/index_e.htm (accessed 11 February 2010).

ATTAC (2009) 'The time has come: let's close down the casino economy', ATTAC Statement on the financial crisis and democratic alternatives, 5 June 2009. Available at www.attac.org/en/campaign/close-down-casino-economy/time-has-come-lets-close-down-casino-economy (accessed 23 March 2010).

Australian Council of Trade Unions (2009) *Jobs and Rights Charter for Working Australians*. Melbourne: ACTU.

Australian Council of Trade Unions (2011) *Climate Change is Union Business*. Melbourne: ACTU.

Baer, P. and Mastrandrea, M. (2006) *High Stakes: Designing Emissions Pathways to Reduce the Risk of Dangerous Climate Change*. London: Institute for Public Policy Research.

Ball, T. and Dagger, R. (2008) *Political Ideologies and the Democratic Ideal*, 7th edn. New York: Pearson Longman.

Bank for International Settlements (BIS) (1996) Quarterly Review November. Available at www.bis.org/publ/r_qt9611.htm (accessed March 2012).

Bank for International Settlements (BIS) (2004) Quarterly Review December. Available at http://www.bis.org/publ/qtrpdf/r_qt0412.htm (accessed March 2012).

Bank for International Settlements (BIS) (2008) Quarterly Review December. Available at www.bis.org/publ/qtrpdf/r_qt0812.htm (accessed March 2012).

Bank for International Settlements (BIS) (2010) Quarterly Review December. Available at www.bis.org/publ/qtrpdf/r_qt1012.htm (accessed March 2012).

Barber, B. (2001) *Jihad vs McWorld*. New York: Ballantine Books.

Bello, W. (1999) *Dark Victory: The United States, Structural Adjustment and Global Poverty*. London: Pluto Press.

Bello, W. (2002) 'What's wrong with the Oxfam Trade Campaign?' Available at www.maketradefair.com/en/index.php?file=03042002121618.htm&cat=3&subcat=2&select=1 (accessed 8 June 2011).

Bello, W. (2005) *Deglobalization: Ideas for a New World Economy*. New York: Zed Books.

Bello, W. (2008) 'How to manufacture a global food crisis', *Development* 51(4): 450–5.

Bello, W. (n.d.) 'Will capitalism survive climate change?' Available at http://focusweb.org/will-capitalism-survive-climate-change-3.html?Itemid=153 (accessed February 2009).

Bello, W. and Baviera, M. (2009) 'Food Wars', *Monthly Review* 61(3): 17–31.

Bhagwati, J.N. (2004) *In Defense of Globalization*. New York: Oxford University Press.

Biel, R. (2000) *The New Imperialism: Crisis and Contradiction in North/South Relations*. London: Zed Books.

Bleiker, R. (2000) *Popular Dissent, Human Agency and Global Politics*. Cambridge: Cambridge University Press.

Bloch, E. (1995) *The Principle of Hope*, 3 vols. Cambridge, MA: MIT Press.

Bourdieu, P. (1990) *The Logic of Practice*. Stanford, CA: Stanford University Press.

Brenner, N. (2004) *New State Spaces: Urban Governance and the Rescaling of Statehood*. Oxford: Oxford University Press.

Brenner, R. (2006) *The Economics of Global Turbulence*. London: Verso.

Bruno, K. (2002) *Greenwash plus 10: The UN Global Compact, Corporate Accountability and the Johannesburg Summit*. San Francisco, CA: Corpwatch. Available at www.corpwatch.org/article.php?id=1348 (accessed May 2009).

Bryan, D. and Rafferty, M. (2006) *Capitalism with Derivatives: A Political Economy of Financial Derivatives, Capital and Class*. Basingstoke, UK: Palgrave Macmillan.

Buechler, S.M. (2000) *Social Movements in Advanced Capitalism: The Political Economy and Cultural Construction of Social Activism*. New York: Oxford University Press.

Carbon Trade Watch (2004) 'The Durban Declaration on Carbon Trading'. Available at www.durbanclimatejustice.org/durban-declaration/english.html (accessed March 2012).

Carroll, W.K. (2007) 'Hegemony and counter-hegemony in a global field', *Studies in Social Justice* 1(1): 36–66.

Castells, M. (1997) *The Power of Identity. The Information Age: Economy, Society and Culture Vol. II*. Cambridge, MA; Oxford, UK: Blackwell.

Castro, J. E. (2008) 'Neoliberal water and sanitation policies as failed development strategy: lessons from developing countries' Progress in Development Studies 8(1): 63–83.

Central de Trabajadoes Argentinos (CTA) (2009a) 'Distribution or poverty', 14 July 2009. Translated by Kevin Wood. Available at www.cta.org.ar/base/article12823.html (accessed 24 November 2009).

Central de Trabajadoes Argentina (CTA) (2009b) 'March for a new model of production'. Translated by Kevin Wood. Available at www.cta.org.ar/base/article13998.html (accessed 24 November 2009).

Central Única dos Trabalhadores (CUT) (2009) 'The census and the common sense: time to invest in family based agriculture'. Translated by Kevin Wood. Available at www.cut.org.br/content/view/17367/ (accessed 2 November 2009).

Chand, R. (2008) 'The global food crisis: causes, severity and outlook' *Economic and Political Weekly*, June 28, 2008: 115–23.

Chossudovsky, M. (1998) '"Financial warfare" triggers global economic crisis', Third World Network website. Available at www.twnside.org.sg/trig-cn.htm

Chossudovsky, M. (2003) *The Globalization of Poverty and the New World Order*, 2nd edn. Pincourt, Canada: Global Research, especially Chapter 6.

Climate Justice Coalition (2007) 'Climate Justice Now! Principles'. Available at www.climate-justice-now.org/principles/ (accessed April 2012).

Climate Justice Now! (2008) Poznan Statement. Available at www.climate-justice-now.org/category/events/cop-14-poznan/ (accessed April 2012).

Coe, K. and Domke, D. (2006) 'Petitioners or prophets? Presidential discourse, God and the ascendancy of religious conservatives', *Journal of Communication* 56: 309–30.

Commisão Brasileira de Justiça e Paz (CBJP) (n.d.) 'Charter of Principles' Available at www.cbjp.org.br/index.php/sobre/carta-de-principios (accessed 24 March 2009).

Conway, J. (2004) 'Citizenship in a time of Empire: the World Social Forum as new public space', *Citizenship Studies* 8(4): 367–81.

Coordenadora de Centrais Sindicais do Cone Sul (CCSCS) (2009) 'Preparing for the 15th United Nations Climate Change Conference Copenhagen: Proposals of the CCSCS to Combat Climate Change'. Translated by Kevin Wood. Available at www.ccscs.org/documentos-ccscs/publicaciones-y-documentos/8/229-camino-a-la-15o-conferencia-de-las-partes-en-copenhague-propuestas-de-la-ccscs-para-enfrentar-al-cambio-climatico (accessed 19 October 2009).

Corpwatch (2002) *Girona Declaration*. Available at www.corpwatch.org/article.php?id=2610&printsafe=1 (accessed 12 August 2009).

Corpwatch (2009) 'Mission and history'. Available at www.corpwatch.org/article.php?id=11314 (accessed 13 May 2009).

COSATU (2009) 'Response to the G20 2 April 2009 London declaration'. Available at www.ituc-csi.org/spip.php?article3170&var_recherche=COSATU (accessed 15 July 2009).

Council of Canadians (2003) 'Vision Statement'. Available at http://www.canadians.org/about/BOD/vision.html (accessed 7 May 2009).

Council of Canadians (2010) 'Real solutions to the climate crisis'. Available at www.canadians.org/energy/documents/climatejustice/real-solutions.pdf (accessed June 2011).

Crotty, J. (2009) 'Structural causes of the global financial crisis: a critical assessment of the "new financial architecture"', *Cambridge Journal of Economics* 33(6): 563–80.

CSIRO (2010) 'Global CO_2 emissions may set a record this year'. Available at www.hannover.csiro.au/news/Global-CO2-emissions-may-set-a-record-this-year.html (accessed June 2011).

Cumbers, P. and Cumbers, A. (2009) *Global Justice Networks: Geographies of Transnational Solidarity?* London: Routledge.

Davis, M. (2005) *Planet of the Slums*. London: Verso.

Della Porta, D. (ed.) (2007) *The Global Justice Movement: Cross-National and Transnational Perspectives*. Boulder, CO: Paradigm.

Della Porta, D., Andretta, M., Mosca, L. and Reiter, H. (2006) *Globalization from Below: Transnational Activists and Protest Networks*. Minneapolis, MN: University of Minnesota Press.

Dembele, D. M. (2009) 'The global financial crisis: lessons and responses from Africa', *Amandla*, 19 March 2009. Available at www.amandlapublishers.co.za/special-features/global-financial-crisis/48-the-global-financial-crisis-lessons-and-responses-from-africa- (accessed 28 August 2009).

Demeke, M.G. Pangrazio and Maetz, M. (2009) *Country Responses to the Food Security Crisis: Nature and Preliminary Implications of the Policies Pursued*. FAO: New York. Available at www.fao.org/fileadmin/user_upload/ISFP/pdf_for_site_Country_Response_to_the_Food_Security.pdf (accessed 21 December 2011).

de Negris, M. (2005) *Defining and Quantifying the Extent of Import Surges: Data and Methodologies, FAO Import Surge Project*. Working Paper No. 2, May.

Depledge, J. (2006) 'The opposite of learning: ossification in the climate change regime', *Global Environmental Politics* 6(1).

Desmarais, A. (2007) *La Vía Campesina: Globalization and the Power of Peasants*. London: Pluto.

Desmarais, A., Wiebe, N. and Wittman, H. (eds) (2011) *Food Sovereignty: Reconnecting Food, Nature and Community*. Halifax: Fernwood.

Dijk, T.A. van (1998) *Ideology: a Multidisciplinary Approach*. London: Sage.

Dunphy, D., Griffiths, A. and Benn, S. (2007) *Organizational Change for Corporate Sustainability*, 2nd edn. London: Routledge.

Eckersley, R. (2009) 'Understanding the interplay between the climate and trade regimes', in Weischer, L. Simmons, B., van Asselt, H. and Zelli, F. (eds), *Climate and Trade Policies in a Post-2012 World*. New York: UNEP, pp. 11–19.

EcoEquity (2008) *The Right to Development in a Climate Constrained World: the Greenhouse Development Rights Framework*. San Francisco, CA: EcoEquity.

ENDA (n.d.) 'L'économie populaire urbaine, levier d'un autre développement [The popular urban economy, lever for another development]', Available at www.enda.sn/ecopole/ecop6.html (accessed 23 March 2010).

Erskine, T. (2002) '"Citizen of nowhere" or "the point where circles intersect"? Impartialist and embedded cosmopolitanisms', *Review of International Studies* 28(3): 457–78.

ETC (2008) *Who Owns Nature?* Ottawa: Action Group on Erosion, Technology and Concentration.

European Trade Union Confederation (ETUC) (2010) 'Position on the financing and management of climate policies'. Available at www.etuc.org/a/7395 (accessed June 2011).

Falk, R. (1999) *Predatory Globalization: A Critique*. Cambridge: Polity Press.

FIAN (2009) 'Introduction – About Us'. Available at www.fian.org/about-us/introduction (accessed 16 January 2009).

Focus on the Global South (n.d.) 'Who we are'. http://focusweb.org/who-we-are.html?Itemid=120 (accessed 4 February 2009).

Focus on the Global South (2007) 'What's missing from the climate talks? Justice!' Available at http://focusweb.org/index2.php?option=com_content&task=view&id=1317&pop=1& (accessed 13 August 2009).

Focus on the Global South (2008) 'The global economic crisis: an historic opportunity for transformation', 15 October 2008. Available at http://focusweb.org/index2.php?option=com_content&task=view&id=1447&pop=1& (accessed 13 August 2009).

FAO (2010) *The State of Food Insecurity in the World: Addressing Food Insecurity in Protracted Crises*. Rome: FAO. Available at www.fao.org/docrep/013/i1683e/i1683e.pdf (accessed 21 December 2011).

FAO (2011a) *Food Price Index*. Available at: www.fao.org/worldfood situation/wfs-home/foodpriceindex/en/(accessed 11 June 2010).

FAO et al. (2011b) 'Price volatility in food and agricultural markets: policy responses', Available at www.oecd.org/document/20/0,3746,en_2649_37401_48152724_1_1_1_37401,00.html (accessed June 2011).

Forum for Food Sovereignty (2007) 'The Nyeleni Declaration', February 2007, Mali. Available at www.foodsovereignty.org/ (accessed 15 January 2012).

Freeden, M. (1996) *Ideologies and Political Theory: A Conceptual Approach*. Oxford: Clarendon Press.

Freeden, M. (2003) *Ideology: A Very Short Introduction*. Oxford: Oxford University Press.

Friedman, T.L. (2000) *The Lexus and the Olive Tree*. London: Harper Collins.

Friedman, T.L. (2005) *The World is Flat: A Brief History of the Twenty-first Century*. New York: Farrar, Strauss and Giroux.

Fukuyama, F. (1989) 'The end of history?' *The National Interest*. Summer 1989: 3–18.

Fukuyama, F. (1992) *The End of History and the Last Man*. New York: Free Press.

Funke, P.N. (2008) 'The world social forum: social forums as resistance relays', *New Political Science* 30 (4): 449–74.

Furet, F. (2000) *The Passing of an Illusion: The Idea of Communism in the Twentieth Century*. Chicago, IL: University of Chicago Press.

G8 (2009) 'Responsible leadership for a sustainable future', G8 Declaration, July 2009, Rome. Available at www.g8italia2009.it/static/G8_Allegato/G8_Declaration_08_07_09_final,0.pdf (accessed March 2012).

General Union of Oil Employees in Basra (2010) Organizational website www.basraoilunion.org (accessed 9 March 2010).

George, S. (1976) *How the Other Half Dies: The Real Reasons for World Hunger*. New York: Penguin.

George, S. (2001) 'A short history of neoliberalism: twenty years of elite economics and emerging opportunities for structural change', in Houtart, F. and Polet, F. (eds) *The Other Davos: The Globalization of Resistance to the World Economic System*. London and New York: Zed Books, pp. 7–16.

George, S. (2004) *Another World is Possible, If …* New York: Verso.

George, S., Barry, K. G., Vander Stichele, M. and Wachtel, H. M. (2008) 'Statement on the G-20 Summit on the Financial Crisis', The Transnational Institute Working Group on the Global Financial and Economic Crisis. 15 November 2008. Available at www.tni.org/detail_page.phtml?act_id=18942&username=guest@tni.org&password=9999&publish=Y (accessed 1 July 2009).

Giddens, A. (2000) *The Third Way and its Critics*. Cambridge: Polity Press.

Gilbertson, T. and Reyes, O. (2009) 'Carbon trading: how it works and why it fails', *Critical Currents* number 7. Uppsala: Dag Hammarskjöld Foundation. Available at www.tni.org/carbon-trade-fails

Gill, S. (2002) *Power and Resistance in the New World Order*. London: Palgrave Macmillan.

Gladstone, R. (2011) 'German official backs tax vetoed by Britain', *New York Times*. 12 December, 2011, available at www.nytimes.com/2011/12/13/world/europe/guido-westerwelle-german-official-backs-tax-vetoed-by-britain.html (accessed March 2012).

Global Progressive Forum (2009a) 'Climate change'. Available at www.globalprogressiveforum.org/article/climate-change (accessed 13 May 2009).

Global Progressive Forum (2009b) 'Introduction of Fair Trade'. Available at www.globalprogressiveforum.org/introduction-fair-trade (accessed 13 May 2009).

Goldman, M. (ed.) (1998) *Privatizing Nature: Political Struggles for the Global Commons*. London: Pluto Press.

Goodman, J. (ed.) (2002) *Protest and Globalisation: Prospects for Transnational Solidarity*. Sydney: Pluto Press, and Vancouver: Fernwood Press.

Goodman, J. (ed.) (2006) *Regionalization, Marketization and Political Change in the Pacific Rim*. Mexico: University of Guadalajara Press.

Goodman, J. (2010a) Interview with Dr Rogate R. Mshana, Director of Justice, Diakonia and Responsibility for Creation, World Council of Churches, 29 November 2010.

Goodman, J. (2010b) Interview with Genevieve Paul, Programme Officer, Globalization and Human Rights, FIDH, 1 December 2010.

Goodman, J. (2010c) Interview with Fiona Dove, Executive Director, Transnational Institute, The Netherlands, 3 December 2010.

Goodman, J. and Ranald, P. (eds) (2000) *Stopping a Juggernaut: Public Interests versus the Multilateral Agreement on Investment*. Public Interest Advocacy Centre, Sydney: Pluto Press.

Goodman, J. and Roberts, E. (2010) 'Is the United Nations' REDDs scheme conservation colonialism by default?', *International Journal of Water*, 5 (4): 419–29.

Government of Brazil (2010) Constitution of the Federative Republic of Brazil, Biblioteca Digital da Camara dos Deputados. Available at http://bd.camara.gov.br/bd/ (accessed 15 January 2012).

Gramsci, A. (1971) *Selections from the Prison Notebooks of Antonio Gramsci*. London: Lawrence and Wishart.

Grassroots Global Justice (2009) 'Stimulating environmental justice'. Statement on sustainable economic development, 16 March 2009. Available at www.ggjalliance.org/system/files/EJ%20Stimulus%20Final%203–16–09.pdf (accessed 27 May 2009).

Grassroots Global Justice (n.d.) 'Mission Statement'. Available at www.ggjalliance.org/print/7 27/ (accessed 27 May 2009).

Greenwald, B.C. and Kahn, J. (2009) *Globalization: The Irrational Fear that Someone in China will Take your Job*. Hoboken, NJ: John Wiley & Sons.

Guehenno, J-M. (1995) *The End of the Nation-State*. Minneapolis, MN: University of Minnesota Press.

Guerrero, M. (2008) 'Who pays, who benefits? GGJ Op-Ed Piece on G-20 Summit'. Available at www.ggjalliance.org/print/33 (accessed 27 May 2009).

Gutierrez, G. (1988) *A Theology of Liberation: History, Politics and Salvation*. New York: Orbis Books.

Hardt, M. (2002) 'Today's Bandung?', *New Left Review* 14, March-April: 112–18.

Harvard Business Review (2010) 'A map to healthy – and ailing – markets', *Harvard Business Review* 88 (1/2) : 30–1.

Harvey, D. (2005) *A Brief History of Neoliberalism*. Oxford: Oxford University Press.

Harvey, D. (2010) *The Enigma of Capital And the Crises of Capitalism*. Oxford: Oxford University Press.

Haselip, J. (2005) 'Renegotiating contracts after an economic crisis and currency devaluation: the case of Argentina', *Electricity Journal* 18(3): 78–88.

Haselip, J., Dyner, I. and Cherni, J. (2005) 'Electricity market reform in Argentina: assessing the impact for the poor in Buenos Aires', *Utilities Policy* 13(1): 1–14.

Hawkes, S. and Plahe, J (2010) *The WTO's Agreement on Agriculture and the Right to Food in Developing Countries*. Monash University Department of Management Working Papers Series, Working Paper 4/10.

Held, D. (1995) *Democracy and the Global Order: From the Modern State to Cosmopolitan Governance*. Cambridge: Polity Press.

Ibase (2009) '13 steps to guarantee the human right to adequate and healthy food'. Translated by Kevin Wood. Available at www.ibase.br/userimages/Relatorio_2.pdf (accessed 10 November 2009).

Instituto Paulo Freire (IPF) (2009) 'About us, what we do'. Translated by Kevin Wood. Available in Portguese at www.paulofreire.org/Capa/WebHome (accessed 6 May 2009).

International Climate Justice Network (2002) 'Bali Principles of Climate Justice'. Available at www.corpwatch.org/article.php?id=3748 (accessed April 2012).

International Forum on Globalization (2009) 'About IFG – Position Statement'. Available at www.ifg.org/about.htm (accessed 26 May 2009).

International Fund for Agricultural Development (2011) *Rural Poverty Report 2011*. Available at www.ifad.org/rpr2011/ (accessed March 2012).

International Trade Union Confederation (ITUC) (2008) 'May Day Declaration'. Available at www.ituc-csi.org/spip.php?article3514 (accessed 30 April 2009).

International Trade Union Confederation (ITUC) (2011) 'UN Environment Talks: Financial transactions tax needed to fund climate action'. Available at www.ituc-csi.org/un-environment-talks-financial.html (accessed June 2011).

Intergovernmental Panel on Climate Change (eds) (2007a) *Climate Change 2007: Impacts, Adaptation and Vulnerability. Contribution of Working Group II to the Fourth Assessment Report of the Intergovernmental Panel on Climate Change.* Cambridge: Cambridge University Press.

Intergovernmental Panel on Climate Change (eds) (2007b) *Climate Change 2007: Mitigation. Contribution of Working Group III to the Fourth Assessment Report of the Intergovernmental Panel on Climate Change.* Cambridge: Cambridge University Press.

Irwin, S.H. and Sanders, D.R. (2010) *The Impact of Index and Swap Funds on Commodity Futures Markets: Preliminary Results.* OECD Food, Agriculture and Fisheries Working Papers, No. 27.

James, P. W. (2006) *Globalism, Nationalism, Tribalism: Bringing Theory Back In.* London: Sage.

Johnston, J. and Goodman, J. (2006) 'Hope and activism in the ivory tower: Freirean lessons for globalization research', *Globalizations* 3 (1): 9–30.

Jones, S. (2011) 'Hedge funds reap post-crisis gains', *Financial Times*, 22 April 2011. Available at www.ft.com/cms/s/0/4fa038aa-6d06–11e0–83fe-00144feab49a.html#axzz1pSyNZhoQ (accessed June 2011).

Jordan, A. (1994) 'Financing the UNCED agenda: The controversy over additionality', *Environment*, 36 (3): 16–30.

Jubilee South (2008) 'JS [Jubilee South] urges governments to guarantee alternative financing for the development of people, not profits'. Available at www.jubileesouth.org/index.php?option=com_content&task=view&id=244 (accessed 18 August 2009).

Jubilee South (2009) 'Banking on change: towards an economic system that works for people and the planet'. Available at www.jubileesouth.org/index.php?option=com_content&task=view&id=239&Itemid=100 (accessed 27 May 2009).

Karam, A. (ed.) (2004) *Transnational Political Islam: Religion, Ideology and Power.* London: Pluto Press.

Kepel, G. (2004) *The War for Muslim Minds: Islam and the West.* Cambridge, MA: Harvard University Press.

Keraghel, C. and Sen, J. (2004) 'Explorations in open space: The World Social Forum and cultures of politics', *International Social Science Journal* 56 (182): 483–93.

Khor, M. (2009) *Analysis of the New WTO Agriculture and NAMA texts of 6 December 2008.* Penang: Third World Network.

Kinealy, C. (1995) *This Great Calamity: The Irish Famine 1845–52.* Dublin: Gill & Macmillan.

Klein, N. (2000) *No Logo.* New York: Picador.

Klein, N. (2007) *The Shock Doctrine: The Rise of Disaster Capitalism.* New York: Picador.

Kokaz, N. (2007) 'Poverty and global justice', *Ethics and International Affairs* 21(3): 317–36.

Korean Confederation of Trade Unions (KCTU) (2009) 'About KCTU'. Available at http://kctu.org/kctu (accessed 9 March 2010).

Kufour, E. (1992) 'South refuses to compromise sovereignty', Statement of the Group of 77, *Earth Island Journal,* Summer 1996, 7 (3): 8.

Kyoto Protocol (1997) Available at http://unfccc.int/kyoto_protocol/items/2830.php (accessed June 2011).

La Via Campesina (1996) 'Food sovereignty: a future without hunger', Conference Statement, November 1996, Rome. Available at www.foodsovereignty.org/ (accessed 15 January 2012).

La Via Campesina (2007) 'The International Peasants' Voice'. Available at www.viacampesina.org/main_en (accessed 28 April 2009).

La Via Campesina (2009a) 'A G8 on agriculture without farmers = more hunger and poverty'. Press release 21 April. Available at www.viacampesina.org/main_en (accessed 9 August 2009).

La Via Campesina (2009b) 'Via Campesina Statement at the UN General Assembly on the Global Food Crisis and the Right to Food'. Available at www.viacampesina.org/en/index.php?Itemid=40&catid=19:human-rights&id=698:via-campesina-statement-at-the-un-general-assembly-on-the-global-food-crisis-and-the-right-to-food&option=com_content&view=article (accessed 9 August 2009).

Leigh, D. and Harding, L. (2011) *Wikileaks: Inside Julian Assange's War on Secrecy.* London: Guardian Books.

Lohmann, L. (2006) 'Carbon trading: a critical conversation on climate change, privatization and power', *Development Dialogue,* 48, September.

Magdoff, F. (2008) 'The world food crisis: sources and solutions', *Monthly Review,* May: 1–15.

Mandaville, P. (2007) *Global Political Islam.* London and New York: Routledge.

Mannheim, K. (1936) *Ideology and Utopia: An Introduction to the Sociology of Knowledge.* London: Kegan Paul, Trench, Trubner.

McDonald, K. (2006) *Global Movements: Action and Culture.* Oxford: Blackwell.

McGregor, I. M. (2011) 'Disenfranchisement of countries and civil society at COP-15 in Copenhagen'. *Global Environmental Politics* 11(1): 1–7.

McGuire, P. and Tarashev, N. (2006) 'Tracking International Bank Flows', *BIS Quarterly Review,* 11 December.

McMichael, P. (2003) *Globalisation.* Cambridge: Cambridge University Press.

McMichael, P. (2004) *Development and Social Change: A Global Perspective.* Thousand Oaks, CA: Sage.

McNally, D. (2011) *Global Slump: The Economics and Politics of Crisis and Resistance.* Oakland, CA: PM Press.

Menezes, F. (2001) 'Food sovereignty: a vital requirement for food security in the context of globalization', *Development* 44 (4): 29–33.

Mills, C. W. (1959) *The Sociological Imagination.* New York: Oxford University Press.

Mittelman, J.H. (2004) *Whither Globalization? The Vortex of Knowledge and Ideology.* London and New York: Routledge.

Moghadam, V. M. (2008) *Globalization and Social Movements: Islamism, Feminism and the Global Justice Movement.* Lanham, Maryland: Rowman and Littlefield.

Moody's Analytics (2012) Homepage. Available at www.moodysanalytics.com (accessed July 2012).

Moody's Corporation (2012) 'About Us'. Avaialable at www.moodys.com/Pages/atc.aspx (accessed July 2012).

Movimento dos Trabalhadores Rurais Sem-Terra (MST) (n.d. a) 'What is the MST'. Available at www.mstbrazil.org/ (accessed 15 January 2012).

Movimento dos Trabalhadores Rurais Sem-Terra (MST) (n.d. b) 'About MST'. Translated by Kevin Wood. Available at www.mst.org.br/ (accessed 11 November 2009).

Movimento dos Trabalhadores Rurais Sem-Terra (MST) (2009) 'National journey of fighting for the land reform'. Available at www.mst.org.br/especials/26 (accessed September 2009).

Nagel, T. (2005) 'The problem of global justice', *Philosophy and Public Affairs* 33 (2): 113–47.

Normand, R. (2003) 'The Declaration of the Poor People's Economic Human Rights Campaign on the Full Realization of Human Rights in the United States'. Available at http://globalization.icaap.org/content/v3.1/10_declaration.html (accessed 18 August 2009).

Nussbaum, M. (1996) 'Patriotism and Cosmopolitanism', in Cohen, Joshua (ed.) *For Love of Country*. Boston, MA: Beacon Press.

Obasi, G.O.P. and Topfer, K. (2000) *Special Report on Emissions Scenarios*. Intergovernmental Panel on Climate Change. Available at www.grida.no/publications/other/ipcc%5Fsr/?src=/climate/ipcc/emission/500.htm (accessed May 2012).

OECD (2009) *OECD-FAO Agricultural Outlook: 2009–2018*. Available at www.agri-outlook.org/dataoecd/2/31/43040036.pdf (accessed June 2011).

OECD (2010) *OECD-FAO Agricultural Outlook 2010–2019*. Available at www.agri-outlook.org/dataoecd/13/13/45438527.pdf (accessed June 2011).

Ohmae, K. (1995) *The End of the Nation-State: The Rise of Regional Economies*. New York: Free Press.

Okereke, C. (2008) *Global Justice and Neoliberal Environmental Governance*. Abingdon, UK: Routledge.

Oxfam International (2002) *Rigged Rules and Double Standards: Trade, Globalisation and the Fight against Poverty*. Report on Global Trade. Available at www.maketradefair.com/en/index.php?file=03042002121618.htm&cat=3&subcat=2&select=1 (accessed 8 June 2011).

Oxfam International (2009) *Suffering the Science: Climate Change, People and Poverty*. www.oxfam.org/en/policy/bp130-suffering-the-science (accessed July 2009).

Palan, R. (2003) *The Offshore World: Virtual Spaces and the Commericalisation of Sovereignty*. New York: Cornell University Press.

Palestinian Grassroots Anti-Apartheid Wall Campaign (PGAAWC) (2008) 'Global Solidarity Commemorates Palestinian Land Day', *Worldwide Activism*. Available at http://stopthewall.org/worldwideactivism/1634.shtml (accessed 27 August 2009).

Patomäki, H. (2009) 'The global financial crisis: causes and consequences', *Local Global* 6(1): 4–27.

Patomäki, H. and Teivainen, T. (2004a) *A Possible World: Democratic Transformation of Global Institutions*. London and New York: Zed Books.

Patomäki, H. and Teivainen, T. (2004b) 'The World Social Forum: an open space or movement of movements?' *Theory, Culture and Society* 21 (6): 145–54.

People's Health Movement (2004) *Mumbai Declaration*. Available at www.phmovement.org/es/es/resources/charters/mumbai (accessed 13 May 2009).

Pearse, R. (2010) 'Making a market? Contestation and climate change', *Journal of Australian Political Economy*, 66: 166–98.

Pieterse, J. N. (1998) 'My paradigm or yours? Alternative development, post-development, reflexive development', *Development and Change* 29 (2): 343–73.

Pieterse, J. N. (2004) *Globalization or Empire?* London: Routledge.

Pleyers, G. (2010) *Alter-Globalization: Becoming Actors in a Global Age*. Cambridge: Polity Press.

Polanyi, K. (1944) *The Great Transformation: The Political and Economic Origins of Our Time*. Boston, MA: Beacon Press.

Poor People's Economic Human Rights Campaign (PPEHRC) (2003) 'The Declaration of the Poor People's Economic Human Rights Campaign on the Full Realization of

Human Rights in the United States'. Available at http://globalization.icaap.org/content/v3.1/10_declaration.html (accessed 18 August 2009).

Public Citizen (2011) 'Table of foreign investor-state cases and claims under NAFTA, CAFTA and Peru FTA', October 2011, Washington D.C. Available at www.citizen.org/documents/Ch11cases_chart.pdf (accessed March 2012).

Quarmby, K. (2005) 'Why Oxfam is failing Africa', *New Statesman,* 30 May. Available at www.newstatesman.com/200505300004 (accessed January 2012).

Reitan, R. (2007) *Global Activism.* New York: Routledge.

Reitan, R. and Gibson, S. (2012) 'Climate change or social change? Environmental and leftist praxis and participatory action research', Paper to the International Studies Association Annual Convention 2012, forthcoming in *Globalizations* 2012.

Responding to Crisis (2011) Workshop hosted by RMIT and UTS in Melbourne, Australia, 1 July 2011. Invited participants from academia, business, government and non-government sectors to discuss preliminary findings of 'Mapping Justice Globalism' Research project. Transcripts available on request.

Ricoeur, P. (1986) *Lectures on Ideology and Utopia.* New York: Columbia University Press.

Riedy, C. and McGregor, I. (2011) 'Climate governance is failing us: We all need to respond', *PORTAL Journal of Multidisciplinary International Studies* 8 (3): 1–9.

Roberts, J. and Parks, B. (2006) *A Climate of Injustice: Global Inequality, North-South Politics, and Climate Policy.* Cambridge, MA: MIT Press.

Robertson, R. (1992) *Globalization: Social Theory and Global Culture.* Thousand Oaks, CA: Sage.

Rodrik, D. (2011) *The Globalization Paradox: Democracy and the Future of the World Economy.* New York: W.W. Norton and Company.

Roisin, C., Stock, P. and Campbell, H. (eds) (2011) *Food Systems Failure: The Global Food Crisis and the Future of Agriculture.* Abingdon, UK: Earthscan/Routledge.

Rosset, P. (2008) 'Food sovereignty and the contemporary food crisis', *Development* 51 (4): 460–3.

Rupert, M. (2000) *Ideologies of Globalization: Contending Visions of a New Order.* London: Routledge.

Sachs, J. (2005) *The End of Poverty.* New York: Penguin.

Sargent, L. (2009) *Contemporary Political Ideologies: A Comparative Analysis*, 14th edn. Belmont: Wadsworth.

Sassen, S. (2001) *The Global City: New York, London, Tokyo.* Princeton, NJ: Princeton University Press.

Sassen. S. (2006) *Territory Authority Rights: From Medieval to Global Assemblages.* Princeton, NJ: Princeton University Press.

Sayer, D. (1989) *The Violence of Abstraction.* Oxford: Blackwell.

Scerri, A. (2011a) Interview with Myrna Maglahus, Community Outreach officer for Africa, IBON/Reality of Aid, Jubilee South Affiliate, 8 February 2011.

Scerri, A. (2011b) Interview with Yvonne Takang, Permanent Secretary, Citizens Association for the Defense of Collective Interests, Africa Trade Network Affiliate, 7 February 2011.

Schutter, O. (2010) *Food Commodities Speculation and Food Price Crises: Regulation to Reduce the Risks of Price Volatility.* UN Rapporteur on the Right to Food Briefing Note 2, September.

Schwab, K. (2008) 'Global corporate citizenship: working with governments and civil society', *Foreign Affairs*, 87 (1): 107–18.

Schwartzmantel, J. (2008) *Ideology and Politics.* London: Sage.

Schweiker, W. (2004) 'A Preface to ethics: global dynamics and the integrity of life', *Journal of Religious Ethics* 32 (1): 13–37.

Sen, J.A. Anand, Escobar, A. and Waterman, P. (2005) *World Social Forum: Challenging Empires*. New Delhi: Viveka Foundation.

Sifry, M. L. (2011) *Wikileaks and the Age of Transparency*. India and USA: OR Books.

Smith, J., Karides, M., Becker, M., Brunelle, D., Chase-Dunn, C., della Porta, D., Icaza Garza, R., Juris, J. S., Mosca, L., Reese, E., Smith, P. (J.) and Vazquez, R. (2007) *Global Democracy and the World Social Forums*. Boulder, Colorado: Paradigm Publishers.

Soros, G. (2008) 'The crisis and what to do about it'. *New York Review of Books* 6 November. Available at www.nybooks.com/articles/archives/2008/dec/04/the-crisis-what-to-do-about-it/?page=1 (accessed 18 May 2011).

Steger, M.B. (2002) *Globalism: The New Market Ideology*. Lanham, MD: Rowman & Littlefield.

Steger, M.B. (2005) 'Ideologies of globalization', *Journal of Political Ideologies* 10 (1): 11–30.

Steger, M.B. (2008) *The Rise of the Global Imaginary: Political Ideologies from the French Revolution to the War on Terror*. Oxford: Oxford University Press.

Steger, M.B. (2009) *Globalisms: The Great Ideological Struggle of the Twenty-First Century*, 3rd edn. Lanham, MD: Rowman & Littlefield.

Steger, M. (2010a) Interview with Cindy Wiesner, Political Coordinator, Grassroots Global Justice, Miami, Florida, 16 February 2010.

Steger, M. (2010b) Interview with Candido Grabowsky, Director, Ibase, Brazil, 19 February 2010.

Steger, M. (2010c) Interview with Alessandro Bento, director, CUT, Rio de Janeiro, Brazil, 24 February 2010.

Steger, M. (2011a) Interview with Paolo Beni, National President, ARCI, Rome, Italy, 11 April 2011.

Steger, M. (2011b) Interview with Rafaele Salineri, Director, Terre des Hommes, Rome, Italy, 12 April, 2010.

Stern, N. (2006) *The Economics of Climate Change: The Stern Review*. Cambridge: Cambridge University Press.

Stewart, H. (2011) 'Robin Hood tax: 1000 economists urge G20 to accept Tobin Tax', *The Guardian*, 13 April 2011. Available at www.guardian.co.uk/business/2011/apr/13/robin-hood-tax-economists-letter (accessed 2 June 2011). The full list of economists is available at www.guardian.co.uk/business/interactive/2011/apr/13/robin-hood-tax-economists?intcmp=239.

Stiglitz, J.E. (2003) *Globalization and its Discontents*, rev. edn. New York: W.W. Norton.

Stiglitz, J.E. (2010) 'Why we have to change capitalism', *The Telegraph*, 23 January. Available at www.telegraph.co.uk/finance/newsbysector/banksandfinance/7061058/Joseph-Stiglitz-Why-we-have-to-change-capitalism (accessed June 2011).

Strange, S. (1997) *Casino Capitalism*. Manchester: Manchester University Press.

Tan, C. (2007) 'The finance and trade nexus: systemic challenges'. Statement on behalf of Third World Network, Informal Hearings of Civil Society on 'Civil society perspectives on the status of implementation of the Monterrey Consensus and the tasks ahead'. High-Level Dialogue on Financing for Development, United Nations, New York, 22 October 2007. Available at www.twnside.org.sg/title2/finance/docs/CTAN-Presentation.doc (accessed 11 May 2011).

Tarrow, S. (2005) *The New Transnational Activism*. Cambridge: Cambridge University Press.

Taylor, C. (2004) *Modern Social Imaginaries*. Durham and London: Duke University Press.

Thematic Social Forum (2012) *Another Future is Possible*. Port Allegre: TSF. Available at http://rio20.net/en/iniciativas/another-future-is-possible (accessed August 2012).

Third World Network (TWN) (2007) 'TWN Statement on Building Blocks Towards Global Action on Climate Change'. Available at www.twnside.org.sg/announcement/Vienna.Climate.talks.29aug07.doc (accessed April 2009).

Thompson, J.B. (1990) *Ideology and Modern Culture: Critical Social Theory and the Era of Mass Communication*. Stanford, CA: Stanford University Press.

Toronto Statement (1988) 'The changing atmosphere: implications for global security, Toronto. Available at www.cmos.ca/ChangingAtmosphere1988e.pdf (accessed March 2012).

Transnational Institute (2010) 'Final Declaration – Asia Europe People's Forum'. Available at http://www.tni.org/print/63062 (accessed 30 May 2011).

Transnational Institute (n.d.) 'History'. Available at www.tni.org/page/history (accessed 30 November 2009).

Tregillis, S. (2011) 'Dark pools, HFT and competition'. Speech to the Stockbrokers Association of Australian Conference, Australian Securities and Investments Commission, Sydney. Available at www.asic.gov.au/asic/asic.nsf/byheadline/Dark+pools,+HFT+and+competition?openDocument (accessed March 2012).

United Nations (2009) *World Economic Prospects and Situation 2009*. Available at www.un.org/en/development/desa/policy/wesp/wesp_archive/2009wesp.pdf (accessed June 2011).

United Nations (2011) *World Economic Prospects and Situation 2011*. Available at www.un.org/en/development/desa/policy/wesp/wesp_current/2011wesp.pdf (accessed November 2011).

UNCTAD (2005) *World Investment Report: TNCs and the Internationalization of R&D*. New York: UN.

UNCTAD (2006) *Latest Developments in Investor–State Dispute Settlement*. International Investment Agreements Monitor No. 4. New York: UN.

UNCTAD (2011) *World Investment Report: Non-Equity Modes of International Production and Development*. Geneva: UNCTAD.

United Nations Department of Economic and Social Affairs, Population Division (2009) 'World Population Prospects: The 2008 Review'. Population Newsletter June, number 87. Available at www.un.org/esa/population/publications/popnews/Newsltr_87.pdf (accessed 7 June 2011).

United Nations Development Program (2008) *Fighting Climate Change: Human Solidarity in a Divided World*. Available at http://hdr.undp.org/en/reports/global/hdr2007-8/ (accessed March 2012).

United Nations Environment Program (2010) *The Emissions Gap Report*. New York: UNEP.

United Nations Framework Convention on Climate Change (UNFCCC) (1992) Available at http://unfccc.int/resource/docs/convkp/conveng.pdf (accessed April 2012).

United Nations Framework Convention on Climate Change (UNFCCC) (2011a) *Compilation and Synthesis of Fifth National Communications*, 23 May. New York: UN.

United Nations Framework Convention on Climate Change (UNFCCC) (2011b) 'The Durban Platform for Enhanced Action', November 2011, Bonn. Available at http://unfccc.int/files/meetings/durban_nov_2011/decisions/application/pdf/cop17_durban-platform.pdf (accessed March 2012).

United States Financial Crisis Inquiry Committee (2011) *The Financial Crisis Inquiry Report: The Final Report of the National Commission on the Causes of the Financial and Economic Crisis in the United States*. New York: Cosimo.

Vittachi, A. (OneWorld UK Director) (2007) 'A call for climate justice'. Available at http://us.oneworld.net/node/147571 (accessed 28 August 2009).

Waterman, P. (2009) 'The global justice and solidarity movement and the world social forum: a backgrounder', in Sen, J. and Waterman, P. (eds) *World Social Forum: Challenging Empires*. Montreal: Black Rose Books.

Waxman, C.I. (ed.) (1968) *The End of Ideology Debate*. New York: Funk and Wagnalls.

Williams, M. (1997) 'The Group of 77 and global environmental politics', *Global Environmental Change* 7 (3): 295–8.

Wilson, E. (2009a) Interview with Claire Courteille, Director, Equality Section, International Trade Union Confederation, Brussels, Belgium, 30 September 2009.

Wilson, E. (2009b) Interview with Juan Moreno, Adviser, European Trade Union Confederation, Brussels, 30 September 2009.

Wilson, E. (2009c) Interview with David Capezzuto, Political Advisor, Global Progressive Forum, Brussels, Belgium, 30 September 2009.

Wilson, E. (2009d) Interview with Wilma Strothenke, Communication and Information Officer, and Anna Maria Suarez Franco, Coordinator of the Justiciability Programme, Food First International Action Network, Heidelberg, Germany, 12 October 2009.

Wilson, E. (2009e) Interview with Joy Chavez, Programme Coordinator – Citizens of the Philippines, and Mary Ann Manahan, Research-Campaigner, Focus on the Global South, Manila, Philippines, 11 December 2009.

Wilson, E. (2009f) Interview with Anuradha Vittachi, co-founder, OneWorld. Copenhagen, 16 December 2009.

Wilson, E. (2009g) Interview with Bob Baugh, Executive Director, AFL-CIO, Copenhagen, Denmark, 16 December 2009.

Wilson, E. (2009h) Interview with Joy Kennedy, Delegate to COP15, World Council of Churches, Copenhagen, 17 December 2009.

Wilson, E. (2009i) Interview with Tamra Gilbertson, Research Fellow, Transnational Institute, Copenhagen, Denmark, 18 December 2009.

Wilson, E. (2011) Interview with Lucien Royer, Director of the International Department, Canadian Labour Congress, Ottawa, Canada, 14 March 2011.

Wittman, H., Desmarais, A. and Wiebe, N. (2011) 'The origins and potential of food sovereignty', in Desmarais, A., Wiebe, N. and Wittman, H. (eds) *Food Sovereignty: Reconnecting Food, Nature and Community*. Oxford: Fahamu Books, pp 1–13.

Wolf, M. (2004) *Why Globalization Works*. New Haven: Yale University Press.

Wolf, M. (2009) 'Seeds of its own destruction', *Financial Times*, 8 March 2009. Available at www.ft.com/intl/cms/s/0/c6c5bd36–0c0c-11de-b87d-0000779fd2ac.html#axzz1uP9chBvW (accessed June 2011).

Woodham-Smith, C. B. (1991) *The Great Hunger: Ireland 1845–1849*. London: Penguin.

World Bank (2000a) 'Energy services for the world's poor'. Energy Sector Management Assistance Programme (ESMAP) Energy and Development Report, Washington. Available at www.worldbank.org/html/fpd/esmap/energy_report2000/front.pdf (accessed March 2012).

World Bank (2000b) 'Poor people in a rich country: a poverty report for Argentina'. Poverty Reduction and Economic Management, Latin America and Caribbean Region, Washington. Available at http://web.worldbank.org/WBSITE/EXTERNAL/TOPICS/EXTPOVERTY/EXTPA/0,,contentMDK:20206704~menuPK:443285~pagePK:148956~piPK:216618~theSitePK:430367,00.html (accessed March 2012).

World Bank (2011) *Responding to Global Food Price Volatility and its Impact on Food Security*. Report Prepared for the WB Development Committee. Available at http://siteresources.worldbank.org/DEVCOMMINT/Documentation/22887406/DC2011–0002(E)FoodSecurity.pdf (accessed June 2011).

World Council of Churches (2001) 'Lead us not into temptation: Churches' response to the policies of International Financial Institutions'. Geneva: WCC. Available at www.oikoumene.org/en/resources/documents/wcc-programmes/public-witness-addressing-power-affirming-peace/poverty-wealth-and-ecology/neoliberal-paradigm/lead-us-not-into-temptation-churches-response-to-the-policies-of-international-financial-institutions.html (accessed March 2012).

World Council of Churches (2004) 'Common ground and differences of view between the Bretton Woods Institutions (IMF and World Bank) and the World Council of Churches', Document issued at a high-level encounter between the three organizations at the Ecumenical Centre, Geneva, 22 October 2004. Available at www.oikoumene.org/en/resources/documents/wcc-programmes/public-witness-addressing-power-affirming-peace/poverty-wealth-and-ecology/trade/common-ground-and-differences-of-view-between-the-bretton-woods-institutions-imf-and-world-bank-and-the-wcc.html (accessed March 2012).

World Council of Churches (2008) 'The Guatemala Declaration'. Available at www.oikoumene.org/...ty-wealth-and-ecology/neoliberal-paradigm/08–10–10-agape-consultation-guate-mala-declaration.html (accessed 27 May 2009).

World Council of Churches (2009a) 'Will the global financial crisis mark the end of "moneytheism"?'. Press release on the global financial crisis. Available at www.oikoumene.org/en/news/news-management/eng/a/browse/7/article/1634/will-the-global-financial.html (accessed 27 August 2009).

World Council of Churches (2009b) 'For a new economic and social model: Let's put finance in its place'. Available at www.oikoumene.org/...c-programmes/public-witness-addressing-power-affirming-peace/poverty-wealth-and-ecology/finance-speculation-debt/for-a-new-economic-and-social-model.html (accessed 2 September 2009).

World Council of Churches (2009c) 'Statement on just finance and the economy of life' Available at www.oikoumene.org/...sources/documents/central-committee/geneva-2009/reports-and-documents/report-on-public-issues/statement-on-just-finance-and-the-economy-of-life.html (accessed 30 May 2011).

World Fair Trade Organization (2009) 'Charter of Fair Trade Principles'. Available at www.wfto.com/index.php?option=com_content&task=view&id=1082&Itemid=334 (accessed 25 August 2009).

World Fair Trade Organisation (2011) 'What is Fair Trade?', World Fair Trade Organisation, Amsterdam. Available at www.wfto.com (accessed 15 January 2012).

World March of Women (2003) 'Declaration of Values'. Available at www.worldmarchof women.org/qui_nous_sommes/valeurs/en (accessed 11 February 2010).

World March of Women (2004) *Global Charter for Humanity*. Available at www.worldmarch ofwomen.org/qui_nous_sommes/charte/en (accessed 9 July 2009).

World Social Forum (n.d) 'Composition of the International Council'. Available at www.forumsocialmundial.org.br/main.php?id_menu=3_2_1&cd_language=2 (accessed 2 February 2009).

World Social Forum (2002) 'Charter of Principles' Available at www.forumsocialmundial.org.br/main.php?id_menu=4&cd_language=2 (accessed 2 February 2009).

World Trade Organization (2001) *Ministerial Declaration: Doha Conference*, 14 November, WTO, Geneva. Available at www.wto.org/english/thewto_e/minist_e/min01_e/mindecl_e.htm (accessed January 2012).

World Trade Organization (2004) *Implementation of the Doha Round, General Council Decision*, July 2004. Geneva: WTO.

Zizek, S. (ed.) (1994) *Mapping Ideology*. London and New York: Verso.

INDEX

Entries are arranged in word-by-word alphabetical order which takes account of spaces, hyphens, dashes and diagonal slashes between words; so 're-democratization' precedes 'Reality of Aid Network'. Locators followed by a 'n' suffix indicate a note, a 't' suffix a table.